THIS BOOK SHOULD BE RETURNED ON OR BEFORE THE LATEST
DATE SHOWN TO THE LIBRARY FROM WHICH IT WAS BORROWED

AUTHOR	CLASS
	942.7

TITLE
The NORTH of England in the age
of Richard III.

The North of England in the Age of Richard III

THE FIFTEENTH CENTURY SERIES
Advisory Editor: Ralph A. Griffiths, Professor of Medieval History, University of Wales, Swansea

THE FIFTEENTH CENTURY SERIES is a tribute to the vitality of scholarly study of the later Middle Ages (and especially of the fifteenth century) and to the commitment of Alan Sutton Publishing to make its conclusions widely available. This partnership, which Charles Ross did much to encourage, has been extraordinarily productive in the quarter-century since the pioneering colloquium on 'The Fifteenth Century, 1399–1509: Studies in Politics and Society' was held in Cardiff and presided over by S.B. Chrimes. The proceedings of that colloquium, edited by S.B. Chrimes, C.D. Ross and R.A. Griffiths, were first published in 1972 and reprinted in 1995. Since 1979 Alan Sutton Publishing has published no fewer than fourteen volumes of papers, invited especially from younger scholars and discussed at further colloquia, which have become a notable feature of the academic landscape in Britain. Aside from the encouragement given to talented young historians, noteworthy features of these volumes are the breadth of topics addressed, the novelty of approaches adopted, and the participation of scholars from North America and the European Continent. The volumes have proved influential and informative, and there is good reason to include future volumes in a major new series, both to recognize the achievements of the present generation of fifteenth-century historians and to consolidate the interest in later medieval history which they have undoubtedly generated.

This third volume in THE FIFTEENTH CENTURY SERIES explores a subject which has attracted increasing attention in the past decade. By focusing on the age of Richard III, who had a special relationship with northern England both as Duke of Gloucester and as king, A.J. Pollard and his collaborators are able to examine some cardinal features of society in the north and the borders. The next volume in THE FIFTEENTH CENTURY SERIES will be:

Courts, Counties and the Capital in the Later Middle Ages, ed. Diana E.S. Dunn.

❖ THE FIFTEENTH CENTURY SERIES NO. 3 ❖

THE NORTH OF ENGLAND IN THE AGE OF RICHARD III

EDITED BY
A.J. POLLARD

ALAN SUTTON PUBLISHING · STROUD
ST. MARTIN'S PRESS · NEW YORK

First published in the United Kingdom in 1996
Alan Sutton Publishing Limited
Phoenix Mill · Far Thrupp · Stroud · Gloucestershire

First published in the United States of America in 1996
St. Martin's Press · Scholarly and Reference Division
175 Fifth Avenue · New York · N.Y. 10010

British Library Cataloguing in Publication Data

North of England in the Age of Richard
    III. – (Fifteenth Century Series; No. 3)
    I. Pollard, A.J. II. Series
    942.7046

ISBN 0-7509-0609-X

The editor and publishers gratefully acknowledge grants towards the
cost of publication from the Richard III and Yorkist History Trust
and the Richard III Society.

Typset in 10/15 Baskerville.
Typesetting and origination by
Alan Sutton Publishing Limited.
Printed in Great Britain by
Hartnolls, Bodmin, Cornwall.

CONTENTS

CONTRIBUTORS

R.B. Dobson is Professor of Medieval History at the University of Cambridge. He has written widely on late medieval ecclesiastical, social and urban history and is the author of *Durham Priory, 1400–1450* and *The Peasants' Revolt, 1381*.

Alexander Grant is Reader in Medieval British History at the University of Lancaster. His writings on the later Middle Ages include *Independence and Nationhood: Scotland, 1306–1469* and *Henry VII*.

Rosemary C.E. Hayes is a Curatorial Officer with the Royal Commission on Historical Manuscripts. She is the author of several pieces on the late medieval Church and the reign of Henry VI.

Jonathan Hughes is Assistant Master for History and English at St Edward's School, Oxford. He is the author of *Pastors and Visionaries: Religion and Secular Life in Late Medieval Yorkshire* and articles on late medieval religion.

Christine M. Newman is a Research Fellow at the University of Durham. In addition to her work on Northallerton, she has published articles on the history of the northern gentry in the fifteenth and sixteenth centuries.

A.J. Pollard is Professor of History at the University of Teesside. His publications include *North-Eastern England during the Wars of the Roses* and *Richard III and the Princes in the Tower*.

Henry Summerson is a Research Editor with the *New Dictionary of National Biography*. He is the author of *Medieval Carlisle* and other works on the history of the west march and the borders in the later Middle Ages.

ABBREVIATIONS

Add. MS	Additional Manuscripts
BIHR	*Bulletin of the Institute of Historical Research*
BL	British Library
Bod. Lib.	Bodleian Library, Oxford
BRUC	A.B. Emden, *A Biographical Register of the University of Cambridge* (Cambridge, 1962)
BRUO	A.B. Emden, *A Biographical Register of the University of Oxford*, 3 vols (Oxford, 1957–9)
CCR	*Calendar of Close Rolls*
CPR	*Calendar of Patent Rolls*
Crowland Chronicle	*The Crowland Chronicle Continuations, 1459–1486*, N. Pronay and J. Cox (eds) (Richard III and Yorkist History Trust, 1986)
DCD	Dean and Chapter Muniments, Durham
EETS	Early English Text Society
EHR	*English Historical Review*
Rymer, *Foedera*	*Foedera, Conventiones, Literae, etc*, Thomas Rymer (ed.), 20 vols (1704–35)
Harley MS 433	*British Library Harleian Manuscript 433*, R.E. Horrox and P.W. Hammond (eds), 4 vols (Richard III Society, 1979–83)
KB	King's Bench
Mancini	Dominic Mancini, *The Usurpation of Richard III*, C.A.J. Armstrong (ed.), 2nd ed. (Oxford, 1969)
NH	*Northern History*
PRO	Public Record Office
Rot. Parl.	*Rotuli Parliamentorum*, J. Strachey *et al.* (eds), 6 vols (1967–77)

SS	Surtees Society
TCWAAS	*Transactions of the Cumberland and Westmorland Antiquarian and Archaeological Society*
Test. Ebor.	*Testamenta Eboracensia*, J. Raine (ed.), 5 vols (Surtees Society, 1836–84)
TRHS	*Transactions of the Royal Historical Society*
VCH	*Victoria County History*
YML	York Minster Library

INTRODUCTION

No student of Richard III in the late twentieth century needs reminding that there was a particular association between the king and the north of England. The 'northernness' of Richard III and the particular associations between northern, especially north-eastern, individuals, corporations, institutions and localities and Richard, as both duke and king between 1471 and 1485, have been thoroughly explored.[1] This collection of essays turns the spotlight from the man on to the region itself.[2] It has the temerity to identify the fifteenth century as the age of Richard III, not only because of the particular association between the north in the later part of that century and its best-known adopted son, but also because it is the product of the fifth triennial conference of the Richard III Society which was held on the weekend of 2–4 April 1993 at University College, Durham.[3] For the society, the fifteenth century *is* the age of Richard III.

[1] See for example R.B. Dobson, 'Richard III and the Church in York', in R.A. Griffiths and J.W. Sherborne (eds), *Kings and Nobles in the Later Middle Ages* (Gloucester, 1986), pp. 130–54; K.R. Dockray, 'The Political Legacy of Richard III in Northern England', in *ibid.*, pp. 205–27; M.A. Hicks, 'Dynastic Change and Northern Society: the Career of the Fourth Earl of Northumberland', *NH*, 14 (1978); *idem, Richard III as Duke of Gloucester: a Study in Character* (Borthwick Paper no. 70, York, 1986); R.E. Horrox (ed.) *Richard III and the North* (Hull, 1986); A.J. Pollard, 'St Cuthbert and the Hog: Richard III and the County Palatine of Durham, 1471–85', in Griffiths and Sherborne (eds), *Kings and Nobles*, pp. 109–29.

[2] The region itself has not been neglected. See, for example, A.J. Pollard, *North-Eastern England during the Wars of the Roses* (Oxford, Clarendon Press, 1990); R.L. Storey, 'The North of England', in S.B. Chrimes, *et al.* (eds), *Fifteenth-Century England, 1399–1509* (Manchester, 1972), pp. 129–44; H. Summerson, *Medieval Carlisle: the City and the Borders from the Late Eleventh to the Mid-Sixteenth Century*, 2 vols, TCWAAS, Extra Series, XXV (Stroud, 1993); and A. Tuck and A. Goodman (eds), *War and Border Societies in the Middle Ages* (1992), a collection of essays focusing on the history of the far north in the later fourteenth century.

[3] Papers from two of these conferences have been published as P.W. Hammond (ed.), *Richard III: Loyalty, Lordship and Law* (Gloucester, 1986), and Rosemary Horrox (ed.), *Fifteenth-Century Attitudes: Perceptions of Society in Late Medieval England* (Cambridge, 1994).

The title of this volume begs another question: what is meant by the 'North of England'? The conventional definition of the region is that it is all of England north of the Trent. But the variations, physical, economic, social and cultural within a region so large have led some historians to doubt whether one can truly speak of it as one. There was a far north, the borders, unvisited by the winter sun, quite different even from the familiar world of Newcastle and Durham, to the 'southern' Aeneas Sylvius Piccolomini.[4] There was a highland north, and there was a lowland north; there was a rural north and an urban north. As Professor Dobson states below, 'a supposedly unitary "north of England" is not a meaningful unit for serious historical analysis'.[5]

Yet the north remains a concept with which contemporaries were familiar in the fifteenth century. What did the north mean to them? It is clear that it meant different things in different contexts to different people. To an administrator in chancery or the duchy of Lancaster it did indeed mean the line of the Trent. To a cleric it meant the province of York, whose boundaries were different. But outside the palace of Westminster and Minster Yard, it was a far more flexible notion. In 1429, as Professor Dobson reveals, disruption of the peace in Northumberland was equated with the disruption of the peace in the country of the north; and yet when, as part of the restoration of that peace, John Maners was banished from the north for seven years he was still permitted to reside as near as York. When John Hardyng stated in his chronicle that the Percies 'had the hearts of the people by north, and ever had', he too was thinking of his own county – Northumberland – not Nottinghamshire, or even Westmorland.[6] To the citizens of Carlisle, the north was Scotland. On the other hand, for the university of Oxford, which divided its students into 'nations' so as to control their boisterous behaviour more effectively, the north began at Northampton on the banks of the Nene. But generally to those who lived in the southern counties

[4] *The Memoirs of a Renaissance Pope: the Commentaries of Pope Pius II*, ed. L.C. Gabel (1960), pp. 35–6. The ideas expressed in this and the following three paragraphs are developed more fully in my 'The Characteristics of the Fifteenth-Century North', in P. Dalton and J. Appleby (eds), *Government, Religion and Society in Northern England, c. 1000–c. 1700* (forthcoming).

[5] Below, p. 3.

[6] *The Chronicle of John Hardyng*, ed. H. Ellis (1812), p. 378.

the north was somewhere vague. Among miscellaneous snippets of news, Sir John Paston reported to his brother on 15 September 1471 that, 'ther is moche adoo in the Northe, as men seyn', and left it at that.[7]

The north, to state the obvious, is a concept of those that live to the south (as is the south to those that live to the north). In the fifteenth century, however, it was also a distinct, but needfully imprecise, cultural construct shared by those who lived in the more populous southern counties of England. Lusty northern students at Cambridge, as Chaucer portrayed them in 'The Reeve's Tale', swore by St Cuthbert and spoke with Geordie accents. It was part of that image that it was distant and unknown, 'far in the north, I cannot tell you where'.[8] It was also cold and unfriendly: the Countess of Oxford finally agreed to surrender her estates to Richard of Gloucester in 1473 when she was offered as an alternative a winter holiday in Wensleydale.[9] And the north was barbarous, lawless and violent; as the propaganda and rumour circulating in 1461, and revived in 1483, exploited to the full. Yet it was also a place where one could be free, in one's imagination, to be one of Robin Hood's merry men, a fearless outlaw under the greenwood tree righting the wrongs of society. In this ballad world, itself of the fifteenth century, the wild north of Barnsdale was the equivalent of the Wild West of modern times. Indeed for Robin Hood read Jesse James; and for the 'northern men', read Red Indians. The power of the image of the north, both frightening and attractive, depended on its being somewhere else, distant, unknown and unvisited; the other. As Professor Richmond has commented, 'The North is a literary locale'.[10] It was created not only by the Robin Hood

---

[7] G. Chaucer, *The Canterbury Tales*, trans. Nevill Coghill (Harmondsworth, 1958), pp. 125–35. It was of course Coghill who brought out the Geordie accents.

[8] *The Paston Letters*, ed. J. Gairdner, 6 vols (1904), vol. 5, p. 108.

[9] M.A. Hicks, 'The Last Days of Elizabeth, Countess of Oxford', *EHR*, C (1988), p. 91. Elizabeth was threatened with imprisonment in Middleham if she did not comply with the duke's demands. As Henry Robson later recalled: 'Wherfor the seid lady consideryng her greate age the greate journey and the grett colde which thenne was of Frost and snowe thought that she cowde not endeure to be conueid theder.'

[10] C.F. Richmond, 'An Outlaw and Some Peasants: the possible significance of Robin Hood', *Nottingham Medieval Studies*, XXXVII (1993), p. 91.

ballads, but also by the 'history' of William of Malmesbury, repeated by Higden and widely circulated thereafter; it was validated by Jeremiah, and quoted famously by the Crowland chronicler ('whence all evil spreads'), who was but deploying a commonplace literary device to reinforce a political standpoint.[11]

It is in the light of this cultural construct that we should approach some recent evaluations of the north of England in the fifteenth century. 'The fifteenth century was the century of the north'; 'the years 1471–1485 were its golden age.' Thus Frank Musgrove. For Musgrove, echoing the recent work of Stephen Ellis, the perimeters of the kingdom became more influential in the fifteenth century: the balance of power between centre, where kings could exercise greater control, and the peripheries of the kingdom, where they depended more on the co-operation of nobles, shifted in favour of the north. The successful exercise of its military power made it for a while, especially in the person of Richard III, the arbiter of politics.[12] Dr Jewell has followed a similar line, but sees the politics of the later fifteenth century as a temporary reverse in the inexorable growth of southern political dominance. Thus, 'when Henry defeated Richard at Bosworth in 1485, a dangerous northern independence was averted'.[13] But we should be wary of these sweeping claims about 'the north'. It was not 'the north', but particular magnates, one a royal duke, who held estates and offices in northern counties, who exercised the military power. They did not want independence; far from it, they sought power at court. And got it. Had Richard III defeated Henry Tudor at Bosworth royal control of 'the north', as it is argued below, would have been more quickly and more effectively reasserted than it in fact was by the early Tudors. It might even be argued, as Dobson suggests below, that the problem in the fifteenth century derived from southern intervention in the northern parts of the kingdom, not

[11] *Crowland Chronicle*, 191, quoting Jeremiah, I:14.

[12] F. Musgrove, *The North of England: a History from Roman Times to the Present* (Oxford, Blackwell, 1990), pp. 155–82, esp. 155, 170; S. Ellis, 'Crown, Community and Government in the English Territories, 1450–1575', *History*, LXXI (1986), pp. 187–204.

[13] H.M. Jewell, *The North–South Divide: the Origins of Northern Consciousness in England* (Manchester, 1994), p. 57.

northern intervention in the south, and that the Tudors destabilised the northern counties, especially the borders.

There is thus a problem of the fifteenth-century north; not, however, the conventional political and governmental problem to be solved by the Tudors, but a problem of cultural meaning and identity and of historical understanding. This collection reflects current caution about the character of 'The North' and its distinctiveness. Historical analysis focuses on particular counties (Cumberland, Durham and Yorkshire), institutions (the crown, the law and the church), individuals (including Richard III) and Anglo-Scottish relations, not on the north as a whole. Yet certain themes emerge which relate directly to the received image of a distant, lawless, rebellious country; the north of the fifteenth-century imagination.

Several essays deal with the questions of the law and lawlessness, order and violent disorder in the northern counties in the fifteenth century. Evaluating the effectiveness of law enforcement and the level of violence throughout late medieval England, let alone the north, is fraught with both evidential and conceptual difficulties. There is a greater quantity of surviving legal evidence for the fifteenth century than for preceding centuries which creates the impression of an increase in crime, especially of violent crime. But this, it must be remembered, is evidence not of an increase in crime itself, but of an increase in the survival of evidence of recorded crime. And, because of the nature of that evidence which is largely made up of indictments, it is primarily evidence of alleged violent crime, not proven violent crime. And the violence, it has been demonstrated, was often fictitious or, if perpetrated, symbolic so as to ensure a speedier course of law. Moreover, while in the twentieth century the use of violence as a means of resolving disputes is condemned, in the fifteenth century it was considered normal, if not desirable. Generally speaking, too, contemporaries were more tolerant of what we call corruption, partiality and favour.[14]

Several chapters in this collection approach the vexed question of the

---

[14] P.C. Maddern, *Violence and Social Order: East Anglia, 1422–1442* (Oxford, Clarendon Press, 1992), pp. 1–110; E. Powell, 'Law and Justice', in Horrox (ed.), *Fifteenth-Century Attitudes*, pp. 29–41.

supposed lawlessness of the north directly from the surviving evidence of the administration of the law, sparse as it is, independently of the contemporary and later preconceptions that the north was particularly unruly. Dr Hayes presents the preliminary conclusions of a research project calendaring 'ancient indictments' touching the north of England between 1461 and 1509. She finds that the level of reported alleged crimes in the counties of Cumberland, Durham, Lancashire, Northumberland and Yorkshire that reached King's Bench was far higher in Yorkshire than in the border counties and higher in the reign of Henry VII than under the Yorkists. How one interprets these findings is problematic. The disparity between Yorkshire and the other counties (Durham excluded, which had its own higher court) might mean that there was less violent crime in the far north, or it might mean that the administration of justice was less effective. The disparity between the Yorkists and Henry VII might mean that the north was more law abiding before 1485 than afterwards. Nonetheless detailed analysis suggests that under Henry VII the law was being enforced more rigorously rather than that the region was becoming more disorderly. In terms of social class it appears that, as in East Anglia earlier in the century, there was a significant degree of gentry involvement in the cases of violent crime referred up to King's Bench. While this suggests that those whose responsibility it was to conserve the peace as justices of the peace were themselves likely also to be major disturbers of it, it is also possible that these cases involving them were more likely to be referred up to the higher court.

In contrast to the indictments before King's Bench which highlight alleged gentry involvement in violent crime, the local courts of a small market town like Northallerton, discussed by Dr Newman, reveal that between 1470 and 1540 the men of local substance, landholders, yeomen, husbandmen and artisans, worked closely together to maintain order, regulate economic activity, control social behaviour and protect the well-being of the local community. While these records reflect the interests of a particular local elite running the town and the liberty under the lordship of the Bishop of Durham, they nonetheless provide a powerful corrective to exaggerated generalisations concerning the lawlessness of the region. They demonstrate that the experience of a small market town and its hinterland in northern Yorkshire was not significantly at variance with the experience of similar towns anywhere further south in the kingdom in these years.

Yet these records too are one-sided. Borough and manorial courts dealt with only the petty and day-to-day regulation of town and country life. By chance, because it was not the formal business of the court, a memorandum concerning a major riot in Northallerton in October 1484, was entered on the borough court roll. One might suppose that Northallerton was on that day the victim of a band of disorderly, discharged soldiers from the recent Scottish wars. Had it not been for this unusual memorandum, such a collapse of order would have passed unrecorded. Moreover, manorial records do not reveal the level or extent of serious crime in which the people of Northallerton might have been involved. An approver's confession before King's Bench in 1473 reveals that the approver himself, William Robynson, a labourer of York, together with two Northallerton butchers, John Metcalf and John Thomson, robbed a man called Stokysley (Stokesley) of £55 8s on Northallerton Moor, just north of the town on 20 December 1470. Robinson admitted to other, later acts of highway robbery, including one in Barnsdale, but it is only through his confession that we discover that otherwise respectable Northallerton tradesmen lived a double life as local highwaymen.

The legal evidence is thus both incomplete and ambiguous. Yet there is nothing in it to lead one to suppose that the north away from the borders was any more lawless and violent than the rest of England in the later fifteenth century. Indeed Dr Summerson suggests that only on the furthest borders in the north-west, in Gilsland and north of the Lyne, was there a serious crisis of law enforcement. And the manner of dealing with two particularly violent disorders in the higher reaches of society detailed in this volume suggests a special desire to preserve the peace and maintain social harmony in the fifteenth-century north. Professor Dobson considers the manner in which the feud resulting from the killing on 20 January 1428 of William Heron of Ford by a servant of John Maners of Etal, close to the Scottish border in Norhamshire (part of the palatinate of Durham), was defused and resolved by Prior Wessington of Durham and a commission of northern clergy acting on the instruction of Bishop Langley of Durham. He suggests that in the north the Church was a respected and effective institution, which, perhaps, played a more prominent role in preserving the peace than elsewhere. If Church involvement represents to modern minds a priest-ridden and backward society, paradoxically such 'backwardness' might also have helped ensure a more law-abiding and less violent society.

The most important case to occupy King's Bench under Edward IV was that of the violent quarrel between the Pilkingtons and the Savilles which was put into the hands of a commission of oyer and terminer which sat at Pontefract under the Duke of Gloucester from 21 to 25 September 1478. This violent confrontation between two leading members of the king's household competing for the domination and rule of the royal lordship of Wakefield which came to a 'head in the spring of 1478 led to more loss of life than the Percy–Neville conflict in Yorkshire from 1453 to 1454. It being a highly political affair, concerning the very core of the Yorkist establishment, the king was anxious to defuse tensions and restore harmony; and this may explain why the hearings were apparently cut short and why there was no great retribution or punishment imposed on the principals. In Yorkshire in the later fifteenth century (in contrast to Norhamshire in the early century), Richard of Gloucester, in the name of the crown, rather than Prior Wessington on behalf of the Church, acted as the healer of wounds. But the aim of restoring peace rather than inflicting punishment was the same. In the light of the successful containment and resolution of these two prominent cases, both of which deeply divided their local societies and were of major concern to the central governments of their day, the more notorious Percy–Neville quarrel of 1453–4, which an emasculated crown failed to stifle, appears less obviously typical of an uncontrollably violent north. Much more depended on the ability and determination of the crown to enforce its authority.

Contrary to common misconception, the crown enjoyed the potential for effective political rule in the north throughout the fifteenth century. Before 1399, it is true, the crown was territorially weak in the northern counties. It perforce depended more than in other parts of the kingdom for the effective exercise of its rule on its deputies, usually one or more of the great quasi-feudal barons of the region. Moreover, the need to defend the border against the Scots and the delegation of this command to the wardens of the marches, again usually drawn from the ranks of greater barons, increased this dependency. But this never meant that the crown was powerless; it always held Carlisle and Inglewood Forest in Cumberland. As Dr Summerson shows, Carlisle may have been a far-flung post of the English crown, but it was still a post. In addition Durham, while constitutionally a quasi-independent palatinate which made its bishop in law the most powerful feudal lord in the kingdom, was, since kings appointed trusted and able servants to the see, in practice throughout the fourteenth century politically an arm of the crown. The Lancastrian usurpation greatly enhanced the direct presence of the crown in the region, bringing as it did the county palatine of Lancaster, four great lordships in Yorkshire and the barony of Embleton in Northumberland under royal control. After 1405, Henry IV and Henry V, through their royal affinity in the region, led by Ralph Neville, Earl of Westmorland, and Thomas Langley, Bishop of Durham, had no difficulty in ruling the north. In this, as in so much else, the unfortunate Henry VI undid what his father and grandfather had achieved. The fateful promotion of Bishop Robert Neville to Durham in 1437 and its consequences for the loss of royal control in the region – a control not recovered until Richard III himself came to the throne in 1483 – are examined in detail in Chapter 4 below. The same pattern is observable in Cumberland, where Henry VI initially conceded power to Richard Neville, Earl of Salisbury, and Edward IV was either unable or disinclined to recover it after 1461. In so far as the fifteenth century witnessed a reverse in the growth of central, royal command over the north, it was the consequence of neither the centrifugal pull of the periphery, nor the resurgent particularism of the region, but the direct result of the policies followed by a particularly incompetent king.

It is in this context that we should understand the kingship, albeit short-lived, of Richard III in the north. As Dr Summerson shows, having benefited as Duke of Gloucester from his brother's generosity (or folly), and avoiding the same mistake as his brother, he kept personal control of Carlisle and the west march. Indeed it is arguable that because he had the benefit of his own ducal following in Carlisle and the county he was able to provide more effective government than Henry VII. Henry VII was able to step easily into his shoes since loyalty lay towards the crowned king, not the individual monarch. He employed the same men, but he did not trust them. Hence he divided authority and powers between Dacre, Salkeld and Musgrave, to a degree setting one against the other, and ultimately retaining his personal control, as he did elsewhere in the kingdom, by the means of recognisances and bonds and the exploitation of his feudal rights. But Henry's policy towards the north-west did not provide a firm basis for a long-term maintenance of royal control; and its shortcomings were revealed when full-scale war with Scotland was resumed in 1513.

The most pressing royal obligation in the north was the defence of the border. Relationships with Scotland were of particular concern to the inhabitants of the northern counties throughout the fifteenth century, who looked for either a stable peace or a successful war. It was one of the elements in Richard III's tragedy that he could not make up his mind whether he wanted to be a peacemaker or a conqueror. The War of Scottish Independence, Dr Grant argues, had effectively come to an end in 1461 when the Scots recovered Berwick, the last English foothold on Scottish soil. But Richard of Gloucester's military ambitions after 1471, encapsulated in the creation of his own principality in south-western Scotland in 1483 and given substance by the recovery of Berwick in 1482, threatened to reopen those wars. Indeed, as Grant stresses, until April 1484 the king seemed to be hell-bent on fighting a war on three fronts. Although he pulled back from the brink, and concluded a truce with Scotland in September 1484, a train of events had been set in motion that led to his defeat and death at the hands of a largely Franco-Scottish force at Bosworth.

The truce of 1484 was of greater significance, however, in its implications for the government of the north of England. In the clauses dealing with procedures, the powers of the wardens of the marches – in 1484 this was in effect solely the warden of the east march, the Earl of Northumberland – were drastically reduced and the responsibilities for maintaining the truce and dealing with breaches transferred from the warden's court to the common law courts and to royal councillors. The truce, which Richard personally negotiated, should be seen in tandem with the establishment of the Council of the North, the retention of the wardenship of the west march and his intervention in the administration of the county palatine of Durham as part of a concerted and co-ordinated plan to retain his personal interest and reassert effective royal control over the north; control which had been lost during the minority of Henry VI. Richard III's plans for the administration of the north, undermined by his political and military failure, were more ambitious and constructive than anything attempted by Henry VII and foreshadowed the reforms introduced by Henry VIII in the 1530s and completed by Elizabeth I. It was Richard III, not Henry VII, who brought the north back under royal control.

Richard III, as a King of England whose roots lay in the north, was well placed to reverse the centrifugal trend of the previous half century; as a man who grew up in the north he professed a piety, as Dr Hughes shows, that was specifically northern in character. He espoused the ideal of the mixed life which had first evolved out of the northern eremitic tradition in the fourteenth century. Through his close links with and patronage of Cambridge-educated northern clergy he became an austere practitioner of the mixed life. The most important manifestation of its development in the second half of the fifteenth century, enthusiastically endorsed and advanced by the northern clergy, was the practice of private prayer. Prayers, focused on books of hours, in which the psalms had a high profile, were of particular assistance in helping the practitioner to cope with the trials, tribulations and sufferings of life. These influences, Hughes suggests, came to bear on his adoption and use of the prayer for delivery from his enemies which he had copied into his own book. While the prayer itself is found elsewhere, Hughes argues that in Richard's hands it does reveal something of his own inner anxieties and fears; anxieties and fears that are also revealed in his royal portrait, which, drawing heavily on the iconography contained in the visions of St Mechtild of Hackeborn, can be read as the presentation of the king's self-image as a misunderstood, suffering, tormented man of prayer, who refused to despair of God's Grace. This tormented spirituality may not be what his Cambridge-educated advisers and confessors anticipated from the practice of private prayer, but it was nevertheless, he concludes, an output of the distinctive religious culture of the fifteenth-century north.

The personal significance of Richard III's prayer is likely to remain highly controversial; but it is worth noting that in his spiritual journey, as in his political career, he was a product of the north of England. It is important to understand the north that shaped him. It was a north, which, these essays show, had greater diversity and shared more in common with the rest of England than some recent writings have allowed. The ease with which the northern magnate

Richard, Duke of Gloucester, became Richard III of England in 1483 should itself warn us against the perception of north and south as two separate worlds. Richard III's own impact was fleeting, but his accession and reign are perhaps significant in that they began the revival of royal authority, or, depending on one's viewpoint, the renewal of royal meddling in the region which was to be the hallmark of the succeeding age.

1

POLITICS AND THE CHURCH IN THE FIFTEENTH-CENTURY NORTH

R.B. Dobson

'I love the Old Castle here: my imagination brings strongly to mind those glorious days when the prince of an independent palatinate lived among us.' Such sentiments, apparently still appropriate for a meeting of the Richard III Society held within Durham Castle in 1993, are of course those of the indefatigable James Boswell.[1] How unfortunate that the words he scribbled into his journal on the evening of 18 July 1788 are evocative but mistaken, a manifestation not of the reality but of the myth of northern England. An 'independent palatinate' the county and diocese of fifteenth-century Durham was certainly, if perhaps regrettably, not.[2] But then we all know that we can never trust a Scot, as we can never trust a northerner himself, when he generalizes about the north of England. Perhaps I am in a worse condition still; for it might be even more naïve to trust a northerner speaking of the north when he is no longer in the north, unexpectedly removed, like Bishop John Fordham in 1388, 'from the flesh-pots of Durham to the more meagre temporalities of Ely'.[3] Indeed my own once strongly held opinions about northern England in the later Middle Ages no longer satisfy myself. Thus, in a lecture of some dozen years ago, I expressed what I then thought was my deepest perception on northern history when I suggested that 'as someone who

[1] *Boswell: The English Experiment, 1785–1789*, eds I.S. Lustig and F.A. Pottle (New Haven, 1986), p. 242; cf. pp. 32, 222, 239–40.

[2] J. Scammell, 'The Origin and Limitations of the Liberty of Durham', *EHR*, LXXXI (1966), pp. 449–73.

[3] T.F. Tout, *Chapters in the Administrative History of Medieval England* (Manchester, 1920–33), III, p. 346; R.B. Dobson, *Preserving the Perishable: Contrasting Communities in Medieval England* (Cambridge, 1991), p. 5.

spent much of his childhood in a farmhouse overlooking upper Teesdale from the late and lamented North Riding of Yorkshire to County Durham, perhaps I can be forgiven for believing that the river Tees may form a much more important internal English frontier than either the Humber or the Trent'.[4] Little though I knew it at the time, this tentative expression of the apparently obvious was shortly to provoke Professor Pollard into writing a remarkable book designed – not too misguidedly – to prove me wrong.[5]

However, this is only a facetious and cumbersome way of making the two preliminary points any medievalist approaching the grand theme of the north of England in the time of Richard III has to make by way of introduction. First, the moment one tries to make the 'north' more than a geographical expression (what Professor Pollard himself calls 'loosely as a province') it becomes a state of mind; and states of mind, however interesting and important, will never lead to unanimity, to agreement on a Platonic ideal of the north.[6] Admittedly, to travel through the north of England may be more interesting than to arrive there. If so, unquestionably the best approach is to follow in the footsteps of Helen Jewell's illuminating article in *Northern History* a couple of years ago – and in particular to trace the concept of the north forward from the Roman *Britannia Inferiora* through Pope Gregory I's famous letter to St Augustine on 22 June AD 601 to the creation (rather late in the day) of the ecclesiastical province of York in 735.[7] If the north of England ever had – or indeed has – any juridical basis, that basis lay in the metropolitan authority of the see of York, a thought which has never of course met with much enthusiasm in this cathedral city of Durham. The second compulsory observation to be made about the north of England, before, during and after the reign of Richard III, is much more important,

---

[4] R.B. Dobson, 'Cathedral Chapters and Cathedral Cities: York, Durham and Carlisle in the Fifteenth Century', *NH*, XIX (1983), p. 17.

[5] A.J. Pollard, *North-Eastern England during the Wars of the Roses* (Oxford, 1990), especially pp. 1–27.

[6] Such seems to be the main argument of J. Le Patourel, 'Is Northern History a Subject?', *NH*, XII (1976), pp. 1–15.

[7] H.M. Jewell, 'North and South: the Antiquity of the Great Divide', *NH*, XXVII (1991), pp. 1–25; and now see Dr Jewell's *The North-South Divide: The Origins of Northern Consciousness in England* (Manchester, 1994), especially pp. 152–84.

much more obvious and much more intractable. Ever since Professor Dickens (the first historian, I think, to make the point explicit), it must seem clear to us all that England north of the Trent (from St Bees to Bridlington, from Liverpool to Lindisfarne) is infinitely more variable – in terms of geography, tenurial conditions, economy, religion and culture – than any comparable area south of the Trent.[8] This is not to deny that (as Professor Pollard's book has again proved) intelligible attempts to 'regionalize' the history of parts of the north can be made, and should be made. But the task is hardly easy. Did travellers from Hurworth-on-Tees feel more at home in Durham or in York during the reign of Richard III? Did the small merchant class here in the city of Durham prefer to trade in Newcastle upon Tyne or in York? Pointless questions no doubt; but they are perhaps not completely irrelevant to analysing the kaleidoscopic mosaics which made up whatever the fifteenth-century north was. Precisely because of such shifting regional patterns, we probably have to disagree – however regrettable it is to do so – with a recent striking assertion that 'The fifteenth century was the century of the north'.[9] That quotation derives from Frank Musgrove's remarkable *The North of England: a History from the Roman Times to the Present*, remarkable not so much because Frank Musgrove taught me history at school while neither of us were interested in northern history at all, but because it is an extraordinary, interesting attempt to do the impossible. The sad fact is that a supposedly unitary 'north of England' is not a meaningful unit for serious historical analysis.

Mr Musgrove's book is more interesting still because it is itself so obviously individual, even at times idiosyncratic, an interpretation of its subject, yet one more demonstration that interest in the history of the north lies more obviously in the eye of the beholder than in the essentials of what the north may actually be. If so, perhaps the political and ecclesiastical history of northern England in the later Middle Ages might be reinterpreted to serve some other prevailing obsessions of the 1990s. I remember that my ex-colleague, Professor John Bossy,

[8] A.G. Dickens, *Lollards and Protestants in the Diocese of York, 1509–1558* (Oxford, 1959), pp. 1–4.

[9] F. Musgrove, *The North of England: A History from Roman Times to the Present* (Oxford, 1990), pp. 154, 155–82.

used to claim – more seriously than not – that the most valid justification for studying history might be to understand why human communities (families, villages, towns, regions, kingdoms, nations, Christendom itself) weren't *always* in a state of perpetual disintegration. To all of us Professor Bossy's dramatized version of Social Contract theory (little as he would accept that definition) must seem more persuasive now than in the days – not long ago – when a Soviet Union and Yugoslavia actually existed. Might it therefore be that the single most important feature of the fifteenth-century north is not its disorder, but rather that it did after all manage to retain its cohesion, both within its own geographical boundaries and as a constituent part of the medieval English realm as a whole?

Why, in other words, did northern England in the age of the Lancastrians and Yorkists fail to be Balkanized? Why was it so relatively tranquil and respectful of authority? Whether or not these are *questions mal posées*, they have certainly not been questions much addressed by most previous commentators on the late medieval north. The latter have almost invariably tended to take a very different tack indeed. In the first year of this century Gaillard Lapsley's pioneering paper on 'The Problem of the North' (a significant title) painted a picture of extreme incoherence, of a 'harsh' and 'brutal' (his adjectives) society which had to be brought to heel by the Council of the North before the kingdom of England could become the England we know.[10] More recent historians have of course taken a progressively less sensationalist view, most interestingly perhaps Professor Storey who (in a paper on 'The North of England' written nearly twenty years ago) argued that – historically speaking – the most interesting feature of the fifteenth-century north was not what happened in the north but what impact events in the north had on the south.[11] For northerners like Professor Storey and myself, this is not an unattractive

[10] G.T. Lapsley, 'The Problem of the North', *American Historical Review*, V (1900), pp. 440–66; reprinted in *idem, Crown, Community and Parliament in the Later Middle Ages* (Oxford, 1952), pp. 375–405.

[11] R.L. Storey, 'The North of England', in S.B. Chrimes, C.D. Ross and R.A. Griffiths (eds), *Fifteenth-Century England, 1399–1509* (Manchester, 1972), pp. 128–9.

thesis; and I only wish I could completely believe it. In fact, however, it would not be too difficult to take an opposite view. Throughout the fifteenth century it was primarily and normally southern 'problems' which were fought out on northern soil rather than vice versa. On this issue at least my sense is that Mr Musgrove strikes the appropriate chords. During the long course of northern history, not only are the 'northerners' (from the Brigantes to the South Yorkshire coal miners) usually the victims, but in the fifteenth century too the northern lords and burgesses are less initiators than allies and supporters who can be courted, exploited and then discarded by those Englishmen who live south of the Humber.[12] To that extent at least it is hard to deny a broad continuity of approach between the treatment of the north under the early Normans and under the early Tudors. Like Mr Musgrove, one might indeed go further still. How ironically appropriate that the late Lord Lieutenant of the county of North Yorkshire should live in the castle of Mulgrave, near Whitby, first built by his ancestor, Peter de Maulay, the most notorious alien active in northern England during the reign of Henry VIII.[13]

However, it is important to avoid succumbing to yet another of the more insidious of the myths which can engulf those who dabble in the waters of northern history in the later Middle Ages. I refer of course to the popular view (partly rooted in Stubbs' vision of the grand sweep of English history as a whole) that the north's inhabitants *had* to be violent in the later Middle Ages in order to be well governed thereafter. Only after suffering the pains of anarchy in the fifteenth century could northerners later appreciate the virtues of good government from Westminster and Whitehall during the early Tudor period and later. Such a stereotype of a northern progress *per ardua ad astra* remains remarkably persistent, even though it is so obviously a myth about the north originally created – during the course of the sixteenth century – in the south. Fully articulated by Gaillard Lapsley in his book on *The County Palatine of*

---

[12] Musgrove, *North of England*, pp. 155–82, and *passim*.

[13] A few ruins (unusually inaccessible) of Peter de Maulay's castle still survive in the grounds of Mulgrave House; but 'no-one without a plan would be able to make sense of it': N. Pevsner, *The Buildings of England: Yorkshire, The North Riding* (Harmondsworth, 1966), p. 260.

Durham, traces of this way of regarding northern history in the fifteenth century are still apparent in the work of such recent modern authorities in the field as Charles Ross.[14] That many northerners of the fifteenth century did have to endure more than their fair share of economic hardship is not in question. However, even here the reason usually put forward for that hardship (military activity by the Scots allegedly always poised to raid from the northern side of the Border) was not necessarily as devastating as is usually supposed: such armed attack was certainly very much less significant under the Lancastrians and Yorkists than it had been under the later Plantagenets.[15] In both periods moreover one generalization usually applies. Not only was the threat of Scottish invasion fairly readily containable after the 1330s (Edward III and James Campbell were surely both right about that); but within the north of England itself serious internal violence, vendetta, rebellion, treason, the revival of 'Northumbrian separatism', was containable too.[16] Richard of Gloucester had few problems in this sphere; and it might even be argued that it was the Tudors not their predecessors who destabilized rather than stabilized the north of England.

At one level the political history of the north in the fifteenth century was accordingly the story of how *rarely* its inhabitants presented much of a threat to tranquillity within its own borders or to the English monarchy south of the Trent (much less of a threat, one might add, than often in the sixteenth century). On the whole, England north of the Trent during the Lancastrian and Yorkist periods seems to be characterized by a series of quasi-military alarms and excursions which, in the end, signified remarkably little. Among the more familiar examples are the abrupt and indeed humiliating collapse of the so-called Archbishop Scrope's rebellion at Shipton Moor in 1405; the failure of the

---

[14] G.T. Lapsley, *The County Palatine of Durham: a study in constitutional history* (New York, 1900); C. Ross, *Richard III* (1981), pp. 44–59.

[15] R.B. Dobson, 'The Church of Durham and the Scottish Borders', in A. Goodman and A. Tuck (eds), *War and Border Societies in the Middle Ages* (1992), pp. 136–48.

[16] J. Campbell, 'England, Scotland and the Hundred Years' War in the Fourteenth Century', in J.R. Hale, J.R.L. Highfield and B. Smalley (eds), *Europe in the Late Middle Ages* (1965), pp. 192–216.

serious dynastic rift between the senior and younger branches of the Neville family to escalate into civil war after the death of their great paterfamilias, Ralph, 1st Earl of Westmorland, in 1425; the similar failure of the skirmish or battle of Heworth Moor between Nevilles and Percies in the suburbs of York to genuinely inaugurate what we call the Wars of the Roses as early as 1453; and, finally, the failure of the so-called Ricardian cause in the north to outlive Richard himself in more than a desultory manner.[17] It would not be difficult to add many more examples of such northern military or political fiascos during the course of the fifteenth century. Although for each of such episodes historians have rightly found a different explanation, one suspects that the single common denominator was usually the political misjudgement (and worse) of the families of Neville and – even more – of Percy. Here again one must beware of an insidious Tudor myth, most notoriously expressed in the deceptive remark that 'the people of the north knew no king but a Neville or a Percy (or Dacre)'. In fact the history of the fifteenth-century north is a commentary on the complete inadequacy of so simple a view of political loyalties north of the Humber. Whether or not, as seems likely, the economic resources and political power of Nevilles and Percies have been much over-valued by modern historians, both families quite clearly suffered chronically, if understandably, throughout the century in not knowing precisely what their political aims actually were, what they really wanted to do.[18] Such uncertainties most obviously reached their climax between the date when Richard of Gloucester became the royal cuckoo in the Neville nest during the 1460s and the battle of Bosworth Field two decades later.[19]

---

[17] See, e.g., R.L. Storey, *The End of the House of Lancaster* (1966), *passim*; R.B. Dobson, *Durham Priory, 1400–1450* (Cambridge, 1973), pp. 188–91; A. Goodman, *The Wars of the Roses* (1981), pp. 86–116; A.J. Pollard, *North-Eastern England*, pp. 245–84.

[18] Whether this problem will ever be satisfactorily solved in the case of the most 'overmighty' subject of them all, Richard Neville, Earl of Warwick, is beginning to seem increasingly unlikely; but see Pollard, *North-Eastern England*, pp. 245–314.

[19] Ross, *Richard III*, pp. 44–55; R.B. Dobson, 'Richard III and the Church of York', in R.A. Griffiths and J. Sherborne (eds), *Kings and Nobles in the Later Middle Ages: A Tribute to Charles Ross* (Gloucester, 1986), pp. 130–5.

However, if the overt political activities of northerners in the fifteenth century are often best interpreted as a series of damp squibs, one would concede that this makes it all the more important to understand the forces of constraint and inhibition which made them so. Perhaps the most general issue facing historians of the period is how outbreaks of northern fractiousness could be curbed and contained when they did occur. Professor Pollard, Dr Hicks and other historians have already begun to analyse some examples of this process. As this paper has space for only one example, let it be a case of extreme fractiousness as northern as it can possibly be, a violent episode which took place in the Northumbrian village of Etal, only a few miles from the Scottish border, in 1428.[20] This *causa de Heron*, the Heron case, as it came to be called, has the additional advantage of being, by late medieval northern standards, exceptionally well documented. Shortly after Prior John Wessington of Durham Cathedral Priory ceased to be the major umpire and peacemaker in the dispute, he deposited a massive file of documents relating to the conflict in his convent's muniments, where they may still be found. So copious are these records that the following account of the Heron case only unravels a few of some very tangled skeins indeed in what looks like the best recorded case of private vendetta to survive from the fifteenth-century north.[21] But here, in brief, is the tale of violence and (even more interesting) the settlement of that violence which the Heron case reveals.

Against a background of long-standing feud between the two Northumbrian families in question, on the morning of 20 January 1428 William Heron of Ford left the Bishop of Durham's Tweed-side castle of Norham with an armed company clearly deliberately designed to attack, or at least to terrorize, the village of Etal, major residence of Lord John Maners. On what seems likely to be the most plausible of various versions of subsequent events, Heron ordered his men to draw their bows; and in retaliation Maners's retainers raised their swords in self-

---

[20] *A History of Northumberland*, ed. K.H. Vickers (Newcastle-upon-Tyne, 1922), XI, pp. 380–1; R.L. Storey, *Thomas Langley and the Bishopric of Durham, 1406–1437* (1961), pp. 142–3; Dobson, *Durham Priory*, p. 197.

[21] Nearly all the items in the large collection of evidences relating to the Heron case are now to be found in Locellus V of the muniments of the Dean and Chapter of Durham (hereafter cited as DCD).

defence, Lord John himself later being accused of killing Heron's servant with the deadly double combination of a 'Scotte axe' and a sword. However, this in itself would have been a matter of comparatively minor significance. Unfortunately at more or less the same moment William Heron himself was killed outright (probably by a spear) in the middle of Etal, thus dividing Northumbrian landed society into two deeply opposed and dangerous factions, led by the two most powerful knights in the county.[22] Sir Robert Umfraville supported the rights for redress of William Heron's widow, Isabel, and her family: Sir Robert Ogle was the principal supporter of Maners and his kindred. Although the royal government appointed commissioners to enquire into the cause of Heron's death on 8 February 1428, neither they nor the sheriff of Northumberland showed any desire to involve themselves in what rapidly showed every sign of becoming an insoluble conflict about reparations.[23] As John Maners pointed out in some detail a couple of years later, the real sticking points and the real dangers were essentially two, and both might have emerged straight out of the Paston's East Anglia of the same date. Firstly, none of the participants in the Heron case were prepared to commit themselves to 'wordes or dedes of humbleness' which might at all detract from their standing or 'wirship' in their county. Secondly, both sides to the dispute were obsessively aware that if they made any attempts to compromise at all, they were likely to be put at risk by 'an unreule word or dede by the ferrest of hys kynn'. By that most characteristic of fifteenth-century ambiguities, the heads of the northern mafiosi families were not in control of events but at the mercy of the hot heads of the ill-advised 'young men' (as Bishop Dudley of Durham liked to call them) of the northern country.[24]

By the beginning of 1429 it had accordingly become clear not only to Bishop Thomas Langley of Durham but also to no less a figure than Cardinal Henry Beaufort himself that 'gude rest and pece to be had in the Cuntre of the north' depended on the breaking of the impasse of the Heron case; and it was therefore at this stage that Prior John Wessington (also under pressure to

---

[22] DCD, Loc. V, no. 44; Loc. XXI, no. 20.

[23] *CPR, 1422–29*, p. 467; cf. Dobson, *Durham Priory*, p. 198.

[24] DCD, Loc. V, no. 48.

become involved by his client Sir Robert Umfraville) was prevailed upon to
intervene in an attempt to bring the Herons and Maners to an amicable and
binding settlement of their dispute.[25] Wessington, together with his junior
colleagues, the Priors of Tynemouth and Guisborough, must often have
regretted his decision to say yes; for although he did finally secure a settlement,
it took him many tedious meetings, many long journeys and approximately two-
and-a-half years to succeed. Needless to say, there is no space here to describe
the often bewildering ups and downs of the tortuous negotiations involved in
the resolution of the Heron affair. Attempting to secure agreement upon the
proper compensation for a prominent individual's death by violence can never
be an easy matter; and in its own small way the retribution exacted for the
murder of William Heron of Ford reminds one not a little of the near-
contemporary wrangling between Valois France and Valois Burgundy over
compensation for the death of Duke John the Fearless at the bridge of
Montereau in 1419.[26] In both cases the issues at stake were in fact substantially
the same – haggling over status, over money, over revenge and (not at all least)
over prayers for the deceased. Here, for instance, is what the Heron family put
forward as their terms for the settlement of the conflict at a fairly early stage of
the negotiations (in April 1429). First, John Maners and his friends were to
appear in person before the Heron kindred and submit themselves humbly to
the award. Secondly, John Maners was to promise to pay all the debts (over
£600) owed by William Heron at the time of his death. Thirdly, and more
remarkably, Maners was to ordain no less than a perpetual chantry at Ford so
that masses could be said there forever for the souls of William Heron and his
servant, Robert Atkinson. Atkinson's mother was herself to be compensated by
an annual pension of 40s; while (most dramatically of all) John Maners and all
others implicated in the homicides were to be required to leave the north of
England (defined, not uninterestingly, as the kingdom of England north of York)
for the next seven years.[27]

---

[25] DCD, Loc. V, no. 47; cf. Bursar's Account Roll, 1428–9 (Expense Necessarie).

[26] P. Bonenfant, *Du Meurtre de Montereau au Traité de Troyes* (Brussels, 1958), *passim*.

[27] DCD, Loc. V, nos. 45, 48, 52, 53; Dobson, *Durham Priory*, pp. 200–1.

Rather disingenuously perhaps, Isabel Heron and her bereaved family put forward these demands as 'thys lytill and esy tretye'; but in fact many months of further protracted negotiation (horse-trading in effect) had to follow before the final ceremony of reconciliation took place at the church of St Nicholas in Newcastle-upon-Tyne on 24 May 1431. Here at last John Maners of Etal publicly swore on the gospels that he was innocent of William Heron's murder and asked for the friendship of his old enemies – 'so that gude love and charite may ever abide amang us'.[28] After the Herons had then received him into their peace, Maners announced his intention of providing for the relief of the deceased's soul – no longer however by the endowment of a perpetual chantry but rather by means of 500 separate masses to be said over the next twelve months. Even this figure was a compromise: in the previous autumn it transpires that Maners had been prepared to pay the almost staggering sum needed to provide no fewer than 1,000 requiem masses during the following year. By the final agreement of May 1431 Maners also agreed to pay the Heron family a cash sum – in instalments – of 250 marks.[29] All in all, no small retribution was here exacted from a Northumbrian lord who had probably committed no murder in the first place and had probably not merited the misfortune of having his residence attacked by a marauding band of neighbouring enemies. Why was John Maners prepared to concede so much? Who can know? The precise moral and legal rights of the Heron case are not now ascertainable and perhaps they never were; but then we have by now all been instructed by Dr Edward Powell and others that the outcome of judicial process (and especially of legal arbitration) in fifteenth-century England had little to do with moral justice but all to do with the healing of wounds to the fabric of society.[30] Perhaps, and after all, the most obvious conclusion to be drawn from the Heron affair is therefore the platitudinous one that (in the extreme north of England as in the extreme south) relationships between gentry

[28] DCD, Loc. V, nos. 45v, 53.

[29] DCD, Loc V, no. 53.

[30] E. Powell, 'Arbitration and the Law in England in the Late Middle Ages', *TRHS*, 5th ser, XXXIII (1983), pp. 49–67.

families, especially when accompanied by that sharp sense of kinship to which
the documents at Durham bear witness, were the decisive force in both
factionalizing and then reharmonizing local politics.

And yet about the Heron case of 1428 to 1431 there is probably something
more to be said, said most cogently in fact by the first historian ever to
encounter the story. I refer, predictably enough, to the indefatigable James
Raine the elder, a much more significant godfather to all historians of the late
medieval north than even his friend and mentor Sir Walter Scott.[31] For James
Raine 'the bitter feud between the powerful families of Heron and Maners
abounds with incident, characterising at the same time the pugnacious state of
the borders, the total absence of everything in the shape of legal redress and
finally the omnipotence of the church'.[32] While conceding that nothing was
more likely to bring forth the founder of the Surtees Society's righteous
indignation more eloquently than the thought of the 'omnipotence of the
church' (especially if such omnipotence should in any way be linked with the
influence of St Cuthbert), Raine is here clearly making a not unimportant
point. The Heron case exposes a serious fracture in Northumbrian society most
interesting of all because that fracture was healed *not* by the Crown, not by the
Crown's agents and officers, not by the machinery of the wardenships of the
march, not by the Percies and Nevilles (who retained a remarkably low profile
throughout the whole course of the affair) and not even by the northern gentry
themselves. For the Herons and the Maners, for the social harmony and
tranquillity of Northumberland, redemption came from elsewhere, in the
unlikely – we might now think – shape of a handful of monastic superiors
operating under the authority of an even smaller group of bishops and invoking
religious, supernatural, means to restore the *status quo*. Might it even be, to
return to the initial premise of this paper, that one of the main reasons why the
north of England was not too insoluble a political 'problem' in the fifteenth
century was that the northern Church and clergy fulfilled their stabilizing role

---

[31] For James Raine's remarkable memoir of his own childhood now see *A Raine Miscellany*, ed.
A. Marsden, SS, CC (1991).

[32] J. Raine, *The History and Antiquities of North Durham* (1852), p. 209.

more effectively here than anyone else? If the political history of the Lancastrian and Yorkist north is primarily (as I have suggested) one of successful containment of dangerous and disruptive pressures, could those ecclesiastics so disliked by James Raine nevertheless have been highly successful practitioners of containment themselves?

Although this may be an unanswerable – and therefore illegitimate – question, perhaps this paper should close by mentioning (however briefly, and among the scores of cognate issues that might and should be explored) three of the main religious themes we have seen present amidst the complexities of the Heron case. I refer, firstly, to the attention devoted in the north to masses for the dead; secondly, to the intervention of monastic prelates in secular affairs; and thirdly to the role of the northern bishop in politics. Of these three issues, it may still be dangerous to say anything of substance about the first. Masses and chantries of all types are probably better documented for the diocese of York (primarily in the probate and other registers deposited in the Borthwick Institute of Historical Research) than anywhere in the country. By contrast, to the north of the Tees and in Cumberland and Westmorland probate records are only too notable for their scarcity or absence. However, and pending the appearance of a detailed study of northern lay piety in the fifteenth century, a few provisional conclusions undoubtedly emerge. The north of England (in Musgrove's words) may have been a 'perimeter'; but all in all its richer inhabitants adopted the contemporary enthusiasm for the perpetual chantry with a fervour which would have been hard to match anywhere in the kingdom. London apart, there can have been no cathedral city in the realm which contained as many as the 150 or so perpetual chantries praying for the souls of northerners day after day in York when the new king, Richard III, rode into his city in September 1483.[33] Half a century earlier, and in the diocese of Durham, Thomas Langley had taken the unusual step of transforming the antiquated greater collegiate churches of Auckland, Lanchester and Chester-le-Street into what amounted to gigantic chantry churches; while in 1412 Ralph Neville,

---

[33] R.B. Dobson, 'The Foundation of Perpetual Chantries by the Citizens of Medieval York', *Studies in Church History*, IV (1967), pp. 22–38.

1st Earl of Westmorland, abandoned his plans to be buried in Durham Cathedral and instead transformed the parish church of Staindrop into a chantry college of no less than a warden, eight chaplains, four clerks, six esquires, six yeomen and six poor men.[34] Seventy years later, Richard of Gloucester's penchant for the collegiate chantry church (notably at Barnard Castle and at Middleham) needs no particular urging. It might also be argued (with tongue slightly in cheek) that perhaps the single most important consequence of the battle of Bosworth was to deprive York Minster from housing the most magnificent chantry chapel in medieval England.[35]

In one of the more interesting chapters of *North-Eastern England*, Professor Pollard has taken these arguments further and deeper, which happily absolves me from the need of trying to do so now. What comparatively little evidence there is certainly points to the exceptional intensity of many northerners' belief in the efficacy of endowed masses for the dead.[36] The implications of such devotional intensity (which clearly still needs testing wherever it can be tested) must naturally have been very considerable, not least on that most seriously neglected of all subjects in fifteenth-century northern ecclesiastical history, the composition of the parish clergy. Whom did John Maners actually expect to sing the 500 (or 1,300) requiem masses for William Heron of Ford in 1431 and 1432? In the absence of more than a handful of the province of York's *Fasti Parochiales* volumes in print, it might be pointless even to guess. However, it seems not at all unlikely that the ecclesiastical deaneries of the north will come to reveal intriguingly different patterns of clerical status, themselves based on highly different types of patron (from Yorkshire magnates in the deanery of Craven to Durham Cathedral monks in Howdenshire and the east coast of Northumberland).[37] What the evidence does not seem to prove – with a few

[34] Storey, *Thomas Langley*, pp. 188–90.

[35] Dobson, 'Richard III and the Church of York', in Griffiths and Sherborne (eds), *Kings and Nobles*, pp. 143–7.

[36] Pollard, *North-Eastern England*, pp. 173–97.

[37] *Fasti Parochiales, Vol. IV: Parishes in the Deanery of Craven*, eds N.K.M. Gurney and C. Clay, Yorkshire Archaeological Society, Record Series, CXXXIII (1971); Dobson, *Durham Priory*, pp. 144–72.

exceptions like the pockets of religious atavism recently revealed to us on the Borders by Professor Goodman – is the existence of that pauperized and near-illiterate northern parish clergy so beloved of (yet again) southern Tudor bishops.[38] All in all, the clerical affinities of the fifteenth-century north cast a fairly fine and thorough net over their parishes, probably capable of 'containing' most of the political and social pressures present at the local level too. If anything, to judge from the startling increase in recruitment of the northern clergy to Oxford and (especially) Cambridge during the course of the century, these clerical cosinages may have become more influential as well as more educated as the middle ages came to a close.[39]

About a second important theme to emerge from the Heron case – the influence of monastic superiors in reconciling lay disputes – this is not the occasion to say much. Thirty years ago, in the introduction to his book on *The English Reformation* Professor A.G. Dickens suggested that 'if the secular clergy have received too little notice from historians of the Reformation, the regulars have perhaps received too much'.[40] A generation later, and now that the great and benevolent shadow of the late Dom David Knowles is beginning to lift, I think that we can begin to see how misplaced that judgement might be. On the whole, it now seems clear that eleventh-hour monasticism in England has been subjected to the wrong – or at least the less interesting and significant – questions. No doubt John Wessington was an exceptional prior of an exceptional monastery, the English Zion itself; but his involvement in the Heron dispute may serve to represent a double development common throughout the monastic life of the late medieval north. First, as the religious houses of northern England were transformed from unitary houses of divine worship into complexes of many mansions, they found more space (in the monastic infirmary, in abbot's and prior's lodgings) to become what might be called the most important 'leisure centres' available to many of the influential local lords

---

[38] A. Goodman, 'Religion and Warfare in the Anglo-Scottish Marches', in R. Bartlett and A. MacKay (eds), *Medieval Frontier Societies* (Oxford, 1989), pp. 245–66.

[39] J. Taylor, 'The Diocese of York and the University Connexion, 1300–1520', *NH*, XXV (1989), pp. 39–59.

[40] A.G. Dickens, *The English Reformation* (London, 1964), p. 51.

and gentry of the north, like the Stanleys at Lytham, the Scropes at Easby, the Ogles at Holy Island, the Homes at Coldingham.[41] No doubt such relationships, often hinging around the tenure of the office of chief steward of a monastery, were frequently based on the acquisitive appetites as much as the religious inclinations of such gentlemen; nor need one labour the point that they carried insidious dangers to the monasteries in question. However, the intervention of the abbot or prior as peacemaker in local lay feuds became an increasingly valued feature of such personal relationships. Paradoxically enough, for a northern abbot or prior who wanted to exercise power outside his monastery, the possibilities were probably never greater than they were by the late fifteenth century. What better example than that client of Richard of Gloucester, Richard Bell, a monk of Durham who almost took over the alien priory of Holy Trinity York in the 1440s, went on to become Prior of Durham from 1464 to 1478 and ended his life as Bishop of Carlisle in 1478–95.[42] Nor was Richard Bell an isolated figure. Indeed he was only the first of the three members of the regular clergy who ruled the diocese of Carlisle for all but six of the forty-two years between 1478 and 1520. By 1500 or so (when Abbot William Sever, a monk of St Mary's, York, became Bishop of Durham) it may have seemed to the intelligent (but mistaken) contemporary observer that the future of the north of England belonged to the monk bishop.

Such an aborted prospect must not however be allowed to detract from the real and neglected importance of the twenty-four prelates (seven Archbishops of York, seven Bishops of Durham and eleven Bishops of Carlisle) who ruled the northern church during the course of the fifteenth century. These two dozen members of the episcopal bench were a motley and at first sight unprepossessing body; and it is doubtful whether any of them found their position a particularly relaxing one. Although a bare majority of the twenty-four were born in the north, in spirit they were nearly all *homines australes*,

---

[41] Dobson, *Durham Priory*, pp. 314, 321–6, 335–41.

[42] R.B. Dobson, 'Richard Bell, Prior of Durham (1464–78) and Bishop of Carlisle (1478–95)', *TCWAAS*, new ser, LXV (1965), pp. 183–221.

deliberately appointed to support the royal cause.[43] Not always successful in their struggles to remain neutral (as the careers of Richard Scrope, George Neville and Thomas Rotherham will always remind us) they were under no illusion that it was their major duty to ensure that 'peace and good rule might be had in this northern country'. All in all, and at times to their own surprise, they were remarkably successful. In particular, and here between the waters of Tees and Tyne, the palatinate of Durham may in many ways have been a legal fiction – but it was nevertheless a steady source of influence and good lordship. If we ask who were the most effective and least dangerous rulers of the north towards the end of the Middle Ages, can there be any doubt? Those prizes must surely go to Bishop Thomas Langley at the beginning of the fifteenth century and Bishop Richard Fox at its close. Fox, the most creative English diplomat vis-à-vis the Scots in the later Middle Ages, has many claims to our memory, not least perhaps because of his precocious view that 'too long continuance in those places at Oxford and Cambridge is an infallible sign of lack of either friends or of learning'.[44] But it may be even more appropriate for us to remember that he was the first Bishop of Durham to begin to transform this 'castle 'gainst the Scot' into the enjoyable residence that the Richard III Society – like James Boswell – will find it to be.

[43] Le Neve, *Fasti Ecclesiae Anglicanae, 1300–1541, VI. Northern Province*, ed. B. Jones (1963), pp. 3–6, 98–9, 108–9.

[44] A.B. Emden, *A Biographical Dictionary of the University of Oxford to A.D. 1500* (3 vols, Oxford, 1957–9), II, pp. 715–19.

2

'ANCIENT INDICTMENTS' FOR THE NORTH OF ENGLAND, 1461–1509[1]

Rosemary C.E. Hayes

'Ancient Indictments' is the Public Record Office's rather archaic title for a class of records of King's Bench, the central criminal court of medieval England.[2] This class comprises indictments originally made against suspected criminals outside the court which were brought into it, either on the initiative of the officials who heard the original indictment, or in response to a writ issued from the central royal administration. For the period and counties described in this paper, some 56 per cent of the indictments from the reigns of Edward IV and Richard III came in as a result of writs, as did

[1] The research for this paper was conducted while I was working on a project directed by Professor Anthony Tuck of Bristol University and Dr Richard Hoyle, now of the University of Central Lancashire. The project's aim is to produce a calendar of ancient indictments for the north of England for the Yorkist and early Tudor period (1461–1509) which, it is hoped, will be published by the Surtees Society. Both I and the project's directors are grateful to the British Academy for funding the research; and I would like to thank Professor Tuck and Dr Hoyle for permission to use the results of some of this research ahead of the calendar's publication. This paper is not, and does not attempt to be, an analysis of crime and/or society in the north during the period under review. It can only claim to be an examination of one source for that subject. By contrast, the records examined by Philippa C. Maddern for her study of *Violence and Social Order: East Anglia, 1422–1442* (Oxford, 1992) include, in addition to the 'Ancient Indictments', King's Bench plea rolls, assize and gaol delivery rolls, manor and borough court rolls, petitions, privy council and town records, letters and literature (pp. 21–2).

[2] It was, of course, more than this. For the court's history during this period, see M. Blatcher, *The Court of King's Bench, 1450–1550. A Study in Self-Help* (1978); and E. Powell, *Kingship, Law and Society. Criminal Justice in the Reign of Henry V* (Oxford, 1989), pp. 54–6. Powell discusses the various categories of indictment in *ibid.*, pp. 66–74. For an early discussion of the class, see B.H. Putnam, 'The Ancient Indictments in the Public Record Office', *EHR*, XXIX (1914), pp. 479–505; and, for the archivist's view, see C.A.F. Meekings, 'King's Bench Files', in J. Baker (ed.), *Legal Records and the Historian* (1978), pp. 97–139.

about 30 per cent of those from Henry VII's reign.[3] A large proportion of these writs were probably issued at the instance of the victims of the alleged crime who were anxious to ensure that their wrongs were avenged; still others may have been issued at the behest of defendants who had secured pardons; and a relatively few may have resulted from the initiative of King's Bench officials, eager to try all serious crimes.[4]

Two main kinds of writ were used, both of which could be issued either from Chancery or more directly from King's Bench. The first was the well-known writ of *certiorari* which could be issued at any stage of proceedings, usually from the king's Chancery. It was this writ which was perhaps most likely to have been initiated by the victim.[5] The less well known writ of *terminari* was usually issued directly from King's Bench, and seems to have gradually overtaken *certiorari* in importance for bringing unfinished cases into the court.[6] A third writ, usually sent to coroners, was the writ *per te,* or *vos, mitti* which followed the form:

> King to coroner '*volentes certis de causis quoddam indictamentum coram te super visum corporis AB nuper captum unde CD et alii in eodem indictamento nominati indicati sunt ut dicitur coram nobis* per te mitti *tibi precipimus quod indictamentum predictum cum*

[3] The writs of *certiorari* and *terminari* are discussed in B.H. Putnam, *Proceedings before the Justices of the Peace in the Fourteenth and Fifteenth Centuries: Edward III to Richard III* (1938), pp. lxiv–lxxvi. See also Maddern, *Violence and Social Order*, pp. 43–6, for a discussion of *certiorari* and its role in bringing cases into King's Bench. Like others (including R.F. Hunnisett, *The Medieval Coroner* (Cambridge, 1961), pp. 78, 99, 195–9, 201), she does not distinguish it from the writs of *terminari* and *per te mitti*; nor does she consider the possibility of King's Bench officials initiating it.

[4] Dr Hoyle certainly considers that the main impetus for issuing these writs came from outside the court. For writs obtained by defendants with pardons, see Putnam, *Proceedings*, pp. lxxii–lxxv. Nevertheless, the statement that 'the Rex side contained only those cases which filtered up, on *certiorari* or *mandamus*, in order to be pardoned or quashed' is too strong (D.J. Guth, 'Enforcing Late-Medieval Law: Patterns in Litigation During Henry VII's Reign', in Baker (ed.), *Legal Records and the Historian*, p. 88).

[5] For a sample writ of *certiorari* for removal into Chancery, see J.H. Baker, *An Introduction to English Legal History* (1979), pp. 445–6.

[6] For an example of this writ, issuing from Chancery, see Putnam, *Proceedings*, pp. 51–2.

omnibus illud tangentibus adeo plene et integre prout coram te nuper captum fuit et penes te iam residet est dictum quibuscumque nominibus predictus CD et alii nuncupentur in eidem coram nobis sub sigillo tuo in crastino Sancti Johannis Baptiste ubicumque tunc fuimus in Anglia mittas una cum hoc brevi ut ulterius inde fieri faciamus quod de iure et secundum legem et consuetudines regni nostri Anglie fore viderimus faciendum'. Attested by the Chief Justice at Westminster.[7]

Despite the distinction in wording and origin between these writs, their effect was the same: to bring indictments into King's Bench for determination there; hence, perhaps, the fact that most scholars refer to them collectively as writs of *certiorari*, without distinguishing between the different types. In addition, a small proportion of the indictments were brought in by writ of error.[8]

The indictments maintain their original arrangement in files in accordance with the four legal terms, Michaelmas, Hilary, Easter and Trinity, during which the court sat. For Edward IV's reign, seventy-nine of a potential eighty-eight termly files survive.[9] At least three of the missing files, those for Trinity term 1464 and for Easter and Trinity terms 1479, can be explained by the failure of the court to sit because of plague in London; and at Easter 1471 there was no

---

7 Translation of writ *per te mitti*: 'Requiring, for certain causes, a certain indictment lately taken before you at the view of the body of AB, in which, it is said, CD and others named in the same indictment are indicated, *to be sent by you* before us, we instruct you to send, under your seal together with this writ, the said indictment with all things touching it, as far wholly and purely as, it is said, it was lately taken before you and now remains with you, with whatever names with which the said CD and others are named in it, before us, on the morrow of the feast of St John the Baptist, wherever in England we might then be, so that we might have done further, in respect thereof, what will then seem to us to need to be done of right and according to the law and customs of our realm of England.' Taken from KB 9/303, m. 10. Unless otherwise stated, all references to original documents relate to records in the PRO.

8 The one case relating to Lancashire appears thanks to a writ of error addressed to Reginald Bray, chancellor of the County Palatine, on the complaint that one Miles Alston had been outlawed erroneously (KB 9/427, mm. 30–3). For a sample writ of error, see Baker, *Introduction*, p. 445. Its use is discussed in Putnam, *Proceedings*, pp. lxiv–lxxiv.

9 KB 8/1, KB 9/293; KB 9/295–318, KB 9/321–348; KB 9/350–363, KB 9/942–948, KB 9/992, KB 9/999, KB 9/1052–1053.

session because of the civil war.[10] Two files, made during the Readeption, are, in fact, described as being of the forty-ninth, or first, year of Henry VI.[11] Two files survive from the short reign of Edward V,[12] and all nine remain for Richard III's reign.[13] At least ninety of a potential ninety-four survive for Henry VII's reign.[14] Most of these files are in the Public Record Office, class KB 9: 'King's Bench Ancient Indictments', although one file for Edward IV's reign and four for Henry VII's reign have strayed into KB 8: 'The *Baga de Secretis*'.[15] As well as the termly files, KB 9 also contains files of indictments made before commissions of *oyer and terminer*. Two of these from this period relate to Yorkshire. One, dating from 1478, is described in some detail below. The other concerns the 1489 Yorkshire rebellion and is outside the scope of this paper.[16]

The files have been examined for cases relating to the north of England, defined as the counties of Cumberland, Durham, Lancashire, Northumberland, Westmorland and Yorkshire. In practice, the bishop of Durham's liberty meant that no indictments were found for that county;[17] and, similarly, only one case, brought into King's Bench by writ of error, concerned the County Palatine of Lancashire.[18] Some 500 relevant indictments were found, fewer than 100 of which related to the Yorkist period, the rest dating from Henry VII's reign (Table 1). In

---

[10] KB 27/813, KB 27/871, note in PRO list for KB 27 (the *Coram Rege* rolls); Blatcher, *King's Bench*, p. 23.

[11] KB 9/293; KB 9/1052.

[12] KB 9/364–365.

[13] KB 9/366–367; KB 9/949–953; KB 9/1000–1001.

[14] KB 8/3/1–4; KB 9/369–380; KB 9/382–389; KB 9/391–449; KB 9/959–962; KB 9/1060–1062. Dr David Crook of the PRO tells me that at least one more has been found but it has yet (October 1994) to appear in the searchroom lists.

[15] KB 8/1 (Trinity term 1477); KB 8/3/1–4 (Michaelmas 1500–Trinity 1501).

[16] KB 9/349; KB 9/381. For the career of the murdered earl of Northumberland and analysis of the 1489 commission, see M.A. Hicks, 'Dynastic Change and Northern Society: the Career of the Fourth Earl of Northumberland, 1470–89', *NH*, XIV (1978), pp. 78–107; and *idem*, 'The Yorkshire Rebellion of 1489 Reconsidered', *NH*, XXII (1986). Both essays are reprinted in M.A. Hicks, *Richard III and his Rivals* (1991), pp. 365–418.

[17] K. Emsley and C.M. Fraser, *The Courts of the County Palatine of Durham from Earliest Times to 1971* (Durham County Local History Society, 1984).

[18] KB 9/427, mm. 30–3.

order to assess what proportion of the whole this represents, some calculations have been made based on the number of membranes concerned with the northern counties as a proportion of the total number of membranes.[19] For the Yorkist period, there are a total of 6,832 in the term files, of which only 145, or just over 2 per cent, relate to the northern counties. For Richard III, the numbers are 479 membranes of which twelve, or 2.5 per cent, concern the north. However, for Henry VII, the total is 6,534 membranes (slightly fewer than the Yorkist total for a very similar period) of which some 575, about 9 per cent, relate to the north.

Thus, during Henry VII's reign, the north not only produced a larger total number of indictments than it had done during the Yorkist period, it also produced a far higher proportion of the whole country's indictments. Why was this? Was it because the north of England was more law-abiding during the Yorkist period, a theory that might appeal to those convinced of the benign influence of Richard, Duke of Gloucester, in the area? Or was it, rather, because the north was *less* under royal control, particularly during the early part of Edward's reign, thus preventing the king's officials from acting properly and sending the results of their work into King's Bench? Perhaps the local courts were not fully functional in all areas. Did Richard's hegemony in the north after 1471 mean that he and his council dealt *directly* with cases that might otherwise have gone into King's Bench? Or again, did stronger government of the country as a whole under Henry VII mean that the south became proportionately more peaceful while a greater number of cases came from the more closely controlled north?[20] Further research is needed before a satisfactory answer to these questions is reached.

[19] Membranes rather than actual indictments were used in this calculation to make use of the fact that the PRO lists record the total number of membranes per file. Each indictment may cover more than one membrane and, similarly, each membrane may concern more than one indictment. However, most membranes are concerned with only one county.

[20] R. Virgoe, 'The Crown, Magnates and Local Government in Fifteenth-Century East Anglia' in J.R.L. Highfield and R. Jeff (eds), *The Crown and Local Communities in England and France in the Fifteenth Century* (Gloucester, 1981), pp. 72–87, touches on 'the increasing control of the crown in the regions through the employment of a more extensive and efficient group of professional administrators' (pp. 81–2). For the development of Henry's power in the north-east, see A.J. Pollard, *North-Eastern England During the Wars of the Roses: Lay Society, War and Politics, 1450–1500* (Oxford, 1990), pp. 367–96, 404.

Table 1

NUMBER OF INDICTMENTS IN FIVE-YEARLY INTERVALS, 1461–1509

Regnal years	Total number of indictments	Number brought in by writ	Number delivered to Justices of Gaol Delivery
1–5 Edward IV one term cancelled because of pestilence	7	3	–
6–10 Edward IV 2 files missing	14	9	–
11–15 Edward IV 1 term cancelled because of civil war 3 files missing	20	11	–
16–20 Edward IV 2 terms cancelled because of pestilence	29	15	–
21 Edward IV – 3 Richard III	19	12	–
1–5 Henry VII 1 file missing	25	16	–
6–10 Henry VII 1 file missing	42	16	14
11–15 Henry VII 2 files missing	79	21	39
16–20 Henry VII	134	38	67
21–24 Henry VII	131	30	51
Totals	500	171	171

Leaving aside the rest of England, what information can be gained from the indictments studied? Turning first to the geographical origins of the indictments (Table 2a), it is not surprising that, throughout the period, cases from the largest county, Yorkshire, and, within Yorkshire, from the West Riding, predominated.[21] During Edward IV's reign the next largest group of cases, although a long way after Yorkshire, came from appeals of king's approvers. These were convicted felons who turned informer in the hope of saving their necks. These men were held in the Marshalsea and gave evidence to a King's Bench coroner, who then passed their indictment to King's Bench.[22] During Henry VII's reign the total number of such appeals drops from ten to three, the last one being recorded in 1489, a reflection of the rapid decline in the use of this system in the fifteenth century.[23]

The other most notable changes in Henry VII's reign are an increase in the number of cases from Cumberland and Northumberland,[24] the brief appearance of Lancashire mentioned earlier, and a large number of cases concerning Westmorland, which had not appeared once during the Yorkist period. The sudden prominence of Westmorland is not easily explained. There are three possible suggestions. One is that the increase in return of coroners' inquests, discussed below, which certainly accounts for most of the increase in numbers from Cumberland, revealed cases that might not have come to the

[21] As well as the three ridings and the city of York, indictments came from the towns of Beverley, Doncaster, Hull, Pontefract and Scarborough and from the liberties of the Archbishop of York, in Beverley, Otley and Ripon, and of St Mary's Abbey, York. There were also some Yorkshire indictments undifferentiated as to riding, particularly in Henry VII's reign.

[22] F.C. Hamil, 'The King's Approvers: a Chapter in the History of English Criminal Law', *Speculum*, XI (1936), pp. 238–58; Hunnisett, *Medieval Coroner*, pp. 69–74. Because these indictments originated from central as opposed to local officials they will not be included in the final calendar. I have considered them here, however, because their cases seem to me to be germane to the question of crime in the north during the period.

[23] Hamil, *Speculum*, pp. 257–8.

[24] The figures for Cumberland include indictments from Carlisle and the Earl of Northumberland's Cockermouth liberty; Northumberland includes indictments from Newcastle, the Earl of Essex's Tynedale liberty, Tynemouth Priory's liberty and the view of frankpledge of the Earl of Northumberland; Westmorland includes indictments from the liberty of St Mary's Abbey, York, and the view of frankpledge of the Countess of Richmond.

Table 2a

SOURCE OF INDICTMENTS: (A) GEOGRAPHICAL

(NB: 'Appeals' are not assigned to a county)

Origin of indictment	Yorkist kings	Henry VII
Appeals	10	3
Direct return to King's Bench	–	1
Cumberland	2	50
Lancashire	–	1
Northumberland	5	29
Westmorland	–	61
Yorkshire: East Riding	5	38
Yorkshire: North Riding	7	26
Yorkshire: West Riding	44	117
Yorkshire: York City	7	8
Yorkshire: Other	9	77
Totals	89	411

notice of King's Bench during the earlier period. Another possibility is that the figures, like those for Northumberland, reflect numerous complaints against sheriffs and other royal officials that may not have come to light during a period of more distant control of the north by the Yorkist kings; or were, perhaps, not necessary until the attainted Cliffords returned to their former control of the shrievalty under Henry VII.[25] Finally, Westmorland seems to have suffered proportionately more than other counties from various kinds of riotous behaviour, perhaps also a reflection of jurisdictional conflicts within the county and dissatisfaction with local royal officials.

[25] R.L. Storey, *The Reign of Henry VII* (1968), p. 142; and see below, p. 110.

The judicial origins of indictments varied as much as their geographical ones (Table 2b).[26] A significant proportion, nearly three quarters during the Yorkist period, and nearly a half during Henry VII's reign, originated in the activities of the justices of the peace.[27] These indictments are variously recorded as having been made at sessions of the peace, special sessions of the peace, or during inquests held before justices of the peace, whether during or outside sessions not being entirely clear. They reveal details of seventeen sessions for Cumberland between 1474 and 1507; two sessions for Lancashire in 1485; thirteen for Northumberland between 1475 and 1507; thirty-one for Westmorland between 1493 and 1508; twenty-eight for the East Riding of Yorkshire between 1475 and 1508; twenty-seven for the North Riding between 1467 and 1508; and 136 sessions for the West Riding between 1461 and 1508.[28] Not only do the indictments give the date of the sessions and where they were held, they also record which justices were sitting, who acted as jurors and which justice, or clerk, of the peace responded to writs issued from Westminster, and delivered the indictments into King's Bench.

These records, then, can be used to supplement the kind of work that has already been done on the composition of commissions of peace[29] with information on who were the active commissioners and what they were doing. Indeed, it should be stressed, given the almost complete dearth of session rolls for the period,[30] how important these indictments are as a source of information

[26] Cf. Maddern, *Violence and Social Order*, table 2.2, for some rather different figures for East Anglia, 1422–42.

[27] Cf. the figure of 90 per cent suggested for the reigns of Henry VI and Edward IV by Putnam (*Proceedings*, p. lxiv).

[28] These figures assume that undefined inquisitions before JPs took place in sessions. If this assumption is wrong, the figures are considerably reduced; but the indictments still give evidence of justices acting as such on this number of occasions.

[29] For example, C.E. Arnold, 'The Commission of the Peace in the West Riding of Yorkshire' in A.J. Pollard (ed.), *Property and Politics: Essays in Later Medieval English History* (Gloucester, 1984), pp. 116–38.

[30] Two survive from Edward VI's reign, for Southampton in 1475, and for Worcestershire in 1477; none survive for 1483–1509 (Putnam, *Proceedings*, pp. 237–74, 424–34). There is also a roll of presentments before the Durham JPs for 1471–3, now published in *Durham Quarter Sessions Rolls 1471–1625*, ed. C.M. Fraser, SS, CXCIX (1991).

Table 2b
SOURCE OF INDICTMENTS: (B) JUDICIAL

Judicial origin	Yorkist kings	Henry VII
Appeals	10	3
Commissions of peace	63	203
Coroners' inquests	10	175
Sheriff's tourn	3	1
Justices for sewers	2	–
Confession of felon in sanctuary to coroner	1	–
Special Commissions	–	5
Justices of Gaol Delivery	–	11
Bills of Presentment	–	10
Court of view of frankpledge	–	2
Delivery by King's attorney	–	1
Totals	89	411

on the activities of justices of the peace.[31] For example, the indictments reveal that Richard, Duke of Gloucester, sat at the North Riding session at Bedale on 6 October 1472; and on three occasions at West Riding sessions at Wakefield and Wetherby between 15 September and 19 December 1479.[32]

The second major source of indictments is the coroner's inquest which had to be held 'upon the bodies of all those who died unnaturally, suddenly or in prison, or about whose death there might or was said to have been suspicious circumstances'.[33] The proportion of indictments originating from this source rose from about 11 per cent in the Yorkist period to 43 per cent, almost equal to

[31] It is, therefore, rather surprising that, despite stressing the dearth of appropriate sources, the class does not appear to have been used for J.R. Lander, *English Justices of the Peace 1461–1509* (Gloucester, 1989). By contrast, they are noted as a source in Putnam, *Proceedings*, p. xvii.

[32] KB 9/330, m. 23; KB 9/351, m. 77; KB 9/352, m. 60; KB 9/355, mm. 28–9; KB 9/356, m. 29.

[33] Hunnisett, *Medieval Coroner*, p. 9.

the commissions of the peace, under Henry VII. This was the direct result of a statute of 1487 instructing all coroners to deliver all indictments for homicide to the justices of gaol delivery, with the added inducement that failure to do so would incur a fine of £5.[34] The justices then tried all suspects who were in gaol and passed all other indictments to King's Bench. The increase in numbers of indictments during Henry VII's reign, most marked for the counties of Cumberland, Northumberland and Westmorland, is almost directly in proportion to the numbers delivered by the coroners to the justices of gaol delivery (Table 1).

Other sources of indictments provide a very small proportion of the total (Table 2b): in descending order, throughout the period, thirteen came from appeals of king's approvers, eleven direct from justices of gaol delivery, ten are undefined bills of presentment, seven came from special commissions, including two from the justices of sewers,[35] four from the sheriff's tourn, two from the courts of view of frankpledge of the Earl of Northumberland and the Countess of Richmond, and one each from delivery by the king's attorney and as a result of a confession, made to a coroner, by a felon in sanctuary.[36]

Much as the indictments reveal about the administrative and judicial history of England, their main content is, of course, information on the activities of the king's subjects, many of whom would not appear in the records of the realm were it not for their criminal acts. Except insofar as the indictments dating from Henry VII's reign provide a contrast, what follows is mainly based on the indictments dating from the Yorkist period (Table 3).[37]

Over a third of these indictments relate to theft of some kind. Of the thirty or so cases of what may be described as 'simple theft', eighteen concern livestock,

[34] 3 Hen. VII, c.2; Hunnisett, *Medieval Coroner*, pp. 115–16, 121–2. See also M. MacDonald and T.R. Murphy, *Sleepless Souls. Suicide in Early Modern England* (Oxford, 1990), pp. 24–5.

[35] For some discussion of the use of such *ad hoc* commissions in the period, see Virgoe, 'Crown, Magnates and Local Government' in Highfield and Jeffs (eds), *The Crown and Local Communities*, pp. 80–1.

[36] For confessions before abjuration of the realm, see Hunnisett, *Medieval Coroner*, pp. 37–54.

[37] Discrepancies between numbers of indictments and numbers of crimes are explained by the fact that one indictment may contain details of more than one crime; and also some crimes produced more than one indictment.

Table 3
INDICTMENTS: 1461–85

Crime	Number of indictments	Percentage of whole
Treason	5	4
Murder	21	17.5
Assault	13	11
Rape	4	3.5
Highway robbery	11	9
Burglary	11	9
Theft	30	25
Expulsion	11	9
Damage	4	3.5
Other	10	8.5
Total	120	100

twelve include objects, and six involve cash. The longest list of goods stolen occurs in a case against seventeen men including three merchants, Edward Blaxton, Thomas Faucus and Robert Clerk, a gentleman, Roland Bere, Brother Robert Crossenside of the Newcastle Austin friary, and eleven assorted tradesmen, who were indicted at Newcastle in 1475 of feloniously despoiling the Yorkshire merchant Laurence Swan of three robes, 'a doblet', two ells each of sanguine and russet woollen cloth, two black 'fresed tippetz', one 'sangwyn bonet', one 'scarlet jaket', eighteen and a half ells of Holland linen, two pairs of thigh boots, three pairs of shoes, one 'wesshyngtowell', two razors, three silk belts harnessed with silver, two rosaries, two silver spoons, a silver ring, a bowl called 'a nutte', a plough share, a lancet, a saw, a spear, a spear head, and other iron tools, all worth £6 8s; a list which serves to introduce one to descriptions and values of all kinds of everyday, and more unusual, objects that might not otherwise be met with.[38]

[38] KB 9/343, m. 34.

There were eleven cases of burglary, some involving violence. For example, John Wrigelyngton, gentleman, and Thomas Knolles, labourer, both late of Cawood in Yorkshire, were indicted at Wakefield in 1467 for breaking in at night to the house of Isabella Watson, a widow, seizing her and Joanna Lytster, her servant, in their beds, tying their hands behind them with cords, and stealing from Isabella 29s 8d in cash, a silk belt harnessed with silver worth 8s, a robe of 'marey colour' cloth worth 6s 8d, and three sheets, and half a cloak of azure cloth, each worth 5s, and, from Joanna, another azure robe worth 5s, a green tunic worth 3s 4d and two lawn veils, worth 16d.[39]

The appeals of approvers reveal a number of men who in later days might have been described as highwaymen. The list of sums they admitted stealing indicates that undetected highway robbery was potentially a very lucrative, if dangerous, career. For example, in 1473, William Robinson, alias Robert Robertson, of York, labourer, confessed that in December 1470 he and two Northallerton butchers had attacked an unknown man on Northallerton moor and stolen £55 8s cash; in October 1469 he and two fletchers had taken £700 from an unknown man walking between Grinton and Marrick Abbey in Swaledale; and in May 1472, with a Nottinghamshire labourer, he had attacked an unknown canon between Pontefract and Wentbridge and stolen a casket worth 2s containing £400 cash.[40] These are enormous sums, comparable to the entire annual income of major landholders.[41]

The next largest group of crimes, after theft, are the twenty-one murders. Many were committed by more than one assailant. Such a case, also exhibiting gentle involvement, and perhaps reflecting something of the politics of the period, was revealed by the inquest taken within the Earl of Essex's liberty of Tynedale in Northumberland on the body of Richard Tweddall. This reveals that, on 23 June 1476, Sir Henry Percy, late of Bamburgh, ten Northumberland

[39] KB 9/317, m. 12.

[40] KB 9/334, m. 152. A marginal note indicates that, despite his appeal, Robinson was sentenced to be hanged. This was the fate of approvers who failed to secure conviction of all those they accused (Hamil, *Speculum*, p. 238). This indictment is printed below, p. 191.

[41] For example, in the fifteenth century, the temporalities of the bishop of Norwich produced an annual income of between £600 and £800 (Norfolk Record Office: EST 15/1/1–2).

esquires and gentlemen, six named yeomen, two named Scotsmen, with 'other unknown Scottish enemies of the king', and 200 others, attacked Tweddall. On the orders of Percy and Giles Thornton esquire, Robert Rogerson, yeoman, struck the back of Tweddall's head with a sword worth 6s; Cuthbert Ogle, gentleman, shot him in the chest with an arrow worth 2d; Thomas Cramlington, gentleman,[42] struck the left side of his head with a sword worth 10s; Edward Carre, gentleman, struck his head with a sword worth 8s; Thomas Galon, yeoman, struck the top of his head with a sword worth 5s; and William Lyon, yeoman, struck his left shin with a sword worth 2s, nearly amputating his foot. As was customary in indictments against multiple persons for murder, all these wounds were described as mortal. Somewhat surprisingly, after such an attack, Tweddall lived for a further three days.[43]

In addition to the twenty-one murders were thirteen assaults, all of which were described, in the common form, as resulting in the victims' lives being despaired of. Richard, Duke of Gloucester, heard the indictment of two of these cases: one in 1472 when Nicholas, Christopher and William Hedlam, gentlemen and servants of the prior of Guisborough in Cleveland, together with sixteen others, ambushed and attacked Sir Richard Strangways, his brother Philip, and two of his servants, injuring Philip with an arrow in his right knee and the two servants with arrows in their chests. Capturing one of the servants, John Preston, they complained to him, 'alas thooreson thi maister Sir Richard Strangways uscaped'. They then made off with two of Philip's spaniels.[44] In 1479, Gloucester received indictments against Sir William and Edward Redman and 100 others who had attacked Sir William Gascoigne at Harewood and were only prevented from killing him by the timely intervention of the town's people.[45] His interest in this case is not surprising: Gascoigne was a leading member of the Yorkshire gentry,

[42] Probably the man who, as heir to George Cramlington, was given custody of the manor of Newsham in Northumberland in 1462 (*Calendar of Fine Rolls, 1461–1471* (1949), pp. 70, 80).

[43] KB 9/343, mm. 70–1. A Giles Thornton, esquire (the same man?) was murdered on 29 July 1477 at Windsor Castle by Thomas Lumley esquire, late of Westminster, abetted by Sir George Lumley of Northumberland (KB 9/345, mm. 8–9).

[44] KB 9/330, m. 23.

[45] KB 9/355, mm. 28–9.

deputy steward of Knaresborough, and, for most of the period, an active JP,[46] and Edward Redman was a lawyer in Gloucester's own service. His action clearly did not stand against him. In 1483, Gloucester appointed him to the quorum of the West Riding commission of the peace.[47]

Further assaults against the person included four rapes. In 1485, a gentleman, Christopher Wentworth, was accused, among other crimes, of breaking into the house of a widow, Alice Scargill, whose surname suggests that she was probably a gentlewoman. He then carried her off to West Burton where he raped her.[48] Given their status, it is possible that this abduction was committed in an attempt to acquire Alice's property along with her person.[49] Nevertheless, Wentworth's indictment and subsequent imprisonment in Pontefract Castle, from which he later escaped, would seem to indicate that Alice was not a willing party to his plans. All three others accused of rape were clerks. Earlier in the century, complaints were made in convocation and parliament about the vexing of clergy by making false indictments for rape against them. It seems possible this was still the case in the Yorkist period.[50]

Apart from simple assault which was a trespass, all the above crimes were felonies and thus punishable by death.[51] One of the largest groups of trespasses

[46] Pollard, *North-Eastern England*, p. 127. At the time of the attack he was not a JP, having been removed in 1475 until his re-appointment in 1481 (Arnold, 'The Commission', in Pollard (ed.), *Property and Politics*, pp. 125–6). He was a retainer and brother-in-law of the Earl of Northumberland (Hicks, *NH* (1978), p. 87).

[47] Arnold, 'The Commission', in Pollard (ed.), *Property and Politics*, p. 127.

[48] KB 9/952, m. 38.

[49] Cf. E.W. Ives, ' "Agaynst taking awaye Women": the Inception and Operation of the Abduction Act of 1487', pp. 21–44 in E.W. Ives, R.J. Knecht, J.J. Scarisbrick (eds), *Wealth and Power in Tudor England. Essays presented to S.T. Bindoff* (1978), especially pp. 22–6; and Maddern, *Violence and Social Order*, pp. 100–3.

[50] R.L. Storey, 'Malicious Indictments of Clergy in the Fifteenth Century' in M.J. Franklin and C. Harper-Bill (eds), *Medieval Ecclesiastical Studies in Honour of Dorothy M. Owen* (Woodbridge, 1995), pp. 221–40.

[51] For the distinction between treason, felony and trespass, see Powell, *Kingship, Law, and Society*, pp. 50–1.

comprised the eleven cases of expelling people from their lands by main force.[52]
One of these indictments, made before Duke Richard in 1479, concerned
Christopher Stansfield of Bingley, gentleman, who, with many others, had
expelled a Richard Gibson from a messuage of twenty acres at Haworth.[53]
More dramatic was the case of John Slyngesby, esquire, who, with forty-four
others, in July 1467 expelled Brian Rouclyff, a member of the quorum of the
West Riding peace commission, from his manor of Cowthorpe. For thirteen
hours Slyngesby kept several members of the family, their guests and two
chaplains, imprisoned, at the same time beating one Thomas Greves, 'so that
his life was despaired of'.[54]

The five cases of treason comprised a king's approver, Lewis Spencer, who
admitted in 1467 that in 1461, at Pontefract, he had plotted with one Thomas
Wood, gentleman, to poison Edward IV; a case of clipping and washing coin by
the gentle Lever family of Bolton, including Giles, vicar of Bolton; and three
cases of forging English coinage.[55] The remaining ten cases include two inquests
on a prisoner dying in York prison; two complaints made before the
commissioners of sewers in Howdenshire that, by failing to maintain drainage,
the Duke of Suffolk had flooded his neighbours' lands; a complaint against a
York master mason for charging more than the statutory daily rate; and two
complaints made by Fountains Abbey: one about the destruction of its hedges in
the parish of Ripon by a large riotous assembly; and one that the steward of the
king's wapentake of Claro in Yorkshire was persecuting it by refusing to accept
the abbot's attorney in the case of a plea of debt.[56]

---

[52] This would seem to argue against the contention that 'very few indictments of forcible entry
appear in the records of the justices of the peace' (Bellamy, *Criminal Law*, p. 60). The development
of the law on forcible entry is traced in *ibid.*, pp. 65–84.

[53] KB 9/531, m. 77.

[54] KB 9/318, mm. 121–2; Arnold, 'The Commission', in Pollard (ed.), *Property and Politics*, p. 124.

[55] KB 9/316, m. 56; KB 8/1, m. 26; KB 9/355, mm. 55–6; KB 9/356, m. 29; KB 9/363, mm.
56–7.

[56] KB 9/355, m. 44; KB 9/363, mm. 21–2; KB 9/327, mm. 17–18; KB 9/334, m. 27; KB 9/325,
mm. 39–40; KB 9/952, mm. 51–2; KB 8/1, mm. 23–4. For three other cases concerning damage to
property, all relating to buildings, see KB 9/321, m. 114; KB 9/353, m. 63; KB 9/948, m. 39.

Of these 120 cases, thirty-eight, or nearly a third, including six murders, involved members of the gentry among the perpetrators, and thirteen, including one murder, involved the clergy. Notwithstanding the relatively few men of gentle status who came before the Durham JPs in 1473,[57] it would seem therefore that, at least for this period and area, the view that 'it is clear . . . that gentry violence rarely appeared in the courts. Few defendants in King's Bench . . . were of gentry status' is not completely unchallengeable.[58] As is clear from the descriptions of thefts and murders cited above, besides telling us who was alleged to have committed what crimes against whom, the indictments are full of incidental details relating to the objects and livestock stolen, together with their values and those of the weapons used, which one should not necessarily regard as fictitious. Such details should make the indictments of substantial interest to economic and social, as well as legal, historians.

There is not space here for a detailed discussion of the 400 or so indictments recorded during Henry VII's reign. As in the earlier period, there are a mass of murders, assaults, thefts and forcible entries. However, it may be of interest to mention briefly a few new types of cases which appear. Sixteen or so riotous assemblies reported suggest the possibility of disorder in the north after Henry's accession.[59] The large number of cases of sheriffs and other royal officials permitting felons to escape may indicate that, in the later years of Henry's reign, all was not well with local royal administration, particularly, it would seem, in Northumberland and Westmorland, both of which incurred special

---

[57] Pollard, *North-Eastern England*, pp. 168–9.

[58] Maddern, *Violence and Social Order*, p. 231. Cf. also Blatcher's claim that 'very few poor defendants made their way into the court'; and her calculation that clerks were about one in twenty of the defendants in Michaelmas 1490 (*King's Bench*, p. 51).

[59] Although none, apart from that which attacked the lands of Fountains Abbey, are recorded for the north during Edward IV's reign, they were not unknown during this period (J.G. Bellamy, 'Justice under the Yorkist Kings', *The American Journal of Legal History*, 9 (1965), pp. 135–55, especially pp. 136–8). Bellamy traces the development of the legal notion of 'riot' and procedures for dealing with it from the mid-fourteenth century, but he barely touches on riotous assemblies that were not connected with forcible entry (*Criminal Law*, pp. 54–89).

commissions.[60] After 1487, coroners' inquests report not only murders but also other untimely deaths. There were ten cases of suicide: three men and three women hanged themselves; two men cut their throats; one man jumped into a 'colepyt' and drowned himself; and one man (perhaps in a suicide pact?) killed his wife and then himself.[61] Incidental details of social life are revealed in the fifteen reported accidental deaths: eleven people drowned, including Brother John Wyllyby who fell into the river at Cockermouth, while drunk; two, including an eight-year-old boy, were killed by runaway carts; and two, including a woman who had fallen asleep behind the butts, died in archery accidents.[62]

Perhaps of most interest to political historians among the new cases in Henry VII's reign are those relating to livery and retaining.[63] Between 1486 and 1503, eight men were indicted for illegally handing out livery and badges.[64] These were Richard Radcliffe, esquire, of Todmorden, Lancashire,[65] Sir Thomas Metham, Sir Thomas Darcy, Sir John Hastings, Sir John Normanville, Thomas Newerk, gentleman, Sir Robert Aske, and the Earl of Derby's sons, Sir Edward and James Stanley, the future Bishop of Ely, who gave out their father's silver eagle's foot badges. Sir Edward was also accused of taking oaths of retaining.

[60] KB 9/440, m. 1, KB 9/441, m. 50a (Northumberland); KB 9/431, m. 1, KB 9/438, m. 105, KB 9/443, mm. 60–2 (Westmorland). It is, of course, possible, that these commissions indicate not that things were especially out of control but that the crown was making a special effort to keep a close eye on its officials. But see S.B. Chrimes, *Henry VII* (1972), pp. 186–7 and Storey, *Henry VII*, pp. 139–44, for complaints against, and measures relating to, sheriffs.

[61] KB 9/423, m. 51; KB 9/435, m. 66; KB 9/438, m. 64; KB 9/442, mm. 39, 40, 45; KB 9/448, m. 70; KB 9/960, mm. 20, 34. Suicide was a felony (Hunnisett, *Medieval Coroner*, p. 21). See also MacDonald and Murphy, *Sleepless Souls*, especially pp. 1, 24–8, 360–6.

[62] KB 9/423, mm. 9, 50; KB 9/427, m. 61; KB 9/438, m. 65; KB 9/442, mm. 43, 45; KB 9/446, mm. 80, 81.

[63] For measures against illegal livery and retaining during the Yorkist period, see Bellamy, *American Journal of Legal History*, pp. 151–4.

[64] KB 8/3/1, mm. 5–7; KB 9/382, m. 1; KB 9/391, mm. 13, 14; KB 9/434, mm. 19, 22, 38. Aske, Darcy, Hastings and Metham were all Yorkshire JPs (*CPR, 1476–1485*, p. 578; *CPR, 1485–1494*, p. 506, *CPR, 1494–1509*, pp. 666–8).

[65] He was a Pilkington supporter in 1478 (see below); and it is interesting that the indictment against him was delivered by John Saville (KB 9/391, mm. 13, 14).

Conversely, in 1502–3, there was a spate of indictments of people alleged to have donned liveries and badges against the wills of the appropriate lords. The men whose liveries were thus abused were the Earl of Derby (again), the Earl of Northumberland, Sir John Hotham, Sir Robert Constable and Sir Edward Savage, although one suspects that their complaints may have been a cover-up for more illegal retaining.[66]

Although it needs further and wider research to establish whether these cases of retaining relate to particular dissatisfaction with Henry VII's rule, these indictment files clearly suggest that the north of England was not a peaceful backwater during his reign; and that the offences covered by the so-called 'Star Chamber' Act were of real concern.[67] However, it would be wrong to conclude from the relative dearth of indictments for the Yorkist period that the area was comparatively peaceful during the reigns of the Yorkist kings in general, and the hegemony of Richard of Gloucester in particular. This caveat may be confirmed by a brief examination of the contents of the *oyer and terminer* file for 1478.[68]

On 5 September 1478 a commission was issued to Richard, Duke of Gloucester, Thomas, Marquess of Dorset, Henry, Earl of Northumberland, Thomas, Lord Stanley, William, Lord Hastings, John, Lord Audley, Sir John le Scrope, Ralph, Lord Greystoke, Walter Devereux, Lord Ferrers, John, Lord Dynham, Sir John Nedeham, Sir Guy Fairfax and Sir Richard Nele (the last three lawyers making up the quorum), to inquire into treasons, insurrections, rebellions, felonies and a long list of other offences in Yorkshire.[69] Richard sat with his fellow justices, at Pontefract, from 21 to 25 September. (Table 4) During this time they received some 200 indictments. One related to an event which took place as long ago as 1445, but the rest covered the period from 1460

---

[66] KB 9/434, mm. 17–22. All of them were Yorkshire JPs (*CPR 1485–1494*, pp. 506–8).

[67] 3 Hen. VII, c.1. The Act specifically mentions livery and maintenance, corruption of sheriffs and riot, all of which it failed to stem (Chrimes, *Henry VII*, pp. 155, 186–93).

[68] KB 9/349.

[69] KB 9/349, m. 223; *CPR, 1476–1485*, p. 145. Nedeham and Nele were justices of both King's Bench and Common Pleas, and Fairfax, a justice of King's Bench was 'one of the leading common lawyers of northern England' (Pollard, *North-Eastern England*, pp. 117–18; Sir John Sainty, *The Judges of England 1272–1990: a List of Judges of the Superior Courts*, Selden Society (1993), pp. 27–8, 70).

Table 4

INDICTMENTS BEFORE THE 1478 COMMISSION OF OYER AND TERMINER

Origin of offence	Number of indictments	Percentage of whole
Saville–Pilkington dispute	34	17
Pilkington crimes	60	30
Bolling crimes	5	2.5
Townley crimes	2	1
Saville crimes	4	2
Stansfield crimes	10	5
Crimes committed by or against Saville or Pilkington supporters	11	5.5
Unconnected crimes	74	37
Total	200	100

to September 1478. They thus received more than twice as many indictments as there are in the term files for the whole of the north of England for the whole Yorkist period. Their proceedings therefore offer powerful evidence of how much criminal activity was never brought to the notice of King's Bench (or possibly any court at all) in the reign of Edward IV. Thirty-four of these indictments relate directly to the probable cause of the commission: an escalating dispute between two Yorkshire gentry families, their clients and supporters, which finally erupted in a pitched battle. So far as can be ascertained,[70] the immediate course of events which prompted the commission's establishment began on 12 April 1478. On that day, Sir John Pilkington of Skipton in Craven (in the words of the indictment)

---

[70] KB 9/349, mm. 12, 14–18, 20–6, 35, 39, 41, 44, 57–62, 80, 82, 84, 88, 93, 100, 104, 119, 158, 160, 200. The affair was discussed in C.E. Arnold, 'A Political Study of the West Riding of Yorkshire, 1437–1509' (unpublished PhD thesis, Manchester University, 1984), pp. 189–91.

'sought to oppose' Sir John Saville of Thornhill and his grandson John Saville, esquire, by taking in maintenance the latter's tenant Richard Elistones who, complaining that Saville had enclosed part of his tenement by raising a hedge on his manor at Elland, enfeoffed Pilkington with the land so that he would maintain him against Saville. The Savilles claimed that they had asked Pilkington in a friendly manner not to do so. Nevertheless, on Sir John Pilkington's instructions, his bastard son, Robert, Leonard Bolling, Thomas Grenehow and Charles Hilton, all Yorkshire gentlemen, accompanied by Richard Elistones and many others, levelled the hedge, in the process, it was claimed, frightening Saville's other tenants off their holdings. The Savilles responded on 14 May. Led by Sir John's son, Thomas Saville of Thornhill, esquire, who took the leadership on himself because of his father's age and illness, and his nephew's being occupied by royal business,[71] they gathered a crowd of 100 who lay in wait at Elland 'ut insidiatores viarum' and attacked Richard Elistones and John Hole, another yeoman, driving both from their homes, and then erecting dykes on the king's common water course thus diverting water over John Hole's land, saying as they did so 'if ther be any man that will pull down this dyke he shall die therfor other elles lose an arm or a legge'.

Undeterred by such threats, on 19 May, Robert Pilkington, together with his uncles, Robert and Edmund and the latter's bastard son Edward, Lawrence Townley, Roger Banaster, Adam Browne, Leonard Bolling, Thomas Grenehow and Charles Hilton, gentlemen, Laurence Bentley mercer, the Elistones, the Holes and 400 others, broke down the hedges and dykes, blowing their horns, the indictment claims, as if to say 'we can do thus' and marched off to Elfletburgh, a Pilkington estate, where they lay in wait for the Savilles. The next day the Savilles, who, like the Pilkingtons, were accused of taking upon themselves royal powers to correct wrongdoers,[72] supported by the Stansfield

[71] KB 9/349, mm. 23, 62.

[72] KB 9/349, mm. 12, 14–16, 18, 20, 26, 41, 82, 88. JPs were authorized to take a posse to the place of a forcible entry or riot and arrest perpetrators (Bellamy, *Criminal Law*, pp. 10–12). Sir John Pilkington was a JP; and Sir John Saville had been one, 1467–75 (Arnold, 'The Commission', in Pollard (ed.), *Property and Politics*, pp. 123–5). Perhaps the indictments were worded thus to prevent them claiming their sons were acting in an official capacity.

family, with between 300 and 500 followers, made up the hedge again and then went to Elfletburgh, as close as they could to John Saville junior's land, blowing *their* horns, mercly, they claimed, to comfort their tenants hiding in their houses, and shouting 'come forth thow Robart Pylkyngton and thy servaunts oute of that place or elles we shall pull it down over your hedes'. They then dined at Halifax, and later claimed that while attempting to return peacefully to Elland they were attacked on Skircote Moor by Robert Pilkington and his 400 men who shot arrows at them shouting 'surrender yourself Thomas Sayvell, surrender yourself or die'.

Battle was joined and casualties were suffered on both sides, with at least eight men being killed.[73] This was followed on 22 May by the intervention of Charles Pilkington of Gaytford, Nottinghamshire, Sir John's brother, who marched on Sandal with three or four hundred men, where they challenged Sir John Saville to come out to fight, before descending on Wakefield. Sir John, Charles and their brother Thomas Pilkington 'machinated and confederated together as to how they might assume the governance of the king's people in his country';[74] and two days later, one of Sir John Pilkington's servants announced, in the chapel of Holmfirth in the lordship of Wakefield, in their names, that all men in the lordship (of which *Saville* was steward) should meet Charles at Almondbury on the 26th to make 'a beleefing' with him, those staying away to do so at their peril. Consequently, the Pilkington tenants came and swore to maintain them against their enemies, the Pilkingtons themselves in the meanwhile fortifying several strongholds. And so the narrative, as far as one can reconstruct it from the indictment file, ends.

It is not clear what was at the root of this vicious quarrel between two

---

[73] At least two on the Pilkington side and six on the Saville side were killed. (Pilkington victims: Robert Wadsworth [KB 9/349, mm. 12, 39, 104], Brownlow [m. 20], other victim(s) illegible [mm. 15, 41]; Saville victims: Roger Clay [mm. 21, 58], Richard Byrkynshawe [mm. 25, 61]; Andrew Sagar [m. 57], George Hopwood [m. 59], William Shyngylton [m. 158], John Howley [m. 160]). The number killed makes this case stand out. Bellamy (*Criminal Law*, p. 10) comments on the usual 'lack of casualties' in the ' "gentlemen's wars" of the later middle ages'.

[74] KB 9/349, m. 100.

families who both enjoyed the king's favour.[75] Saville had been steward of the duchy of York's lordship of Wakefield since 1442 when he was probably knighted by Duke Richard. Pilkington was made an esquire of the body in 1461, gained greatly from Yorkshire attainders in the 1460s, and was rewarded for his support of Edward IV during the Readeption by a knighthood after the battle of Tewkesbury.[76] His brother Charles was also a member of the king's household; and both were closely associated with Gloucester.[77] Carol Arnold considers that the root of the quarrel lay in a land dispute between the Pilkingtons and the *Stansfields* of thirty years' standing. It is possible that the Savilles' attitudes to the Pilkingtons were further soured by King Edward's grant to Pilkington of a reversion of Saville's offices at Sandal and Wakefield; and by Saville's removal from the peace commission in 1475.[78] Certainly, John Saville junior was later to disappoint Richard III,[79] but it does not seem that high politics was at the root of the quarrel. Nevertheless, the commission that it provoked certainly discovered enough to give Richard cause for concern about the kind of people chosen to serve on the Yorkshire commission of the peace.

In addition to the indictments related to the nub of the dispute, there were sixty dating back as far as 1460 concerning other crimes of the Pilkington family, the bastard Robert in particular. About twenty of these related to cases of forcible entry, including one against the Savilles and three against the Stansfields. They also record about fifteen livestock thefts, including two from

---

[75] Pollard describes them as 'two of the king's right-hand men' (*North-Eastern England*, p. 337).

[76] Arnold, 'Political Study', pp. 8, 45, 46, 59–62, 159–61, 175–8.

[77] Sir John Pilkington's will, dated 28 June 1478, clearly reveals his connection with Gloucester (P.W. Hammond and A.F. Sutton, *Richard III: The Road to Bosworth Field* (1985), p. 75); and Charles was later one of 'Richard's trusted agents in the murder of Hastings' (C.D. Ross, *Richard III* (1981), p. 156). See also R.E. Horrox, *Richard III: a Study of Service* (Cambridge, 1989), p. 45.

[78] Arnold, 'Political Study', p. 178; *eadem*, 'The Commission', in Pollard (ed.), *Property and Politics*, p. 125.

[79] Richard appointed him captain of the Isle of Wight in 1484 but, refusing permission to exercise this office by deputy, removed him from the stewardship of Wakefield in favour of Sir Richard Ratcliffe. Saville was an early supporter of Henry VII (Arnold, 'Political Study', pp. 198–201; Pollard, *North-Eastern England*, pp. 347, 374).

the Savilles and four from the Stansfields; six assaults, four against Stansfields; five cases of imprisoning for ransom, three against Stansfields; two of extortion from the Stansfields; several of criminal damage; one of appropriating the income of Almondbury rectory which belonged to Master Robert Fleming, then dean of Lincoln cathedral;[80] and two of murder. One of these murders dispels any doubt as to the quality of Robert Pilkington's character. On Shrove Tuesday 1477, one Leonard Metcalf was playing football at Pontefract when he accidentally hit Pilkington with his ball. Pilkington drew his dagger (worth 20*d*), and Leonard apologized profusely. Thinking they had made their peace, he turned back to his game only to be knifed to the heart and killed.[81]

As well as the many complaints against the Pilkingtons, there were four indictments against the Savilles, one for cattle theft and three for expulsion;[82] ten against their main supporters the Stansfields, comprising assaults, thefts and extortions and three cases of destroying houses, one of which involved the murder of the householder, John Wadsworth, and the taking of his wife, Alice, for ransom. Not surprisingly, several Wadsworths were named as being among the Pilkington followers in the main dispute. One of them, Robert, was killed.[83] The Pilkington supporters, the Bollings and Townleys, were indicted for five and two crimes respectively,[84] Leonard Bolling also being involved in a number of crimes in which the Pilkingtons were the main perpetrators. About a dozen cases involved other supporters of the leading figures either as perpetrators or victims.

Finally, there are over seventy indictments which do not appear to concern

[80] KB 9/349, m. 191; KB 9/349, mm. 110, 174, 182; KB 9/349, mm. 113, 154; KB 9/349, mm. 53, 99, 110, 114, 141; KB 9/349, mm. 52, 110, 114, 140, 141; KB 9/349, mm. 111, 115, 146; KB 9/349, mm. 7, 99; KB 9/349, m. 43; John le Neve, *Fasti Ecclesiae Anglicanae 1300–1541,* I, *Lincoln Diocese,* compiled by H.P.F. King (1962), p. 4.

[81] KB 9/349, mm. 78, 108. The game, and Metcalf's part in it, may not have been as completely innocent as the indictment makes it appear. Cf. John Bossy's statement in discussing Shrove Tuesday and carnival: 'Somewhere between symbolic and genuine violence one must put the carnival games, which included early forms of football, then as now a satisfying outlet for collective hostility' (*Christianity and the West 1400–1700* (1985), p. 44).

[82] KB 9/349, mm. 134, 164, 177, 180.

[83] KB 9/349, mm. 5, 8, 12, 13, 32–4, 39, 85, 86, 89, 90, 104.

[84] KB 9/349, mm. 42, 70, 71, 97, 118 (Bolling); KB 9/349, mm. 81, 149 (Townley).

the principals in the dispute at all.[85] Among these were more than twenty murders. Two contain particularly vivid accounts. One concerned Richard Cowper, a monk of Whitby Abbey, who had administered poison to his abbot, a fellow monk and three others, one of whom died.[86] The other contains a very detailed account of the murder of his wife by the adulterous William Bellamy.[87] In addition, there were recorded many cases of assault, livestock and crop theft, and criminal damage; and one or two each relating to forgery, buying wool with false weights, rescuing distrained goods, the misdeeds of Ralph Hastings, the king's escheator in Yorkshire, and rape.[88]

The *oyer and terminer* file indicates that juries were empanelled and that Gloucester dealt with the adulterous murderers, the forgers, a gang of highway robbers, and three of the livestock thieves, all of whom were sentenced to death.[89] One of the latter was a William Botre who was accused of stealing a horse and twelve sheep from Sir Thomas Witham of Cornburgh. It seems likely that this was the same man as William Buttree, his 'instaurator' whom Sir Thomas had remembered in his will three years earlier.[90] Another man sentenced to hang was Richard Saville, gentleman of Elland, who had reportedly stolen two of Thomas Meryng's oxen.[91] He was not, however, among the Savilles indicted for activities concerning the main dispute. In fact, none of these seem to have been dealt with while the commission sat. Marginalia, '*mar.*', '*po. se.*', '*ff.*', etc., indicate that various of those indicted were dealt with at some

---

[85] Cf. Arnold's calculation that 93 per cent of the surviving indictments were a direct result of the quarrels ('Political Study', p. 91). None of those named in the seventy-four indictments I cite were mentioned in the central indictments; but her deeper knowledge of the area and men may have enabled her to identify more connections than I can make.

[86] KB 9/349, m. 77.

[87] KB 9/349, m. 159.

[88] KB 9/349, mm. 46, 136; KB 9/349, m. 126; KB 9/349, mm. 72, 130; KB 9/349, m. 49; KB 9/349, m. 66. The main complaint in the rape case seems to have been, that by raping Katherine Bull, servant of Thomas Copley (one of the Savilles' supporters), Thomas Beaumond had injured her so badly that he deprived her master of her service for four months.

[89] KB 9/349, mm. 201–38.

[90] KB 9/349, mm. 161, 162; Pollard, *North-Eastern England*, p. 64.

[91] KB 9/349, m. 134.

stage, as does the endorsement, '*billa vera*', on most of the indictments; but their fates are not recorded in the enrolment.[92] Two Pilkingtons were sentenced to be hanged, the bastard Robert, not for the battle but for his murder of Leonard Metcalf and for cattle theft associated with setting fire to a chapel in which one of the Stansfields was attempting to hide from him;[93] and Thomas Pilkington for stealing livestock including 142 rams belonging to one Isabella Saville.[94] Both claimed benefit of clergy, Robert, at least, successfully.[95] It may be that Arnold is right to suggest that Edward IV, who was in Pontefract, decided that enough was enough, calling an abrupt halt to the proceedings on 26 September.[96] Certainly, Gloucester seems to have felt able to continue to work with two of the main protagonists: he knighted both Charles Pilkington and John Saville junior during the war with Scotland in 1481.[97]

Clearly, there is more to be learnt about the causes and consequences of the Saville–Pilkington dispute than the *oyer and terminer* file alone can tell us; and further research is needed before any firm conclusion can be reached. However, there is one almost inescapable conclusion, given the contents of this file, and

[92] Those recorded as being in the Marshalsea and placing themselves on the country included Leonard Bolling, Richard Elistones, Charles and Edward Pilkington, Henry and Thomas Saville, and Geoffrey, Henry, Peter and Thomas Stansfield. Edward Pilkington escaped in, or just before, Hilary term 1479 and was finally outlawed in 1497 (Blatcher, *King's Bench*, p. 75). None of those recorded to have made fines were involved in the main dispute.

[93] KB 9/349, mm. 114, 141.

[94] KB 9/349, mm. 113, 154, 225. This particular crime occurred in 1461, an indication of the long time span of the vendetta.

[95] KB 9/349, mm. 206, 225. Thomas's claim for benefit of clergy was challenged as he was reported to have been married more than once which, if proved, would have annulled his benefit. Apparently, this counter-plea of bigamy was not unusual (Bellamy, *Criminal Law*, p. 116). Bellamy discusses the whole question of benefit of clergy in the fifteenth and sixteenth centuries (*ibid.*, pp. 115–72), a useful supplement to the pioneering, but flawed, work of L.C. Gabel, *Benefit of Clergy in England in the Later Middle Ages* (USA, 1928–9).

[96] 'Political Study', p. 191. She calculated that a higher proportion of indictments against the Pilkingtons were endorsed '*billa vera*' than against the Savilles. However, if she is right in her contention that the commission was aborted before it had completed its task, there may be no malign significance in this.

[97] *Ibid.*, p. 43.

the generally high level of gentry involvement with crime, as revealed through the term files. Perhaps the greatest indictment against those attempting to rule in this period, be they Yorkist or Tudor, is that those who should have been conserving, and indeed were, in many cases, actually commissioned to conserve, the king's peace, were the very ones who disturbed it the most.[98] Despite recent, and convincingly argued, claims to the contrary, this examination of one source for an admittedly limited area and period seems to suggest that the gentry were indicted for violence, and for real violence, not just the legal fiction which might be associated with property claims, more often than was good for a society in which they played a leading part.[99]

This may be too negative a view. Records relating to crime, and indictments in particular, inevitably expose the seamier side of a society; and, because they reflect the bias of only one side of the legal process, they should not be taken at face value.[100] Nevertheless, it should be clear, even from this brief and necessarily shallow examination of a small section of the 'ancient indictments', that they provide a vivid, if incomplete, glimpse of crime and society in later medieval England, together with an insight into the personnel and administration of the criminal justice system, and snippets of information about hundreds of individuals, the lives they led and the property, real and personal, that they owned. They are a source that historians interested in any of these subjects cannot afford to ignore.

[98] Lander (*English Justices of the Peace*, pp. 93–155, 161–7) discusses these failings and the crown's, usually unsuccessful, attempts to rectify them during this period.

[99] For a more subtle view of this question, and a review of much relevant literature, see Maddern, *Violence and Social Order*, pp. 1–26. The level of violence revealed by the King's Bench indictments examined here would seem to be higher than the proportion she perceived in her examination of King's Bench records, even on the Rex side (*ibid.*, pp. 31–67). My general conclusions on violence may have been distorted by the nature of this source. Maddern looked at a great many more sources. However, for the north, in this period, it would not be correct to cite King's Bench indictments in support of her claim that 'all court statistics show allegations of non-violent crimes vastly outnumbering accusations of violence against the person' (p. 226).

[100] For essential caveats about legal records, see Powell, *Kingship, Law and Society*, pp. 91–7.

3

ORDER AND COMMUNITY IN THE NORTH: THE LIBERTY OF ALLERTONSHIRE IN THE LATER FIFTEENTH CENTURY

Christine M. Newman

The latter half of the fifteenth century is often seen as an era of political upheaval and dynastic struggle. Moreover, there are few places in England more closely associated with this turbulent image than the north wherein lay the strongholds of the most 'over-mighty' magnates of the period. Indeed, a region so closely identified with the magnate houses of Neville and Percy and one which further provided the territorial power-base of Richard III, as Duke of Gloucester, could scarcely avoid the reputation as a centre of political intrigue. Moreover, the vilification campaign against Richard, which began almost immediately after his death, was not slow to besmirch the image of the region of his greatest support and there can be few fifteenth-century historians who are unaware of the Crowland chronicler's famous description of the north as a region, '. . . whence every evil spreads . . .'.[1] Yet to what extent was this image of an unruly, troublesome region a fair reflection of the nature of northern society, as a whole, during the later decades of the fifteenth century? Was the social fabric as disordered and turbulent as the political annals suggest or was there another, less dramatic side to everyday life in the age of Richard III? Certainly the picture which is beginning to emerge from the study of one small northern community, that of Allertonshire in the North Riding of Yorkshire, presents a strikingly different perspective. Indeed, the degree of stability and continuity that the

---

[1] *Crowland Chronicle*, p. 191.

sources reveal stands in sharp contrast to the more usual (and perhaps, more romantic) image of the untamed north. What emerges instead is the impression of a closely regulated, predictably ordered and almost sleepy rural society which existed almost on another level from (and certainly in spite of) the high political tumults of the age.

The liberty of Allertonshire was one of the Yorkshire possessions of the bishopric of Durham and, in extent, encompassed much of the old Domesday wapentake of Allerton. The liberty had been granted to Bishop William de St Calais, by William II, in the closing years of the eleventh century although the connection between the see of St Cuthbert and this part of the North Riding of Yorkshire certainly pre-dated the Conquest.[2] Indeed at the time of the Domesday survey, the bishop of Durham was already in possession of the Allertonshire vills of Deighton, Girsby, Winton, Foxton and Brompton. Beyond the confines of that wapentake, he also held lands in the North Riding vills of Knayton, Hutton Sessay, Hutton Conyers, Holme, Holgrave and Norton Conyers, which were also subsequently incorporated into the bishop's Allertonshire liberty.[3] In extent the liberty comprised more than thirty small townships and vills together with the market town of Northallerton, the focal point of administrative, economic and social activity within the liberty. The bishop's status in respect of Allertonshire was that of a tenant-in-chief of the king. As such he was unable to exert the palatine privileges he enjoyed in the bishopric of Durham. Nevertheless, within the liberty, he still enjoyed a

[2] *Symeon of Durham*, ed. T. Arnold (Rolls Series, 1882), vol. 1, p. 127; *Historiae Dunelmensis Scriptores Tres*, ed. J. Raine, SS, IX (1839), p. ccccxxv; *Early Yorkshire Charters*, ed. W. Farrer (Edinburgh, 1915) vol. 2, p. 266; K. Emsley, 'The Yorkshire Enclaves of the Bishops of Durham', *The Yorkshire Archaeological Journal*, 47 (1975), p. 103; C.J.D. Ingledew, *The History and Antiquities of North Allerton* (1858), pp. 92–6.

[3] *Victoria History of the County of York: North Riding*, ed. W. Page, vol. 1 (1914, reprinted 1968), p. 397; vol. 2 (1912, reprinted 1974), pp. 314–15. A surviving terrier, pertaining to the Allertonshire lands of the bishop and dating from the early years of the twelfth century, suggests that the bishop's pre-Conquest holdings also included lands in the Allertonshire vills of West Harlsey, Osmotherley, Ellerbeck and Kirkby Sigston although these were not noted as such in the Domesday survey. These vills were all later incorporated into the liberty of Allertonshire (*Early Yorks Charters*, II, pp. 269–72).

considerable degree of authority. Indeed, by the early fourteenth century, alongside the essentially minor privileges of free warren, waif and stray, right of infangenthef and the amendment of the assize of bread and ale, the bishop was claiming a variety of hundredal privileges. These included return of writ and estreat, the authority to hear pleas of replevin, the right to issue (through his bailiff) precepts to summon and attach defendants other than those involved in crown pleas and the entitlement of holding the bi-annual view of frankpledge and tourn.[4]

In geographical terms, the liberty of Allertonshire lay approximately twenty-five miles north of York and extended, in a long strip, from some three miles north of Thirsk up to the banks of the River Tees at High Worsall, near Yarm. To the west it was bounded by Richmondshire and to the east by that area of the North Yorkshire Moors known, during the period under consideration, as Blackamore.[5] This was a region of mixed economy, flanked as it was by moorland yet nestling between the fertile vales of Cleveland and York. Indeed, the Tudor antiquarian John Leland, who journeyed into the liberty during his travels of the early 1540s, noted how, 'There is goode Corne in Northalverton, yet a great Peace of the Ground that I saw at hand betwixt Northalverton and Smithon Bridge [to the north] is low Pasture and Mores, wherof Part beere sum fyrres.'[6] As a result the raising of cattle, sheep and pigs went hand in hand with the growing of crops

[4] *Registrum Palatinum Dunelmense*, The Register of Richard de Kellawe, Lord Palatine and Bishop of Durham, ed. T.D. Hardy (London, 1875), vol. 3, pp. 48–9; Emsley, 'Yorkshire Enclaves', p. 103.

[5] T. Langdale, *A Topographical Dictionary of Yorkshire* (Northallerton, 1822) p. 3. Several of the townships actually lay beyond the strict confines of the liberty. Indeed, the vills of Norton Conyers, Hutton Conyers and Holme-with-Holgrave were nearer to Ripon and the East Riding boundary whilst those of Sessay and Hutton Sessay were situated to the south of Thirsk.

[6] A.J. Pollard, *North-Eastern England during the Wars of the Roses* (Oxford, 1990), pp. 31–2; *The Itinerary of John Leland, in or about 1535–1543*, Part I to III, ed. L. Toulmin Smith (1907), p. 67; 'The Yorkshire Portion of Leland's Itinerary', *Yorkshire Archaeological and Topographical Journal*, X (1889), pp. 327–8.

such as wheat, barley, rye and oats. This agricultural diversity is nicely illustrated by the details given in the inventories of several Allertonshire residents of the period. In 1486, for instance, the Northallerton husbandman, William Eryam, left, in crops, some eight acres of wheat and unquantified amounts of oats, barley and peas and, in livestock, four oxen, six horses, two cows, two geese, a cock and twelve hens. The Northallerton smith, John Stevenson, who died in 1498, similarly left quantities of wheat, rye, barley, peas and hay in his lathe and, in his field, one horse, three cows, sixteen sheep, two old swine and four young ones.[7]

As Professor Pollard has illustrated, the late fifteenth century was a time of continued economic constraint within the north-east of England, unlike parts of the south which, following the demographic and economic upheavals of the fourteenth and earlier fifteenth centuries, had begun to show signs of economic re-growth and prosperity.[8] The accounts of the Allertonshire receiver survive only from the early 1490s. However, from these it seems clear that the liberty was experiencing the same degree of economic stagnation as the rest of the region. Indeed, if the continuingly high arrears totals shown in the accounts are taken as an indication of the administration's difficulties in collecting revenues, then this state of affairs continued until well into the 1520s, with little movement in rent or farm values throughout the period.[9] This economic stagnation may well also have inhibited population growth during this time. Indeed, as a study of the north-eastern city of Newcastle has indicated, its late-medieval population possibly reached its 'nadir', in the 1470s and 1480s.[10] A similar state of affairs may have existed in Allertonshire. When comparisons of population estimates are made between the 1377 Poll Tax figures and those

---

[7] University of Durham Library, Archives and Special Collections Dept, Dean and Chapter Muniments, Locellus VIII, nos 6, 9; Pollard, *North-Eastern England*, p. 70.

[8] Pollard, *North-Eastern England*, pp. 78–80.

[9] The Allertonshire receivers' accounts are held in the University of Durham Library, Archives and Special Collections Dept, C(hurch) C(ommission) Bishopric (Deposit).

[10] A.F. Butcher, 'Rent, Population and Economic Change in Late-Medieval Newcastle', *NH*, 14, (1978), p. 76.

derived from Tudor demographic sources, it seems clear that, even by the
1530s, the liberty's population had barely risen beyond that of its fourteenth-
century level.[11] The subsidy returns of 1524–5, generally regarded by historians
as the most comprehensive of the period, are badly under-assessed in respect of
Yorkshire and provide little realistic demographic evidence. The returns for the
subsidy granted in 1543, whilst providing the slightly more realistic figure of
some 500 tax-payers for the liberty, still seem unrepresentative in terms of the
population as a whole. The most promising source is an undated muster return,
possibly drawn up in the 1530s. Yet this too confirms the overall impression of
stagnation for it suggests that, even some fifty years after the period in question,
during a period of probable demographic upturn, the liberty's population was
still lingering below the 3,000 mark.[12]

The population size of Northallerton is not certain, although it probably
boasted no more than 500–600 inhabitants during the period under

[11] The 1377 Poll Tax returns for Allertonshire are printed in B.J.D. Harrison, 'The 1377 Poll Tax
Returns for the North Riding', *Cleveland and Teesside Local History Society Bulletin*, 10, (Sept. 1970),
p. 8. As regards the multiplier necessary to estimate the late fourteenth-century population, from
the Poll Tax figures, both Professor Phythian-Adams and Professor Palliser have adopted Professor
Postan's suggestion of doubling the number of taxpayers, rather than that of J.C. Russell, who
proposed an increase of only 50 per cent. C. Phythian-Adams, *Desolation of a City. Coventry and the
Urban Crisis of the Late Middle Ages* (Cambridge, 1979), pp. 33–4. D.M. Palliser, 'Urban Decay
Revisited', in J.A.F. Thomson (ed.), *Towns and Townspeople in the Fifteenth Century* (Gloucester, 1988),
p. 9. Some 1,306 people are listed in the Allertonshire returns of 1377 although the returns cover
only eighteen of the liberty's townships and vills, so this figure is by no means comprehensive.
Nevertheless it suggests that the liberty had a late fourteenth-century population of at least 2,600
inhabitants.

[12] J. Sheail, 'The distribution of taxable population and wealth in England during the early
sixteenth century', in J. Patten (ed.), *Pre-Industrial England* (Dawson 1979), pp. 59–60. PRO
E179/212/107; E179/212/112; E179/212/160; E179/212/183. The Allertonshire Muster Roll
gives details of some 636 men of musterable age (i.e. between 16 and 60) within the liberty. PRO
E101/549/22. Dr Schofield has estimated that men of this age comprised between $22\frac{1}{2}$ per cent
and 30 per cent of the total population during this period and, if his suggested multipliers of
between $3\frac{1}{3}$ and $4\frac{1}{2}$ are used upon the muster figures, this gives a total estimated population of
between 2,100 and 2,800 in the 1530s. R. Schofield, '1542 Muster Rolls', *Local Population Studies*, 6
(Spring 1971), pp. 61–5.

consideration.[13] The town was ancient, with tradition suggesting that it had been built upon the foundations of a Roman settlement. Its borough status was acknowledged as early as the twelfth century, as a reference in an early Exchequer roll, dated 1196–7, to 'the town of Aluerton' illustrates. Moreover, it sent two representatives to the Parliament of 1298, although this privilege was thereafter discontinued and no more MPs were returned until the right to representation was restored in 1640. The privileges of the burgesses were enshrined in the findings of a royal inquisition, taken in 1334, which was set up to investigate the townsmen's appeal against unjust financial exactions made by the bishop and by the crown during vacancies of the see of Durham. This inquisition found that the men of Northallerton were free and of free condition and that they held the town, together with the market and fair and all profits arising from the same, of the bishop in fee of forty marks. Also confirmed by the inquisition was the privilege of holding the borough court wherein a panel of townsmen was empowered, in conjunction with the bailiff of Allertonshire, to adjudicate in all pleas pertaining to lands and tenements within the borough.[14]

Leland, writing some forty or so years after the period under consideration, came upon Northallerton from the York road and encountered a town which lay '. . . yn one fair long Streate lying by South and North . . .'. On the outskirts he passed the twelfth-century hospital dedicated to St James. As he proceeded into Northallerton he noticed several other substantial buildings; the house of the Austin Friars which lay on the eastern side of the high street; the parish

[13] The chantry certificate for the parish of Northallerton (which encompassed several outlying vills in addition to the borough) noted the existence of some 700 howseling people (i.e. communicants) in 1548. If this figure is adjusted upwards by some 25 per cent in accordance with the calculations made by Wrigley and Schofield, to take account of those below communicant age, a figure of 875 is reached. This again compares unfavourably with late fourteenth-century estimates. Indeed, in 1377, the town alone had some 372 taxpayers, suggesting a total population of around 750. *Yorkshire Chantry Surveys*, II, ed. W. Page, SS, vol. XCII (1895), pp. 123–4; E.A. Wrigley and R.S. Schofield, *The Population History of England 1541–1871* (1981), pp. 565–6; Harrison, *op.cit.*, p. 8.

[14] Ingledew, *North Allerton*, pp. 6, 96, 98–103, 127; J.L. Saywell, *The History and Annals of Northallerton* (1885), pp. 84–5. *CCR, 1333–37*, pp. 189–90.

church which he considered to be large, although somewhat deficient in its lack of noble tombs and, to the west, a little way from the church, the bishop's palace or manor-house which was '. . . strong of building and welle motid . . .'.[15] Indeed, during the period under consideration regular provision was made, in the Allertonshire receivers' accounts, for the purchase of oats for the winter feeding of the swans which apparently graced the moat.[16] Slightly to the north-west of this were the '. . . diches and the Dungeon Hille wher the Castell of Alverton sumtyme stoode . . .', although by Leland's time this had been ruinous for some 350 years.[17] Within the high street, also, stood the tollbooth (a two-storey building with shops on the ground floor), the shambles, the market cross and the stocks. A maison dieu, established to provide for the relief of thirteen poor persons, also stood on the eastern side of the high street, not far from the church. The details of various properties granted to this institution by the Northallerton draper, Richard Moore, sometime before 1476 further point to the existence of at least one hostelry, 'The Swan', within the town.[18] This, then, was the economic and administrative hub of the liberty. Here the courts were convened. Here, too, the weekly market and the annual fair were held whilst further commerce and manufacture took place in the shops and workshops of the resident craftsmen and tradesmen who provided a variety of services, both for their fellow townspeople and for the inhabitants of the surrounding countryside.

Much of the administration in Allertonshire was undertaken in one or other of the liberty's courts for, in addition to the aforementioned tourn, the bishop also enjoyed the usual feudal and tenurial powers of lordship in his liberty which were exercised through the medium of regularly held court sessions. As a

[15] 'The Yorkshire Portion of Leland's "Itinerary"', *Yorkshire Archaeological and Topographical Journal*, X, p. 327.

[16] See, for example, C.C. Bishopric, nos 190127; 189358.

[17] 'The Yorkshire Portion of Leland's "Itinerary"', *Yorkshire Archaeological and Topographical Journal*, X, p. 327; Ingledew, *North Allerton*, p. 115.

[18] Ingledew, *North Allerton*, pp. 260–9. Several other hostelries are mentioned in the records, but these are all referred to by the names of their proprietors.

consequence, sittings of the baron court and the halmote took place on a regular basis. For the town of Northallerton a regular borough court was convened, jointly, by the bishop's bailiff and by freeholders of the borough.[19] An annual forestermote was also held to deal with matters pertaining to the administration of the bishop's wood of Clack and Cotcliffe and this, together with the tourn, brought the total number of separate courts sitting within the liberty to five.

It is primarily from the records of these that evidence pertaining to everyday life in Allertonshire is drawn, for many aspects of social and economic interaction within the town and liberty were controlled by, and thus recorded in the rolls of, the local courts.[20] Indeed, scarcely a week went by without the holding of one or another of these. The tourn, which by this period was concerned primarily with cases of minor misdemeanour and the failure of vills to perform public obligations such as the maintenance of ditches and roads, was held twice yearly as was the halmote which supervised the tenurial affairs of the customary tenants. Sessions of these usually met just after Michaelmas and at Easter. Chief sittings of the baron and borough courts were also convened at these times but, additionally, ordinary sessions of both were held frequently throughout the year. On average the baron court met every three weeks, but the borough court was apparently convened on an ad-hoc basis and often between thirty and forty sittings took place during the year. Much of the business of both courts was concerned with small-plea litigation (most commonly, actions for debt, trespass, detinue and contract-breaking) thereby providing the bishop's tenants with a local and probably inexpensive means of settling small-scale

[19] W. Hutchinson, *History and Antiquities of the County Palatine of Durham*, vol. 3 (Newcastle 1794), p. 425; *VCH North Riding*, 1, p. 422.

[20] I have discussed the Allertonshire courts in some detail in my article, 'Local Court Administration within the Liberty of Allertonshire: 1470–1540', *Archives*, XXII, no. 93 (1995), pp. 13–24. Much of this and the following paragraph is based upon this study. The rolls of the Allertonshire courts, which are held in the North Yorkshire County Record Office, have been reproduced onto microfilm and it is the references to these, prefixed ZBD in accordance with the NYCRO calendar, which will be used in this article. The relevant frame numbers, when applicable, will also be given.

disputes and grievances.[21] The baron court probably originated as a court for the bishop's free tenants but, whilst these were still obliged to pay suit at the chief Michaelmas sitting, in other respects the court had, by the late fifteenth century, taken on the appearance of a general court of small pleas for the liberty. Similarly whilst chief sessions of the borough court were concerned with the regulation and government of all aspects of Northallerton town life, the bulk of the business in this court, too, was taken up with the minor suits of the townsmen.

Nowhere in the court rolls is the sense of regulation, order and control more evident than in matters pertaining to trade and economic activity. Naturally, given its position at the centre of the local economy, much of the evidence relates to the town itself. Late fifteenth-century Northallerton boasted a considerable array of tradespeople and artisans. Alongside the more usual callings of butcher, baker, brewer and smith existed a variety of other skilled occupations including those of plumber, wheelwright, slater, mason and plasterer. The further presence of craftsmen such as tanners, shoemakers, glovers and sadlers bore witness to the leather-working trade whilst that of tailors, weavers, shearmen and litsters or dyers indicated the extent of the town's involvement in the cloth trade. Economic activity within the town came under the close scrutiny of the borough court. Indeed, chief sessions of this court, which were held twice yearly at Michaelmas and Easter, sought to impose a variety of trading and marketing regulations. By the closing decades of the fifteenth century the townsmen had come to enjoy jurisdiction over the assizes of bread and ale and over forestallers. As a result, all those accused of forestalling, regrating, selling short measures or adulterated or unfit provisions within the borough were presented before the court. Two supervisors, or custodians, of the assize of bread and ale were elected annually, at Michaelmas.

[21] From the evidence of individual pleas it appears that both courts were competent to hear only actions for claims worth under 40s, in accordance with the provisions of the 1278 Statute of Gloucester. For this see *Select Pleas in Manorial and other Seignorial Courts*, ed. F.W. Maitland, Selden Society (London, 1889), vol. 2, p. lvi; H.M. Cam, *The Hundred and the Hundred Rolls* (London, 1963), p. 182.

These officials were obliged to make regular circuits of the town in order to oversee the operations of the (predominantly female) brewers and bakers and to present before the court all those who failed to comply with the regulations.[22] Indeed, between 1490 and 1510 (a period when the records were particularly well-detailed), the names of between twenty and thirty women, several the wives of prominent tradesmen, appeared regularly in the presentments for contraventions of the assize.[23] Two further supervisors were appointed, similarly, to oversee the sale of meat and fish. Thus presentments, such as those made before the chief borough court at Easter 1499, when six of the town's butchers were called to account for selling at excessive prices and trading after hours, were not unusual. At this particular sitting an ordinance was also made directing the supervisors to ensure that no butcher killed any pregnant ewes between the feast of St Andrew the Apostle (30 November) and lambing time.[24] Further economic regulation was, indeed, sometimes imposed through the agency of such ordinances, which were underpinned by the imposition of fixed penalties for non-compliance. Weights and measures seem often to have been regulated by this means. In 1497, for instance, an ordinance was issued decreeing that bushell weights within the town should conform to the standard measure laid down by the crown, on pain of a fine of 3s 4d.[25] Similarly, in 1499, an ordinance was laid down obliging the town's millers to abide by the regulations in respect of grain measures and payments for the grinding of corn, upon pain of farm-breaking and a fine of 6s 8d.[26] In terms of economic control, the competence of the borough court extended to all of those, townsmen and outsiders alike, whose trading activities within the confines of the borough contravened regulations. Thus outsiders, such as Henry Smyth of Eston in Cleveland or Richard Robynson of Rudby (some eleven or so miles from Northallerton), who were both presented in 1505 for selling unfit fish in the

---

[22] ZBD 52/24 (189272), fr. 7, 9.

[23] See, for example, ZBD 52/25 (189449), fr. 3, 4; 52/26 (189450), fr. 11.

[24] ZBD 52/24 (189272), fr. 7, 9.

[25] ZBD 52/21 (189585), fr. 7.

[26] ZBD 52/25 (189449), fr. 5.

town's market, were as liable to restriction as the Northallerton brewers or butchers.[27] Indeed, if anything, the participation of outsiders in the trading life of the town was even more closely regulated than that of the townsmen. Custom dictated, for instance, that on the day of the market, the cornbell should be rung between the hours of twelve noon and one o'clock, during which time only inhabitants of the town could purchase merchandise; outsiders wishing to buy corn and other commodities were forced to wait until after that time.[28] It is not clear whether, as in some boroughs, the burgesses of Northallerton were exempted from paying market tolls.[29] However, outsiders travelling into the town to trade were certainly penalized. Indeed, from the details of an ordinance laid down in 1497 it appears that a toll of one halfpenny was imposed upon each single waggon-load of coal, hay and whynnes (gorse) brought into the market whilst the sum of fourpence was levied upon the same quantity of goods purchased in the town but then carried outside.[30]

Economic activity within the surrounding vills and townships was supervised by the tourn with presentments probably being made by the vill constables. Often these pertained to infringements against the assize of ale, with the names of women from the vills of Hutton Conyers and Osmotherley appearing from time to time.[31] Occasionally a more serious trading infringement was dealt with. One such case was brought in 1496 when John Bowman, the miller of Heton mill, was presented by the vill of Birkby for charging excessive prices for the grinding of grain. As a consequence Bowman was ordered to make amends to those concerned on pain of the quite substantial fine of 20s.[32] Such instances were, however, rare, for cases pertaining to trading and economic infringements

[27] ZBD 53/4 (189588), fr. 2.

[28] ZBD 53/2/189587, fr. 2.

[29] The burgesses of Colchester, for instance, were exempted from paying tolls on both purchases and sales. R. Britnell, *Growth and Decline in Colchester, 1300–1525* (Cambridge, 1986), p. 37.

[30] ZBD 52/21 (189585), fr. 2.

[31] Three of the Osmotherley ale-wives presented in 1495, for instance, were still appearing before the tourn in 1500. ZBD 52/17 (189699), fr. 1–2; 52/27 (189543), fr. 1.

[32] ZBD 52/17 (189699), fr. 7.

were not presented before the tourn with anything like the same degree of frequency as those in the borough court. This suggests either that such activity was less strictly monitored in the vills or else (and more probably), since most lay within reasonably close proximity to Northallerton, that it was simply uneconomical to enter into serious trading activity within the smaller localities.

Away from official scrutiny, a further means of economic control was imposed by the inhabitants of the liberty themselves who were able to regulate their own minor trading and economic concerns through the medium of small plea litigation, undertaken in the baron and borough court; a process designed, as Marjorie McIntosh has suggested in respect of Havering, in Essex, to '. . . channel friction into confined and non-violent forms'.[33] Indeed, as I have demonstrated elsewhere, suits for debt formed the largest category of pleas terminated in both courts during the period under consideration.[34] In some cases, particularly those that were settled without dispute, the initiation of such pleas may well have been, as in Havering, little more than a convenient means of registering a particular transaction.[35] In other cases, the progression of the suit through the court was a lengthy, drawn out procedure, indicating a matter of real dispute. Moreover, such suits often involved tradesmen and their suppliers, suggesting that this means of settlement was an accepted and integral part of everyday trading activity. In 1483, for example, Laurence Hunter, a Northallerton weaver, was sued for a debt of 10s 0d, the price of six bundles of linen purchased from one Thomas Jackson of Bedale.[36] In similar vein, during the administrative year 1489–90, eight out of a total of nineteen pleas of debt terminated in the borough court were prosecuted against two Northallerton butchers, Robert Symson and Robert Brown; in each case the debt related to a transaction concerning the purchase of livestock.[37] However, sometimes

[33] M.K. McIntosh, *Autonomy and Community: The Royal Manor of Havering, 1200–1500* (Cambridge, 1986), p. 191.

[34] Newman, 'Local Court Administration', pp. 19–20.

[35] McIntosh, *Autonomy and Community*, p. 198.

[36] ZBD 52/1/189269, fr. 1.

[37] ZBD 52/11/189539.

tradesmen were forced to resort to litigation in order to exact payment for goods or services rendered. In both 1496 and 1497, the Northallerton tailor, Laurence Grey, prosecuted pleas of debt in the baron court against local countrymen over their failure to pay for various items of clothing ordered from and made up by Grey.[38] Not only tradesmen and the more substantial members of society took advantage of the process of small plea litigation, which was apparently viewed as a means of redress by the whole of local society. In some cases, indeed, it was the poorer members of the community who took advantage of the process. In 1497, for instance, a plea of debt was initiated in the baron court by one John Nicholson, a swineherd of Allerton, who sued the entire vill of Brompton (represented by the vill pledge, Christopher Staney) for 2s 4d, his stipend as the common pasturer of animals. A similar case occurred some years later, in 1502, when the Northallerton shearman, Richard Hopton, was sued over the alleged non-payment of wages by Ralph Curle of nearby Ellerton-on-Swale who claimed Hopton had hired him to full cloth.[39]

The increasing assertiveness and independence of the local courts in this period has been discussed by several historians.[40] Indeed, as Anne DeWindt has pointed out, local juries were far from being the 'passive tools' of their landlord and were, in fact, bodies which, '. . . wielded genuine power . . .' within the sphere of local judicial administration.[41] Certainly, in late fifteenth-century Allertonshire the courts appear to have been firmly under the control of the local community. Admittedly, it was the bishop's officers who presided over the various sessions. The twice-yearly tourn, for instance, was convened by the

---

[38] ZBD 52/19/189541, fr. 3; 52/22/189447, fr. 4.

[39] ZBD 52/19/189541, fr. 7; 52/26 (189450), fr. 10.

[40] See, for example, Marjorie K. McIntosh, 'Local Change and Community Control in England, 1465–1500', *Huntingdon Library Quarterly*, 49 (1986), pp. 231–2; E. Searle, *Lordship and Community: Battle Abbey and its Banlieu, 1066–1538* (Toronto, 1974), pp. 415–16; Anne Reiber DeWindt, 'Local Government in a Small Town: A Medieval Leet Jury and its Constituents', *Albion*, 23, no. 4 (Winter 1991), pp. 627–54.

[41] DeWindt, 'Local Government', p. 628. The influence of local jurors in the manorial courts of the estates of the bishopric of Worcester has been discussed in, C. Dyer, *Lords and Peasants in a Changing Society* (Cambridge, 1980), pp. 329, 368–9.

steward of the liberty. However, from the 1480s until his death in 1521, this office remained in the hands of Sir James Strangways, a prominent member of local gentry society and the bishop's leading resident free tenant within Allertonshire. The tourn 'jury of great inquisition' seems also to have been comprised of substantial or influential Allertonshire tenants. A particularly detailed list of jurors sworn in the tourn of Michaelmas 1510 included the names of several free tenants, described variously as either gentry or armigeri; four men who were designated 'frankleyns' and one other, William Watson, who held customary land in Knayton and was, at that time, serving as the reeve of that vill.[42] In similar vein, as an analysis of borough court jurors has established, these were drawn from the town's freeholders (whose names were usually listed at the head of the borough court roll). Moreover, the bailiff of the liberty, whose duty it was to represent the bishop's interests in the court, seems also to have been drawn from the same freeholding group. Thus townsman John Hopton, named as bailiff in 1492–3, was succeeded in the office by fellow Northallerton freeholder, Edmund Scarlett, who apparently retained the position until at least the mid-1520s.[43] Control within the liberty was, therefore, to a great extent in the hands of the local men of substance. For such men (for no women sat as jurors) the maintenance of order within their community was of prime importance. As a result the Allertonshire courts strove to enforce order, through the agency of regularly elected constables who regularly presented small-time troublemakers and those who transgressed against the numerous ordinances and penalties designed to control and restrain social behaviour.

Whilst everyday life in medieval Allertonshire may not have been perpetually turbulent and disordered, the liberty was not without its troublemakers and mischief-makers. As a consequence, a regular procession of presentments for unruly or socially unacceptable behaviour came before the chief borough court and the tourn. Many of the presentments were for minor disturbances and

---

[42] For the Strangways family see A.J. Pollard, *North-Eastern England*, pp. 90–1; J.S. Roskell, 'Sir James Strangways of West Harlsey and Whorlton', *Yorkshire Archaeological Journal* 34 (1958). ZBD 53/12 (189522), fr. 1.

[43] See, for instance, C.C. Bishopric, nos 190127; 189375.

affrays although occasionally matters of greater import were recorded in the rolls. One such incident occurred in October 1484 when some 300 armed men, led by one Thomas Redman and his associate Christopher Ratcliffe, riotously entered the liberty and proceeded to Northallerton where they began to abuse and insult the town's inhabitants to such an extent that a 'great affray' then ensued. During the course of this four leading townsmen, John Vale, John Jackson, John Bynkes and Robert Founder were attacked, maltreated and injured. No further record of this incident, which was detailed in the rolls of the tourn, appears to exist and the reasons behind this apparently unwarranted intrusion into the liberty and indeed any subsequent ramifications regarding the affair remain intriguingly obscure.[44] The Anglo-Scottish Treaty of Nottingham had been agreed only in the September of that year and it is possible that the miscreants were soldiers, recently discharged from the border-garrison of Berwick, who were making their rowdy way home. Alternatively, since the names of the leading protagonists were those of families closely associated with the regime of Richard III, these may have been dissatisfied or disaffected cadet members of the Redman and Ratcliffe families who were seeking to air their grievances at a time when, as Professor Pollard has suggested, some northerners were beginning to have 'second thoughts' about their king. The competence to adjudge a disturbance of such proportions properly fell under the aegis of a higher authority than the bishop's tourn, which dealt only with minor misdemeanours, and it is possible that this was, in fact, the record of an incident which was to be handled by the newly constituted Council in the North which had been given specific authority to deal with incidents such as this.[45] Indeed, whilst this incident was reported by the Northallerton constables, no one was actually presented before the tourn for their part in this affair. Certainly this was the only occurrence of such proportions to be reported in the liberty's court

[44] ZBD 52/3 (189413), fr. 9. The alleged day of the incident, given as Saturday, 26 October, 2 Ric. III, is incorrect for in 1484 the 26th was a Tuesday. However, the month and year are clearly detailed in the records.

[45] Pollard, *North-Eastern England*, p. 365. I am indebted to Professor Pollard for discussing with me the various possibilities surrounding this incident.

rolls during the period in question (and indeed beyond) and the fact that it was considered sufficiently noteworthy for its details to be included in the court rolls suggests that incidents of this magnitude were unusual.

Indeed, for the most part the affrays and disturbances recorded appeared to have been of a relatively minor nature. A fair share of disputes and squabbles presumably occurred as the result of economic and trading grievances and, indeed, the Wednesday market provided a perfect venue for the settling of such matters. A trading dispute undoubtedly lay behind the market day attack made by the Northallerton butcher, Christopher Coupland, upon John Tiplady of Kirkby Sigston, the details of which came before the Easter 1490 session of the chief borough court. Indeed, during the previous autumn Coupland had been the defendant in two private suits – one for debt and one for trespass – brought by Tiplady over the sale and pasturing of two cows.[46] Several other incidents bore great similarity to those involving William Sampson who, at Michaelmas 1499, was presented before the borough court on two occasions, firstly for causing an affray in the shop of one William Wydowson and secondly for assaulting Robert Helmesley in the open market.[47]

While prominence of status was no guarantee of good behaviour neither did it provide exemption from presentation before the court. Indeed, the names of several leading members of local society appeared in connection with cases of unruly or disorderly behaviour. One unusually serious case concerned members of two prominent Northallerton families, the Vales and the Fewlers, who in 1490 were presented before the Michaelmas session of the tourn for brawling in the fields beyond the town (and therefore beyond the jurisdiction of the borough court). The heads of both families, John Vale and John Fewler (who were both apparently involved in the incident), were freemen of the town who sat regularly as jurors during the 1480s and 1490s and, indeed, Vale was a member of the tourn jury which heard the case. This did not prevent him from being fined 1s for his misdemeanours and, indeed, the seriousness with which the court viewed the affair can be judged by the fact that, in all, amercements totalling 3s 8d were

---

[46] ZBD 52/11 (189539) fr. 2, 7.
[47] ZBD 52/25 (189449), fr. 3, 4.

levied from the offending parties.[48] The correction of such men probably provided the dual benefits of reinforcing the overall authority of the court while, at the same time, embarrassing the offender before the whole of the community.

The bad behaviour of women, although less frequently reported, was also a matter of concern for the courts. In 1485, for instance, the wives of John Hog and Richard Baxter were presented for scolding and inciting their menfolk to make an affray.[49] Several years later, in 1490, the wife of John Bowes was presented before the borough court as an ill-governed petty thief and slanderer and, as such, ordered to leave the vill. At the following (Easter) session of the court she was again presented, however, for tarrying in the town with her husband who was also presented for harbouring her. As a result both were ordered to leave before Pentecost upon pain of a fine of 6s 8d each.[50] Moral behaviour was, primarily, a matter for the church courts and before the 1490s there is little evidence of prostitutes being presented or disciplined by the courts (although after this time such women were increasingly named and ordered to remove themselves from the town or vill). However, the harbouring of such women and the keeping of bawdy houses was always a matter of concern to the court. Certainly, from the records it appears that the town had at least one or two houses of ill-repute. In 1476, for instance, one Thomas Brayn, the keeper of a 'bordelhous', was accused of giving hospitality to scurrilous persons and ordered to desist. In 1484 John Hert was penalized for receiving prostitutes and ill-governed females; Robert Braine (perhaps a relative of Thomas) was similarly presented in 1489, while in 1490–1 both Elenor Heton, alias Chapman, and John Blakey were brought before the court for receiving divers prostitutes, vagabonds and scurrilous persons.[51]

In common with their counterparts in other regions, the Allertonshire jurors began in the later fifteenth century to take a greater interest in the control of social behaviour.[52] As a consequence presentments concerning the receiving

[48] ZBD 52/13 (189357), fr. 1.

[49] ZBD 52/5 (189583), fr. 1.

[50] ZBD 52/11 (189539), fr. 7; 52/14 (190118), fr. 1, 6.

[51] ZBD 221658 fr. 2; 52/11 (189539), fr. 1; 52/11 (189539), fr. 2, 6, 7.

[52] Searle, op.cit., pp. 414–15; McIntosh, Autonomy and Community, pp. 255–61.

and harbouring of vagabonds, Scots, prostitutes and other undesirables as well
as those pertaining to gaming and drinking became much more prevalent in
the court rolls as the century drew to a close. As Marjorie McIntosh has
pointed out, the increased concern of manorial courts with matters of social
control was particularly evident, from the 1460s onwards, due to increases in
poverty and geographical mobility. Such concerns were especially noticeable in
parts of the more prosperous south-east, where expanding local economies
attracted high levels of poor migrants whose presence naturally created
tensions within their host communities.[53] Problems relating to economic and
demographic upswing were, as has already been discussed, clearly not the issue
in the north. Nevertheless, poverty and vagrancy were creating problems in the
region. Northallerton possessed a well-founded maison dieu for the relief of
the town's poor, the trusteeship of which passed into new hands in 1746.[54]
Moreover, the growing number of presentments, after 1490, for the harbouring
of outsiders, particularly Scots, suggests that the issue of employment-seeking
itinerants was becoming as acute in the north as in other parts of the country.[55]
The fact, too, that Northallerton lay on the main route between York and the
north probably exacerbated its problems in this respect, for the town
undoubtedly provided a convenient stopping point for southward-bound
travellers. Thus it is likely that, in the economically depressed north, as in the
more prosperous south, the gap between the poorer and wealthier sections of
local society was widening.

[53] McIntosh, 'Local Change', pp. 227–33.

[54] Ingledew, *North Allerton*, pp. 260–70. For Yorkshire maisons dieu in general, see P. Cullum, 'For
Pore People Harberles' in *Trade, Devotion and Governance*, D.J. Clayton et al (eds) (1994), pp. 36–54..

[55] Itinerant Scots were probably doubly suspect, for not only did they add to the growing
vagrancy menace but, in an era of continuing Anglo-Scottish hostility, they also belonged to the
nation regarded as the traditional enemy. Northallerton was sufficiently far north for its menfolk to
play a major part in the defence of the region against Scottish depredations. Indeed, in December
1496, during a phase of open Anglo-Scottish warfare, a series of leases granted by the borough
court made the provision that, for every four oxgangs of land held, the farmer thereof should make
himself available, '. . . able arrayed as wele in harness as in horse . . .' to do the service of the king
and the bishop, when required. ZBD 52/20 (189542).

Admittedly presentments for socially undesirable behaviour in the Allertonshire courts began to increase significantly in the 1490s, the era of the first Tudor initiatives against vagabonds and beggars. As such it is likely that the influence of government legislation played a significant role in this sphere.[56] Nevertheless it is possible that more localized considerations were also at work. Indeed there is much evidence to suggest that, despite the stagnant nature of the local economy, living standards amongst the better-off sections of north-eastern rural society, even down to the level of yeomen and husbandmen, were comparatively comfortable.[57] Within more urbanized areas the same was possibly true of local tradesmen. Indeed, as has been shown, the Northallerton draper Richard Moore had been sufficiently wealthy to be able to endow the town's maison dieu. Under the circumstances it seems feasible that the Allertonshire jurors, who were drawn predominantly from the better-established sections of local society, would almost certainly have closed ranks to prevent the erosion of their living standards by the encroachments of the poor and outsiders. The borough court plea of trespass entered by the shearman, Richard Hopton (a Northallerton freeman who regularly sat as a borough court juror), in 1500, neatly illustrates this concern. Hopton claimed damages of 20s from one John Wightman of nearby South Ottrington who had come into the town and had set himself up in the 'sherman' or 'walkercraft', contrary to the statutes and ordinances of the craft and to the detriment of the plaintiff.[58] Undoubtedly, therefore, a combination of factors, inspired by both local and national concerns, prompted the Allertonshire courts to address the issue of social control with increasing vigour. As a result it is probable that, by the closing decades of the fifteenth century, everyday life within the liberty was coming under an ever greater degree of control and scrutiny.

[56] The 1495 Act against Vagabonds and Beggars (11 Hen. VII, c. 2), was the first of eleven such statutes to be passed by the Tudor regime. A.L. Beier, *The Problem of the Poor in Tudor and Early Stuart England* (1983), p. 39.

[57] Pollard, *North-Eastern England*, pp. 70–1.

[58] ZBD 52/25 (189449), fr. 12. Hopton appeared as a juror from 1489–1506; see for example, ZBD 52/11 (189539), fr. 1; 53/6 (189453), fr. 1.

The view of small town and rural life within the late fifteenth-century north, as portrayed in the Allertonshire records, is one of coherence and relative stability. Admittedly, by their very nature, sources such as court rolls do tend to impose a heightened and probably exaggerated sense of order and control upon the issues with which they deal. Moreover, the limitations of the bishop's jurisdiction within his liberty meant that only relatively trivial cases were dealt with by his courts. Indeed, whilst the list of the bishop's free tenants within the liberty, bearing the names of such as Scrope of Bolton, Greystoke, Danby, Conyers, Ingleby, Burgh and Strangways, does tend to read like a 'Who's Who' of the northern affinity of Richard III, there is little of the political activities of these men in records which, in format, convey a sense rather of continuity than transition.[59] It is, in fact, the case that the court rolls for the reign of Henry VII follow on, without any sense of change or disruption, from those of Richard's reign. Nevertheless, despite such shortcomings, the Allertonshire records still serve to convey the overriding impression of a well-regulated and relatively stable community wherein individuals were far more likely to settle their disputes through the sophisticated medium of small-plea litigation than through recourse to violence. Certainly, if the evidence pertaining to late fifteenth-century Allertonshire is representative of other local communities within the north, then it presents a far different perspective from that of the region as a centre of disorder and turbulence. Indeed, what emerges instead is the notion of coherence and continuity in a society where, for the great majority of the population, the unremitting round of everyday economic and social activity carried on regardless of the political upheavals of the age.

[59] ZBD 52/3 (189443), fr. 1.

4

THE CROWN AND THE COUNTY PALATINE OF DURHAM, 1437–94

A.J. Pollard

Ll who approach the peninsula at Durham by Prebends Bridge will stop and admire the magnificent view of the cathedral and notice carved in stone on the parapet the lines of Sir Walter Scott in its praise: 'half house of God; half castle 'gainst the Scot'. His words are hardly true of the cathedral itself; but they do encapsulate the explanation given by the crown in 1311 for the special privileges enjoyed by its bishop in the land between Tees and Tyne as 'a bulwark against the Scots'.[1] In 1311 this justification was immediately relevant, but by the mid-fifteenth century it was no longer so pertinent. In so far as the Bishops of Durham maintained a castle against the Scots, this lay at Norham (North Durham), sixty miles to the north on the south bank of the Tweed. Bishops of Durham continued to play a part in the defence of the border; their constable at Norham held a petty wardenry, their tenants were still required to serve in the event of war, and the banner of St Cuthbert was still unfurled to protect them. For the most part, however, the bishopric, as the land between Tees and Tyne had already come to be called, was like any other county of England, albeit with a distinct constitution. This constitution and the special relationships between crown and bishop in its formative years have been fully explored by historians.[2] Indeed the county

---

[1] K. Emsley and C.M. Fraser, *The Courts of the County Palatine of Durham from Earliest Times to 1979* (Durham, 1984), p. 93; *Registrum Palatinum Dunelmensis* (ed. T.D. Hardy), I (Rolls Series, 1873–8), pp. 73–5.

[2] C.T. Lapsley, *The County Palatine of Durham: a study in constitutional history* (Cambridge, Mass, 1900); J. Scammell, 'The Origins and Limitations of the Liberty of Durham', *EHR*, LXXXI (1966); R. Lomas, *North-Eastern England in the Middle Ages* (Edinburgh, 1992), pp. 75–84.

palatine in the early fifteenth century under the energetic Bishop Langley, as
well as the priory serving the cathedral, have found their recent historians, as
has the region in the sixteenth century.[3] Several specialist essays on particular
aspects of the history of the palatinate after 1437 have been written,[4] yet one
important topic, the relationship between crown and bishop in these years, has
remained largely unexplored and no study has been made of the bishops and
the character of their episcopacies between Langley who died in 1437 and
Richard Fox who was provided in 1494. This is perhaps not surprising since on
the whole the four bishops, Robert Neville (1437–57), Laurence Booth
(1457–76), William Dudley (1476–83) and John Shirwood (1483–94), made no
particular impact on public affairs. Perhaps, too, Durham has been seen as little
more than a backwater during the confusion and upheavals of the Wars of the
Roses.[5] But the period is of some significance precisely because these four
bishops were for the most part overshadowed by powerful lay subjects of the
crown even within their own palatinate, the last of whom was Richard, Duke of
Gloucester, before he became king.

Strictly speaking, as was made explicit in the Quo Warranto proceedings of
1297, Durham was a liberty within the county of Northumberland. In
challenging episcopal privileges or rights of lordship, as Sir William Eure and

---

[3] R.L. Storey, *Thomas Langley and the Bishopric of Durham, 1406–1437* (1961); R.B. Dobson, *Durham
Priory, 1400–1450* (Cambridge, 1973); M.E. James, *Family, Lineage and Civil Society: a study of Society,
Politics and Mentality in the Durham Region, 1500–1640* (Oxford, 1974); *The Last Principality: Politics,
Religion and Society in the Bishopric of Durham, 1494–1660*, D. Marcombe (ed.) (Nottingham, 1987).

[4] R.B. Dobson, 'Richard Bell, Prior of Durham (1464–78) and Bishop of Carlisle (1478–95)',
TCWAAS, new series, 65 (1965); M. O'Regan, 'Richard III and the Monks of Durham', *The
Ricardian*, IV (1978); A.J. Pollard, 'St Cuthbert and the Hog: Richard III and the County Palatine of
Durham' in R.A. Griffiths and J.W. Sherborne (eds), *Kings and Nobles in the Later Middle Ages*
(Gloucester, 1986). Particular families and individuals have been studied in, for example, W.E.
Hampton, 'John Hoton of Hunwick and Tudhoe', *The Ricardian*, VII (1985); C.M. Newman, 'The
House of Bowes and the Wars of the Roses', *Medieval History*, 1, no. 3 (1991); and J. Petrie, 'The
Nevilles of Brancepeth and Raby, 1429–99', *The Ricardian* (1982).

[5] See, for instance, F. Musgrove, *The North of England: a history* (Oxford, 1990), ch. 7 *passim*, in which the
hypothesis that a shift in power towards the northern 'perimeter' of the kingdom in the fifteenth century
became a threat to the centre takes no cognizance of the palatinate of Durham. See also above, p. 17.

his allies did in 1433, and Richard Neville, Earl of Salisbury, did in 1439, the
bishop's rivals resorted therefore to the technical device of securing royal
commissions to make enquiry into the county of Northumberland, thus in effect
temporarily suspending the liberty in the matter at issue. Indeed in 1461 Robert
Rhodes, the lay steward of the priory, claimed that he had committed perjury
before an Inquisition Post Mortem in 1439 by stating that Barnard Castle lay in
the county of Northumberland, to the harm of the 'liberty and title of the
church of St Cuthbert'. The territorial extent of the liberty was still in dispute in
the mid-fifteenth century; in particular the overlordship of Barnard Castle and
Hart (which included Hartlepool), confiscated from Baliol and Bruce for their
'rebellion' by Edward I, was contested between crown and bishop. Bishop Bek
and his successors claimed that the crown had no right of forfeiture. In the case
of Hart he was eventually successful, Edward IV recognizing in 1461 the right
of Bishop Booth to take possession from the Cliffords. And it was Bishop
Shirwood who restored Lord Clifford in 1485. But the crown remained overlord
of Barnard Castle until it became part of the royal demesne itself with the
accession of Richard III in 1483. In strict law, therefore, the lordship did not lie
within the palatinate, even though it would appear that the bishop's justice was
administered therein throughout the later Middle Ages.[6]

The dispute over bounds aside, after 1433 there was no challenge by either
crown or subject to the regality of the bishop within his palatinate. This
included his own chancery, exchequer, mint and courts; the issuing of his own
original writs and the exclusion of the king's writ; and the appointment of his
own justices (of assize and of the peace), sheriff, escheator, coroners and other
officers. Durham was not represented in parliament and did not pay taxes to
the king. However, the bishop had no power to make or alter law: the common
law was administered and statutes enacted in parliament were obeyed. The
regality did not extend to the making of war and peace. A sophisticated system

[6] For the Eure case see Storey, *Thomas Langley*, pp. 116–34; and for Barnard Castle see A.J.
Pollard, *North-Eastern England during the Wars of the Roses: Lay Society, War and Politics, 1450–1500*
(Oxford, 1991), pp. 147–9 and 'The Title and Right to Barnard Castle in the Later Middle Ages',
T(eesdale) R(ecord) S(ociety) J(ournal), 3rd series, 2 (1994), pp. 8–16.

of administration had been established, based on Palace Green in Durham and separate from the bishop's own household, maintaining its own records. Routine administration was conducted by the bishop's council, which was composed of his principal officers: his lay chancellor and receiver-general (by the second half of the century usually the same man), chief auditor, chief justice, sheriff (appointed during pleasure and not annually) and steward. These same officials dominated the commission of the peace. The bishop's steward, his deputy as the head of the civil government of the palatinate, presided over the council. The steward was either one of the great laymen of the palatinate or a trusted servant of the bishop.[7] The bishop thus possessed the potential through his regalian powers and bureaucracy to exercise considerable independent power.

Potential, however, was not the same as actuality. The real power exercised by Bishops of Durham in their palatinate had declined markedly since the days of Bishop Puiset, who, it has been said, dominated his bishopric in solitary splendour.[8] One limitation was placed collectively by the bishop's subjects in the name of the community of the bishopric, or, as it was called in a charter of King John, the 'Haliwerfolk', who had over the centuries secured significant concessions from him. These 'liberties' had most recently been invoked by Sir William Eure and his allies in their challenge to Bishop Langley in 1433. But thereafter the Bishop's subjects never challenged him as a body. Their sense of identity focused on the cult of St Cuthbert, and found expression from time to time in the coronation of a new bishop or such events as the gathering of five knights, fifty-one esquires and eighteen others in the cathedral on 23 September 1434 to take a solemn oath not to maintain lawbreakers. The bishop's principal tenants seem to have had a voice as a body, but in the absence of any record of its routine articulation this remains an imprecise and perhaps always insubstantial entity.[9]

[7] The best modern summary discussion of the constitution and administrative system of the palatinate is to be found in Storey, *Thomas Langley*, ch. 2 *passim*. The administration is further discussed in Pollard, *North-Eastern England*, pp. 160–3.

[8] Scammell, *EHR*, LXXXI, p. 471.

[9] Storey, *Thomas Langley*, pp. 121–7; Scammell, *EHR* LXXXI, pp. 461–2; Pollard, *North-Eastern England*, pp. 153–4.

The leading subjects of the bishop themselves provided more of a threat to his authority individually, especially if they also held substantial estates in neighbouring counties and entered the services of the king. Sir William Eure was such a man. But most of the leading gentle families of the palatinate, such as the Bowes, Claxtons, Conyers of Sockburn, Hiltons and Lumleys themselves prospered through episcopal service. The dominant lay family of the palatinate, and the only alternative focus of power and influence, was Neville of Raby and Brancepeth, since 1397, Earls of Westmorland. So important were they considered to be that in 1476 Prior Bell advised the incoming Bishop Dudley that if 'your lordship and they stand as one ye may rule and guide all other that inhabit the country'. And certainly most of the leading gentry of the county traditionally served the Nevilles as well as the bishop, successive heads of the Claxton family being particularly prominent.[10] Ralph, 1st Earl of Westmorland, who died in 1425, with estates in Yorkshire and Cumbria as well as Durham, and his close connection with the house of Lancaster, had undoubtedly been a power to reckon with. But he had been no threat to Langley since they were both dedicated servants of the dynasty and had worked closely in partnership in its interest. The subsequent partition of the Neville estates, however, greatly weakened the Earls of Westmorland, so that while they remained socially pre-eminent within the palatinate, for the rest of the fifteenth century they were politically of little weight.

The principal constraint on independent episcopal authority, exemplified in Bishop Langley, was that after Edward I's struggle with Anthony Bek, the Bishop of Durham had almost invariably been a senior clerical administrator and civil servant who owed his promotion to royal patronage. Langley was the fifth successive bishop who had been keeper of the privy seal. That the bishop should be an experienced administrator and civil servant was, given the sophistication of palatine government, sensible. That he should also be a confidant of the king, of unquestioning loyalty to him, was essential. As

---

[10] *Historia Dunelmensis Scriptores Tres*, J. Raine, SS, IX (1839), cclxxiv, p. 359; Pollard, *North-Eastern England*, p. 138.

Professor Dobson has commented on the late fourteenth-century bishops, none 'could have contemplated using the financial and military resources of Durham, except in furtherance of policies pursued by the royal master to whom they owed their very appointment'.[11] By the early fifteenth century the bishopric of Durham had come to be ruled on behalf of the king by his nominee the bishop. Thus while in theory the bishop retained his regal prerogatives, in practice they were exercised for the crown by its deputy. This custom, as it had become by 1406, ensured that the crown had a much greater presence in north-eastern England than the distance from Westminster and the absence of a significant landed estate north of the Tees would at first suggest. Moreover, the Bishop of Durham, as the king's agent in the far north, could, if necessary, exercise his authority as a counterweight to ambitious subjects who might be tempted to use their might to their own advantage. Under Langley, and then again under the early Tudor bishops beginning with Richard Fox, and culminating in Thomas Wolsey, this was successfully achieved. The palatinate of Durham provided, therefore, at one remove, an important extension of royal authority into the far north-east of the realm. What sets the years 1437–94 apart is that this system collapsed, royal control was abandoned and the financial and military resources of the palatinate were put at the disposal of local magnates; and the loss of royal control over Durham in the mid-fifteenth century was an important element in the events that led to the Wars of the Roses and helped to shape the world which Richard of Gloucester entered in 1471.

The key to what happened lies in the particular political circumstances both at court and in the palatinate on Bishop Langley's death on 20 November 1437. In the autumn of 1437 Henry VI was emerging from his minority and the royal council was caught up in the tricky stage of transition between acting on behalf of a king too young to be able to exercise power himself and being the servant of a king old enough to be king in deed as well as in name. Precisely when Henry VI

---

[11] R.B. Dobson, 'The Church of Durham and the Scottish Borders, 1378–88', in *War and Border Societies in the Middle Ages*, A. Goodman and A. Tuck (eds) (1992), pp. 130–1. See also the comment of Dr Scammell (*EHR*, LXXXI, pp. 471–2) that the bishop was 'the most amenable of the northern magnates' whose privileges were only 'as long as the king's temper'.

achieved his majority is a matter of current debate. That he did so by stages is apparent, but the significance of those stages is not entirely clear, partly because of the obscurity of the sources and partly because it was already apparent that the sixteen-year-old youth was not very interested in being a king. The council itself was of several minds. On the one hand it represented and sustained a tradition of serving collectively and indifferently the needs of the kingdom; on the other it was riven by faction, particularly between Humphrey, Duke of Gloucester, and Cardinal Beaufort, each seeking to profit from the king's coming of age. On 12 November 1437 the relationship between the king and the council and their respective powers was redefined. This may or may not have marked the formal end of the minority; but it certainly represented a triumph for Beaufort.[12] And the strengthening of the Beaufort grip on the conduct of affairs was marked by the swearing in of the cardinal's nephew, Richard Neville, Earl of Salisbury, on the same day.[13]

In November 1437 Salisbury had recently returned from a year's service in France. His major concern was to secure the terms of his father's will which had made over the Neville inheritance to him after the death of his mother, Joan Beaufort, the cardinal's sister. She was in possession of Raby and Brancepeth in Durham. Until Langley's death the dowager countess and Salisbury, who had headed the commission of the peace in the palatinate since 1427, had received the whole-hearted backing of the bishop in Durham and Cardinal Beaufort at court. There was little that the Earl of Westmorland could do against such influence.[14] Langley's death on 20 November revived his hopes. But Beaufort

<hr/>

[12] J.L. Watts, 'When Did Henry VI's Minority End?', in D.J. Clayton *et al.* (eds), *Trade, Devotion and Governance* (Stroud, 1994), pp. 116–31, esp. 127–9; R.A. Griffiths, *The Reign of King Henry VI* (1981), pp. 232–5, 275–8; B.P. Wolffe, *Henry VI* (1981), pp. 91–2; G.L. Harriss, *Cardinal Beaufort: a Study of Lancastrian Ascendancy and Decline* (Oxford, 1988), pp. 276, 292–5.

[13] R. Virgoe, 'The Composition of the King's Council, 1437–61', *BIHR*, XLIII (1970), p. 141. Salisbury was in the following five years one of the better attenders among the lay lords of the council (*ibid.*, 157).

[14] Harriss, *Cardinal Beaufort*, pp. 267–8; Dobson, *Durham Priory*, pp. 185–90; E.F. Jacob, *The Fifteenth Century* (Oxford, 1961), pp. 322–5, drawing upon the unpublished doctoral research of Charles Ross.

and Salisbury acted swiftly to protect the family interest. A week later the king recommended to Pope Eugenius IV that Robert Neville, one of Joan Beaufort's own sons, be translated from the bishopric of Salisbury and at the same time the keeping of the temporalities during the vacancy was committed to the Earl of Salisbury himself.[15] Neville was duly provided by the Pope, was elected by the prior and convent on 27 January 1438 and translated in February. By mid-May Robert was fully installed in his new diocese and the position of the countess, whose commanding tone in correspondence with her son the bishop suggests the nature of the relationship between the two, was apparently stronger than it had ever been.[16]

In his letter to the Prior and chapter of Durham, ordering them to elect Robert Neville, the king, in words of barefaced cynicism, no doubt penned by Cardinal Beaufort, stressed the value to the bishopric of his nominee's birth and kinsmen which were of great and notable estate. For good measure too he added that it was necessary to appoint such a notable and mighty person as bishop since the diocese was 'nygh unto the marches of Scotland' and he could 'puissantly kepe thayme best to the honnour of god and defence of this oure Royaume'. In the light of the recently ended northern war and the difficulty the government had faced in finding a warden of the east march there is something to be said for this, but one wonders whether the new bishop had as 'grete vertues, connyng and discrete providence' in spiritual matters, and doubts that he was the 'moost convenient, soufficant and hable prelate' available, as the king's letter claimed.[17] In truth, of course, the promotion of Robert Neville was an act of naked factionalism in the pursuit of Beaufort family aggrandisement. It reflected neither the personal will of the king nor the will of the council seeking to appoint a capable royal servant to the palatinate to exercise the king's will on his behalf. The keeper of the privy seal, William Lyndwood, remained neglected as Archdeacon of Oxford and

---

[15] Harriss, *Cardinal Beaufort*, pp. 267–8; Dobson, *Durham Priory*, p. 188; Griffiths, *Henry VI*, p. 234.

[16] Dobson, *Durham Priory*, pp. 187, 224–6.

[17] DCD, Locellus xxv, no. 96. See Appendix. For doubts concerning Neville's intellectual calibre see Dobson, *Durham Priory*, p. 225.

his predecessor, William Alnwick, a much more likely candidate, stayed at Lincoln.[18]

The promotion of Bishop Neville was a defining moment in the history of Durham in the fifteenth century, perhaps also in the history of Henry's majority. It led immediately to violence, as the Earl of Westmorland led 'great routs and companies upon the field'. Archbishop Kemp attempted and failed to arbitrate a settlement; and twice in 1439 both parties were summoned before the council. It was not until three years after the death of Countess Joan in 1440, however, that a settlement was possible under which Salisbury made the significant concession of surrendering Raby and Brancepeth to the Earl of Westmorland in exchange for his uninterrupted possession of Middleham, Sheriff Hutton and Penrith.[19] Thus a partition was made of the great Neville inheritance between the two branches of the family. Salisbury may well have calculated that with his pliant brother installed as bishop he had less need for the Durham lordships.

By 1443 the administration of the palatinate had already been infiltrated by his kinsmen and servants. One brother, George, Lord Latimer, then still of sound mind, had been appointed chamberlain for life with a fee of £40 p.a. in December 1438 and another, Edward, Lord Abergavenny, granted an annuity of 40 marks at the same time. Salisbury himself was granted an annuity of £100 on 10 June 1439. Two years later, on 12 April 1441, the fifth brother, William, Lord Fauconberg, was appointed lay steward for life and additionally, without precedent, 'governor and ruler of all our tenants and men in time of peace and war' during pleasure, thus giving some substance to the justification for Neville's promotion in 1437. Although Fauconberg was much engaged in the war in France, when in England he occasionally presided over the halmote courts of the bishop's manors, as in October 1443 and October 1447. When he was

---

[18] Alnwick, who had been keeper of the privy seal from 1422 to 1432, was also a member of Beaufort's circle. Only a year earlier he had been translated to Lincoln, but he was still the most obvious candidate for Durham in 1437. In 1439 he was one of the arbiters appointed by the crown who failed to find a lasting solution to the Neville dispute. See Harriss, *Cardinal Beaufort*, pp. 268, 272.

[19] Harriss, *Cardinal Beaufort*, p. 268; Dobson, *Durham Priory*, p. 191.

absent, his deputy, Salisbury's second son, Sir Thomas (who succeeded him in
1448), frequently sat for him. All four brothers of the bishop were justices of the
peace in the palatinate until the end of the pontificate. Moreover, Bishop
Neville's first chief justice was Salisbury's retainer, Sir James Strangways, who
was succeeded by another, Robert Danby, who had been attorney-general since
1438.[20]

The consolidation of Durham as a fiefdom of the junior Nevilles in the late
1430s makes all the more puzzling the attempt by Bishop Neville to seize
Barnard Castle, which he occupied 'with a great multitude in manner of riot
and war' following the death of Richard Beauchamp, Earl of Warwick, in the
spring of 1439. Perhaps he considered this to be the quid pro quo owing to him.
If so he miscalculated badly, for, as he must have known, the new Earl of
Warwick, although a minor, was Salisbury's son-in-law and Salisbury would not
tolerate the loss of any of his daughter's prospects or offend a potentially
powerful ally at court. A royal commission under Salisbury's presidency was
established shortly before Christmas 1439 to report on the petition submitted to
the crown by the late earl's feoffees, of whom Salisbury was also one. A month
later, even before the commission had reported, the king ordered the restoration
of the lordship to the feoffees. Chastened by the experience, Bishop Neville
seems never again to have attempted to assert his independence. Certainly he
made no effort to reassert his claim when the then Duke Henry of Warwick
died in June 1446, leaving a two-year-old daughter, and Salisbury's
granddaughter, Anne, as his sole heiress. The custody of Barnard Castle was
granted, by the crown, to Salisbury. After her death in 1449 the lordship, with
all the estates of the earldom of Warwick, passed to her aunt, Anne, and her
husband, Salisbury's eldest son and heir, Richard.[21]

Durham under Bishop Neville thus became part of the hegemony of the Earl
of Salisbury in northern England. For twenty years its resources were at the
disposal of the earl and its bishop acted not as the agent of the crown but as the

[20] Pollard, *North-Eastern England*, pp. 161, 251–2.
[21] Pollard, *TRSJ*, 2, pp. 9–10.

lackey of one of its overmighty subjects. In October 1453 he was presumably Salisbury's nominee (the Earl of Westmorland represented the Earl of Northumberland) to the team of mediators which, under the Archbishop of York, appears to have averted a pitched battle between the two earls and their forces at Sand Hutton. But in May 1455 the military strength of the palatinate seems to have been placed fully at Salisbury's disposal. According to one account of the first battle of St Albans, Sir Robert Ogle, a retainer of the earl who was also constable of the bishop's castle of Norham, led the assault with 600 men of the Scottish marches which seized the market place and decided the conflict. Thus ultimately did the puissance of the noble Bishop of Durham come to be deployed not against the king's enemies as intended but against his friends.[22]

Robert Neville died on 8 July 1457, bringing to an end almost twenty years of factional rule in the palatinate. The immediate provision of Laurence Booth as his successor on 22 August is usually seen as equally factional. It is true that Booth was a close associate of the queen, Margaret of Anjou, whose chancellor he had been since 1451. But he was also keeper of the privy seal, a position he had held since September 1456. Thus his promotion can also be seen as a return to tradition and an attempt to restore the palatinate to effective royal control. In normal times this would undoubtedly have been the case. But these were not normal times. By 1457 England was deeply divided, the king little more than a cypher and his court once again firmly under the control of a faction now given a lead by the queen herself. The appointment of her chancellor to Durham, notwithstanding his position as privy seal, was as much a move to curtail the power of the Earl of Salisbury in the north as a reassertion of royal will.[23]

Nevertheless the circumstances in 1457 demanded that Booth follow a conciliatory line. In November the king himself presided over a Great Council at Westminster, possibly convened on his own initiative, at which he first attempted to persuade the lords to come to terms. This first attempt at

---

[22] Pollard, *North-Eastern England*, pp. 257, 264.

[23] See Griffiths, *Henry VI*, pp. 777, 783; R.L. Storey, *The End of the House of Lancaster* (1966), p. 181; Pollard, *North-Eastern England*, p. 267.

reconciliation between the victors and victims of St Albans failed, but the conference was reconvened in January 1458 in an atmosphere of great tension in London, and, after protracted negotiation, on 24 March an agreement was reached and a settlement made between the Dukes of Somerset and York, and the Nevilles and the Percies. The royal arbitration was solemnly marked by a 'love-day' at St Paul's on the following day and the end of discord and the restoration of civil peace was celebrated by a round of jousting, feasting and other entertainments until May. The settlement of March 1458 proved to be shallow and short-lived, but it nevertheless reflected a determined effort to find a peaceful solution to the gathering crisis in which the keeper of the privy seal and new Bishop of Durham was deeply involved.[24] This would seem to explain the conciliatory approach he took in the palatinate itself. True, most of the annuities granted by his predecessor to his Neville kinsmen were cancelled. And Sir Thomas Neville, Salisbury's second son, was replaced as steward by his namesake Sir Thomas Neville of Brancepeth in a move which clearly indicated that the family of the Earl of Westmorland would be restored to favour. But by no means were all the traces of the preceding regime removed. The new chancellor, Henry Preston, had served Neville in the same office in 1452–6 and he had been constable of Durham Castle since 1438. Likewise the sheriff, Geoffrey Middleton, appointed for life by Neville, remained in office for the time being and the chief justice, Robert Danby, was retained. Furthermore Salisbury, his brother, William, Lord Fauconberg, and his retainer, Sir Thomas Lumley, were all reappointed as justices of the peace. Above all Salisbury continued to enjoy his grant of Stanhope Park which he had held in the later years of his brother's pontificate in lieu of his annuity of £100.[25] It was not in fact until after Ludford and the attainder of Salisbury and his principal retainers in the Coventry parliament in 1459 that all traces of his influence in the palatinate were removed and the restoration of the Nevilles of Raby completed. Then Booth also stepped in, no doubt with royal assent, himself to confiscate Barnard Castle from the Earl of Warwick, even before he was

---

[24] Griffiths, *Henry VI*, pp. 805–7; Pollard, *North-Eastern England*, pp. 268–9.

[25] Pollard, *North-Eastern England*, pp. 267–8.

attainted of treason, and thus to exercise the right of forfeiture that had been denied to his predecessors.[26]

Booth's pontificate thus began in faction and civil war. But Booth himself proved to be no puppet. For one, it would seem, he came to identify himself closely with the traditions, privileges and prerogatives of his palatinate and sought to exploit the weakness of the crown and the political divisions of the kingdom to reassert them.[27] There are several indicators of Booth's ambition to be another Anthony Bek or Hugh Puiset. He soon came into conflict with his priory at Durham over its claim to archidiaconal jurisdiction over its appropriated churches and his insistence on exercising his feudal prerogatives over its lands.[28] He revived the mint which had been in decline throughout the century, and the revival culminated in 1473 with a royal grant to coin episcopal halfpennies as well as pennies. Booth's policy proved profitable, for the income from the mint rose from £1 10s at the beginning of his pontificate to £33 6s 8d at its peak in 1473–4.[29]

Booth's ambition to reassert his independence might also be reflected in his reform of the stewardship. When in 1466 the last great lay steward, John Neville, then Earl of Northumberland, stepped down, he was replaced not by another prominent political figure, but by a professional lawyer, Thomas Morslaw, retained for half the customary fee. Although for a brief while in 1476 at the very end of his pontificate Booth retained Ralph, Lord Neville, as steward for the old fee of £40, it is apparent that this was a sinecure and that his new deputy, Thomas Middleton, like Morslaw a lawyer, continued to exercise the office. Morslaw, Middleton and their successors ceased to act as head of the civil government, restricting themselves to the presidency of manorial courts and

[26] Pollard, *TRSJ*, 2, pp. 10–11.

[27] Professor Loades' comment (Marcombe, *Last Principality*, p. 2) that the bishop 'was seldom tempted, even during troubled periods like the mid-fifteenth century, to display the independence of his lay contemporaries' is not borne out by Booth's pontificate.

[28] Dobson, *TCWAAS*, ns 65, pp. 205–7; R.L. Storey, 'The North of England', in S.B. Chrimes et al. (eds), *Fifteenth Century England* (Manchester, 1972), pp. 140–1.

[29] A.G. Woolley, 'The Bishop of Durham's Estate in the City of Durham in the Fifteenth Century' (University of Durham, MA thesis, 1991), ch. 9 *passim*.

other legal responsibilities. In place of the steward, Booth turned to his chancellor, Henry Gillowe, a senior clerical administrator, to head the civil administration of the palatinate. This reform was no doubt modelled on the kingdom, but it might well have also reflected Booth's desire to reassert personal control over the palatinate once he had escaped from the enforced tutelage of the Nevilles.[30]

But above all Booth's preoccupation with the prerogatives of his palatinate is revealed in his single-minded pursuit of the right to forfeiture of Barnard Castle. At Durham in April 1461, in the aftermath of Towton, both he and the Earl of Warwick pressed their claims to the lordship, which Booth had been occupying since November 1459, to the victorious Edward IV. Not surprisingly, on this occasion, Edward restored it to Warwick. But in June 1470, after Warwick had rebelled against Edward IV, Booth pressed his claim again. In his petition he stressed the point that the lordship had been wrongly forfeited to Edward I, a wrong recognized in the first parliament of Edward III but never rectified. The king now acceded to his request and granted that 'ye occupy, have and enjoy the said manor and castle with all the appurtenances according to your rights and title'. It is not surprising that Booth's insistence on his prerogatives created enemies, particularly the Nevilles of Middleham, who had lost control of the palatinate in 1457.[31]

In 1461, however, Booth was quickly reconciled to the new king, Edward IV.[32] Immediately after Towton he made a formal submission, was received into the king's grace and became his confessor. In the following eighteen months he served his new king loyally. Troops raised by him defeated his one-time steward, but now rebel, Sir Thomas Neville of Brancepeth, who raided the bishopric in June 1461. He participated in the negotiations with Queen Mary of Scotland which culminated in the agreement of a truce in July 1462. He was rewarded in February 1462 with the joint custody of Wressle and four days later was granted

---

[30] Pollard, *TRSJ*, 2, pp. 8, 11, and *North-Eastern England*, pp. 295–6.

[31] This and the following four paragraphs draw on Pollard, *North-Eastern England*, pp. 295–8 where fuller references are to be found.

[32] Pollard, in *Kings and Nobles*, pp. 109–15.

the alien priory and manor of Tooting Bec in Surrey. Yet on 7 December of the same year, Edward IV then being at Durham, the king took the temporalities of the diocese, that is to say the palatinate and the episcopal estates, into his own hands and removed Booth himself to house arrest in Pembroke College, Cambridge.

The received explanation of the sequestration of Durham in 1462 is that Booth had been revealed to be a traitor, communicating with his one-time patron Margaret of Anjou who at the end of October had recovered control of the Northumberland castles of Alnwick, Bamburgh and Dunstanburgh. The threat from this Lancastrian invasion was the reason for Edward's presence in Durham in early December at the head of a large army. There is no knowing whether Booth had communicated with Margaret of Anjou. It is not implausible, given the circumstances. But the occasion for the seizure of the temporalities was the receipt of information that the Scots intended to invade in force. The only remaining castle on the border then in loyal English hands was Norham. It was imperative that this was secure; indeed it was besieged in the following year. Thus if there were any doubts about the bishop's loyalty, it was necessary to secure direct royal control of Norham; and if the bishop were unwilling to surrender part of his palatinate voluntarily to the king, sequestration of the temporalities was the only course.

It is probably wrong, however, to assume that the initiative was the king's; it is more likely that Booth was the victim of Neville vindictiveness. The disposition of offices during the fifteen months when the temporalities were in royal hands reveals that the Nevilles were the principal beneficiaries. One of the three guardians to whom the king committed them, Thomas Colt, was in fact a councillor of the Earl of Warwick. Two of Bishop Neville's appointees were restored: John Lound as lay chancellor and Geoffrey Middleton as sheriff. Warwick's brother, John Neville, Viscount Montague, took up the all-important post of steward and both he and Warwick were appointed for the first time to the commission of the peace. While a significant proportion of the revenues of the bishop's estates were transferred to the royal coffers, the exercise of power in the palatinate passed back once more into the hands of the Nevilles at Middleham.

Booth was released from house arrest on 15 April 1464; on 17 April the temporalities were restored to him. Ten days earlier Edward IV had appointed commissioners to treat for peace with Scotland. It would appear that the imminence of peace with Scotland, even though the Lancastrians still occupied the Northumberland castles, paved the way for the restoration. But Booth now trod warily. He put in his own chancellor and sheriff, but continued to retain John Neville, soon to be created Earl of Northumberland, as his lay steward until December 1466. Not until after the destruction of Warwick and his brother in 1471 was Booth to be fully free of their unwelcome attention.

Thus when Richard of Gloucester stepped into Warwick's shoes in the summer of 1471 he found himself face to face with a Bishop of Durham who had established his own independence in his palatinate, was determined to brook no interference and was anxious to retain possession of Barnard Castle which he had been granted for a second time in 1470. The story of Booth's difficult relationship with Gloucester until his translation to York in 1476 has been told elsewhere.[33] Although he was willing to placate the duke in other matters, and later, as archbishop of York, worked amicably with him, as far as the palatinate of Durham was concerned, even though in the end he was obliged to surrender Barnard Castle yet again, he remained its undisputed ruler, promoting the family of the Earl of Westmorland yet again. In many respects for the remaining five years of his pontificate, now that civil war and faction seemed to have been brought to an end, Booth played the traditional role of Bishop of Durham as the king's loyal and trusted agent in the north. He played a prominent role in the negotiations that culminated in the Treaty of Edinburgh in 1474, served as chancellor for a year in 1473–4, and sat on the council in Westminster during the king's expedition to France in 1475.[34] York was a just reward for a bishop whose stature was far greater than has generally been recognized.

---

[33] Pollard, *North-Eastern England*, pp. 231–2, 330–1; C.L. Scofield, *Edward the Fourth* (1923), vol. II, p. 125. According to the well-placed second continuator of the Crowland Chronicle, Booth 'became weary and tired by the endless task' of managing parliamentary business (*The Crowland Chronicle Continuations, 1459–86*, N. Pronay and J. Cox (eds) (Richard III and Yorkist History Trust, 1986), p. 133.

[34] Pollard, in *Kings and Nobles*, pp. 117–20.

The king's nominee to replace him was William Dudley, who was duly provided and elected. Again the keeper of the privy seal was ignored; John Russell, Bishop of Lincoln, and his predecessor, Robert Stillington, were both overlooked. Dudley was a strange choice. He had no experience of public administration. But he was dean of the royal chapel; the senior clergyman of the royal household. His promotion was thus in tune with the general tenor of Edward IV's preference for household government and one might suppose that the king anticipated that he would admirably fill the role of his agent in the diocese. Whether he was happy for him rapidly to become the tool of his brother, Richard of Gloucester, one cannot tell; for that is what happened. Initially, it was to be expected that Gloucester would be given his part in the affairs of the palatinate that Booth had denied him. Close cooperation with the duke, who already dominated northern England, was to be encouraged. Thus Gloucester was immediately added to the commission of the peace. But before long he acquired a more prominent role. Within a year the bishop was sending to London to assure himself of the duke's good disposition on affairs in the palatinate. Several of his councillors were Gloucester's servants. A string of offices and annuities were granted to his retainers. And in May 1479 Gloucester himself was granted for life the forest of Weardale and Stanhope Park, together the equivalent of an annuity of £100. This is precisely the arrangement that had existed earlier in the century between Bishop Neville and his brother, the Earl of Salisbury. Moreover, Gloucester, even though he was the heir to Middleham Nevilles, successfully patched up the quarrel with the Earl of Westmorland and his family, by securing a formal release of their claim to the lost Yorkshire lordships and bringing Ralph, Lord Neville, the heir to the earldom, who had been highly favoured by Bishop Booth, into his service. By 1480, when on the outbreak of war with Scotland he was made the bishop's lieutenant, Gloucester was in truth the man who, cherishing the Nevilles, and standing as one with them, had the rule of the palatinate. And it was to him, not the bishop, to whom its inhabitants turned for favours and justice.[35] Once

[35] *Ibid.*, pp. 120–1.

again, perhaps even more completely than during the pontificate of Robert
Neville, the palatinate had fallen into the pocket of the Lord of Middleham. It is
hard to believe that this was Edward IV's intention; but so dominating a person
was his brother, and so weak a man and so inexperienced a politician was
Dudley, that the effect was almost exactly the same as the promotion of Robert
Neville forty years earlier.

It is hardly surprising, therefore, that Dudley was a willing supporter of
Richard of Gloucester's succession to the throne in 1483. It may have been a
disappointment to the new king that Dudley died in November 1483. But
Richard III made a characteristically original choice for his successor in John
Shirwood, Archdeacon of Richmond, a member of his own clerical affinity and
a scholar. But perhaps Shirwood's greatest attraction to the king was that he
had spent most of his recent life in Rome. He had returned to England for the
coronation, but at the time of his provision he was back at the curia. Indeed he
did not visit his diocese until 1490. His absence gave Richard III the
opportunity to retain the temporalities in his own hands until 6 August 1485.
Although regrettably the administrative records of the palatinate are defective
for the period 1483–90, it is apparent that it was governed by its council directly
in the king's interest.[36] One cannot know for certain, but it is likely that Sir
Richard Ratcliffe was appointed steward, for late in 1483 or early in 1484
Robert Ebbchester, prior of the convent, referred in an undated letter to the
'great rule that he beareth under the King's Grace in our country'.[37] Under
Richard III the palatinate in effect ceased to exist. And there is nothing to
suggest that Henry VII reversed his predecessor's policy in the early years of his
reign. Only when he was able to promote Richard Fox, his keeper of the privy
seal, to the palatinate in 1494 was the traditional pattern of provisions and
customary relationship between crown and loyal servant fully restored.

The story of the relationship between the crown and the palatinate between
1437 and 1494 is instructive in several ways. It is revealing about the character
and policies of successive kings. The promotion of Robert Neville in 1437 was

[36] Pollard, *North-Eastern England*, pp. 374, 388–9.
[37] DCD, Registrum Parvum, III, f. 188v.

symptomatic of the descent into factional rule at the end of Henry VI's minority; the inability of the adult king subsequently to curtail the absorption of the palatinate into the larger hegemony created by Salisbury in the north is entirely at one with the character of his rule before 1453; and the promotion of Booth, even though more obviously qualified for the post, is in keeping with the factionalism choking his reign in its later years. One perhaps should feel some sympathy for Margaret of Anjou in 1457, for it was not she who first made the appointment to Durham factional and there was every justification for rectifying the situation. Edward IV, as in so much else, found his hands tied behind his back in his first reign and perhaps had little choice but to bow to concerted Neville pressure in 1463 to restore the status quo ante 1457. Only after 1471 was he fully free to act as he would wish, and it is to be noted how quickly he re-established the traditional relationship with Bishop Booth. But the promotion of Dudley raises once more the question of Edward's judgement. Whether intended or not, it led directly and swiftly to the surrender once again of authority in the palatinate to the heir to Neville of Middleham, albeit that this now was his own brother Richard. In promoting so obviously an unsuited candidate as Dudley, did he give in to Richard's importuning to be given a free hand in Durham? Or did he fail to foresee the consequence? Richard III himself took the opportunity of Dudley's death to maintain and extend his personal authority in the palatinate. The palatine council became, in effect, a sister body to his council in the north; had he lived it is likely that he would have anticipated, in deed if not in law, Henry VIII's reform of the palatinate by some fifty years. His was a truly novel departure.

The history of these years is also revealing about the role of the Nevilles in the palatinate. Despite Prior Bell's judgement on the importance of the Earl of Westmorland's family in 1476, it is apparent that the second earl, who died in 1484, was never a force to reckon with. This was primarily because of the partition of his estates, but it is also because he was himself no more than a figurehead, described as being 'homo innocens' by one contemporary,[38] and

---

[38] William Worcester, *Itineraries*, J.H. Harvey (ed.) (Oxford, 1969), p. 345.

because his own son and heir died in 1451. The family was represented
therefore for most of the period by his kinsmen – his younger sons or his
eventual heir and nephew, Ralph, Lord Neville. Even so, apart from brief
periods at the beginning and end of Booth's pontificate, not even these
members of the family were showed much favour. They were largely
excluded from palatinate affairs. And in the first year of Richard III's reign,
be it remembered, it was Sir Richard Ratcliffe, not Ralph, Lord Neville, who
had the rule of the country under the king's grace. Henry VII was no more
generous to the third and fourth earls than Richard III.[39] In so far as the
later Earls of Westmorland enjoyed a greater degree of local power and
influence in the mid-sixteenth century this was by nature a revival of the
situation as it had been before 1425 rather than a continuation from the later
fifteenth century.

For, during the fifteenth century, it was the junior branch of the Neville family
which dominated and quite eclipsed the earl and his family. What the Earl of
Salisbury and his mother had gained through court favour in 1437 by the
promotion of Robert Neville, Warwick recovered by the sequestration of the
temporalities in 1463 and Richard of Gloucester, as his political heir, received
by gift of his brother, the king. There is no question that these three men, who
dominated the north from 1437 to 1483, were overmighty subjects. They took
more for themselves than their kings should wisely have allowed, made
themselves free of royal control and did not scruple, when they judged their
positions were threatened, to turn that power against the crown itself (or, in the
case of the third in 1483, to take the crown for himself). A critical element,
arguably perhaps the single most important, in what happened is that both
kings, Henry VI and Edward IV, surrendered control of the palatinate of
Durham to them.

Furthermore this story is instructive about the relationships between court
and country, the centre and the provinces in fifteenth-century politics. As
Bishop Russell intended to declare in one of his draft sermons for the opening
of the parliament that did not meet in 1483, politic rule, or successful

---

[39] Pollard, *North-Eastern England*, pp. 371, 391.

government, depended on the nobles exercising the will of the sovereign.[40] Because of its distance from Westminster, because of the need to delegate military power and authority on the borders to the magnates and because the crown itself was territorially weak in the far north, it was more difficult for the crown to ensure that the nobles in the region did in fact act on its behalf. Recently there has been a tendency to suggest that in the fifteenth century it became impossible to sustain this control. But there was nothing inevitable about what happened. The crown always had Durham at its disposal. It was not forced in the fifteenth century to surrender control over the palatinate, or to abandon the practice of promoting its own trusted servants. Rather what happened between 1437 and 1494 was the result of a sequence of specific, inter-connected events at court and in the region. That it was not inevitable or irreversible is revealed by the ease with which Edward IV and Laurence Booth were able to restore the traditional relationship between crown and bishop in 1471–6.

Finally the story throws light on the career and actions of Richard III. What happened in the three and a half decades before he succeeded to the Kingmaker's estates in northern England provided a tradition and example of aggrandisement for him to follow. Salisbury and Warwick had both sought to dominate the palatinate; he understandably sought to do the same as Duke of Gloucester. But as king he grasped the wisdom of using the palatinate as an extension of his own authority. It is not simply that he did not wish to surrender the personal control over the palatinate which he had secured between 1476 and 1483; it is also that on 24 June he ceased to be a subject and became a king. In his brief reign the palatinate became a direct arm of royal government in the north. He learnt as much from the failures of his predecessors as kings as he copied from his Neville precursors as lords of the north.

---

[40] *Grants Etc from the Crown during the reign of Edward V*, J.G. Nichols (ed.) (Camden Society, old series, LX, 1854), pp. xiii–xiv.

5

CARLISLE AND THE ENGLISH WEST MARCH IN THE LATER MIDDLE AGES

Henry Summerson

Early in the summer of 1461 John Paston received yet another letter. The new king, Edward IV, he was informed, 'because of the siege about Carlisle, changed his day of Coronation to be upon the Sunday next after St John Baptist [28 June] to the intent to speed him northward in all haste; and howbeit, blessed be God, that he hath now good tidings, that Lord Montague hath broken the siege and slain of Scots 6000 and two knights, whereof Lord Clifford's brother is one, yet notwithstanding he will be crowned the said Sunday . . .'[1] The opening of Parliament, too, had had to be postponed because of the threat to Carlisle.[2] The scarcity of sieges of towns during the Wars of the Roses has several times been remarked upon by historians.[3] But Carlisle in 1461 was an important exception to this rule. The attackers were a force of Lancastrians and Scots, said to have been led by Queen Margaret, who had promised to surrender the city to the Scots if they would help her to capture it, and by northern Lancastrians such as Humphrey Dacre, Richard Tunstall and Henry Bellingham.[4] Subsequent payments for repairs to the walls, damaged during 'le Sege', suggest that they had siege-engines, perhaps even some light guns.[5] They ravaged the suburbs and

---

[1] *The Paston Letters*, ed. J. Gairdner (Edinburgh, 1910), vol. 2, p. 13.

[2] *CCR, 1461–1468*, p. 60.

[3] E.g. C. Ross, *The Wars of the Roses* (1976), p. 163 – 'No major English town was looted or pillaged, or even systematically besieged'. Also A. Goodman, *The Wars of the Roses: Military Activity and English Society, 1452–97* (1981), p. 181; J. Gillingham, *The Wars of the Roses* (1981), p. 27.

[4] For the background to the siege, see H. Summerson, *Medieval Carlisle: the city and the borders from the late eleventh to the mid-sixteenth century*, Cumberland and Westmorland Antiquarian and Archaeological Society, Extra Series, vol. 25 (1993), pp. 446–7.

[5] C(umberland) R(ecord) O(ffice), CA/4/138.

exerted a pressure so tight that some of the citizens deserted to them – three years later it was decided that burgesses who had gone over to the enemy during 'le Segetyme' should be put out of the franchise.[6] The siege probably began in May, and certainly continued into June, and it would appear that in the end the invaders broke into the city – in December 1461 Carlisle Priory was licensed to acquire lands worth £20 'on account of the devastation of their possessions in Carlisle by the rebels'.[7] The situation was saved first by Sir Richard Salkeld, a Neville retainer, who was later said to have performed 'eminent services' which included 'rescuing the city and castle of Carlisle from the rebels',[8] and then by Lord Montague, who brought up a relieving army large enough to challenge the queen's forces. The number of reported casualties may be doubted, but there appears to have been a battle outside Carlisle.

To Yorkists and Lancastrians alike, Carlisle was an important place – 'one of the chief keys and fortresses to the defence of this our realm', as it was described in 1498.[9] It was not large. Sir Gilbert de Lannoy, passing through in 1431, rather patronizingly called it 'a very pretty little town, enclosed with walls and possessing a very fine castle and cathedral',[10] and it seems unlikely that its population during the fifteenth century at any time rose much, if at all, above 1,500.[11] But it was important by reason of its functions, as a commercial entrepôt for the produce of its region, as the centre of a diocese, and as the county town, where assizes and gaol deliveries were supposed to be held (in fact they were often held at Penrith), and where the sheriff of Cumberland had his office, while with its castle and walls it was of fundamental importance to the

---

[6] *The Royal Charters of the City of Carlisle*, ed. R.S. Ferguson, Cumberland and Westmorland Antiquarian and Archaeological Society, Extra Series, vol. 10 (1894), pp. 114–15.

[7] *CPR, 1461–1467*, p. 87.

[8] *CPR, 1467–1477*, pp. 25–26.

[9] CRO, Ca2/105.

[10] O.H. North, 'The Travels of Sir Guilbert de Lannoy in the North of England and elsewhere 1430', in *TCWAAS*, 2nd Series, vol. 21 (1921), p. 46 (these travels are misdated by a year in this article).

[11] For discussions of Carlisle's population in the later Middle Ages, see Summerson, *Medieval Carlisle*, pp. 302–8, 412–14, 506–15.

defence of the English west march against the Scots. This last function was vital, for it was this which more than anything else engaged the interests of the crown. The effectiveness of royal power was greater in some parts of the north of England than in others. But it was certainly real in much of Cumberland (a point rehearsed in greater detail below), a fact which would make it less inappropriate than might otherwise be the case for this analysis of the fortunes of Carlisle and Cumbria to be presented largely from the point of view of the English central government, even had the accidents of archival survival not made a heavy reliance on records originating at Westminster unavoidable anyway.

The inevitable accompaniment of such a viewpoint is the danger that the north-west will consequently be seen in too exclusively a remote, and southern, perspective, in the light which caused the Crowland Chronicler to refer to 'the North, whence all evil spreads . . .'.[12] To the government of the realm, as situated at Westminster, the control of the north did indeed pose problems, but it should be stressed that they were problems caused primarily by distance, compounded by the proximity of a recurrently hostile national frontier. The latter was responsible for the only institution of government to be found only in the north, the march days and warden-courts responsible for the enforcement of border law.[13] Those apart, society in the north-west was very much like society everywhere else in late medieval England, though climate and terrain, *and* the effects of war, undeniably helped to make it relatively poor, to the extent that it sometimes found it hard to feed itself. In February 1482 the large numbers of troops stationed on the west march led to what was described as 'daily increasing dearth and scarcity of victuals', with the result that quantities of food had to be imported from outside the region.[14] The habits of force, of familiarity with arms and speedy response to attack, generated by a warlike ambience,

[12] Quoted in A.J. Pollard, *North-Eastern England during the Wars of the Roses* (Oxford, 1990), pp. 25 7.

[13] See H. Summerson, 'The Early Development of the Laws of the Anglo-Scottish Marches, 1249–1448', in T.D. Fergus and W.M. Gordon (eds), *Legal History in the Making* (1991), pp. 29–42.

[14] *Calendar of Documents relating to Scotland*, vol. IV, *1377–1509*, ed. J. Bain (Edinburgh, 1888), no. 1472.

probably did make the northern shires more violent, less law-abiding, than those further south. But only on the furthest borders, in Gilsland and the parts north of the River Lyne, does there seem to have been a serious crisis of law-enforcement, and that, by the early sixteenth century, seems to have been exacerbated by a growth in population, which intensified competition for scarce resources and encouraged sheep and cattle stealing as part of that competition.[15]

Another response to population pressure was emigration. This was particularly common from Cumbria to York, and since those who went south often kept in touch with their homeland,[16] and might eventually return there, such movement of people also helped to counteract the region's isolation, though this tends to be exaggerated anyway. The men of Carlisle and its region traded with Scotland – in spite of repeated prohibitions – and with Newcastle, Kendal and York. Some of the Kendal merchants who came to Carlisle also traded south to Southampton, while by 1518 Carlisle merchants were joining the Corpus Christi gild at Coventry.[17] Robert Bell, formerly Prior of Durham but from 1478 Bishop of Carlisle, in around 1490 bought iron and wine in Newcastle, more wine at Hull, 'three images of the lord' at York, and fish from Jarrow.[18] The fact that the principal lords of the region had lands elsewhere, principally in Northumberland and Yorkshire, would likewise have served to keep the north-west in touch with the rest of the north of England, and of the realm.

The same would doubtless have been true of the city's ecclesiastical functions, the result of its having been a cathedral city within the province of York, and still more, perhaps, of its role as a place of pilgrimage, with a noted cult of the Virgin. In 1414 the King of Arms for Ireland specified in his will that after his death a man should make a pilgrimage in his name to St Ninian's in Scotland, travelling there by way of a number of important shrines – starting in London, he was to go successively to St Mary of Walsingham, St John of Beverley,

---

[15] See A.J.L. Winchester, *Landscape and Society in Medieval Cumbria* (Edinburgh, 1987), pp. 51–5.

[16] Summerson, *Medieval Carlisle*, pp. 578–9, 585.

[17] Ibid., pp. 419–20, 567–86.

[18] CRO, DRC/2/16, m. 1d; DRC/2/14, m. 9; DRC/2/28.

St John of Bridlington, St William of York and St Mary of Carlisle, before crossing into Scotland.[19] In 1472 the rector of Heslerton in East Yorkshire ordered that a pilgrim, or pilgrims, should go in his name to a total of eighteen shrines, the Blessed Mary of Carlisle among them.[20] People made pilgrimages to Carlisle, and also from Carlisle and the rest of Cumberland, particularly into Scotland, to the shrines of St Ninian at Whithorn and St Kentigern at Glasgow. It has been plausibly suggested that Richard of Gloucester acquired his apparent attachment to the cult of St Ninian through his interests in north-west England.[21] It would certainly have been easy for him to have done so. In 1427 James I laid down regulations for pilgrims coming to Whithorn from England, including the badges they should wear,[22] and they were still travelling thither a century later, when a kinsman of Lord Dacre was kidnapped on his way back, even though he had a safe conduct from the King of Scots.[23] And reverence for St Kentigern, or Mungo, is attested not only by the Christian names of Cumbrian men,[24] but also by lines in the verse chronicle of the Northumbrian John Hardyng, advising Edward IV (in the course of a three-year programme for the conquest of Scotland) that after he, or his representative, had captured Stirling, he should then go on to Glasgow – 'Ere twenty mile and four to Mungo's shrine Where with offering ye shall to him incline . . .'.[25] Carlisle and its regions were not isolated, either to north or south. Many Scots traded with north-west England, and many came to work there, especially as agricultural

---

[19] BL, Add.MS 9010, ff. 10, 10v. The will refers to 'St Ronan's', for whose being identical with St Ninian, see J. Sledd, 'Canterbury Tales, C310, 320: "By Seint Ronyan"', *Medieval Studies*, 13 (1951), pp. 226–33.

[20] *Testamenta Eboracensia*, III, ed. J. Raine, SS, XLV (1865), pp. 199–201.

[21] D. Palliser, 'Richard III and York', in R. Horrox (ed.), *Richard III and the North*, University of Hull Studies in Regional and Local History, no. 6 (1986), pp. 60–1; R.B. Dobson, 'Richard III and the Church of York', in R.A. Griffiths and J. Sherborne (eds), *Kings and Nobles in the Later Middle Ages* (Gloucester, 1986), pp. 141–2, 145–6.

[22] *Registrum Magni Sigilli Regum Scottorum*, II, *1424–1513*, ed. J.B. Paul (Edinburgh, 1882), no. 107, p. 20.

[23] *State Papers*, vol. IV (Record Commission, 1836), pp. 503–4.

[24] A. Goodman, 'Religion and Warfare in the Anglo-Scottish Marches', in R. Bartlett and A. Mackay (eds), *Medieval Frontier Societies* (Oxford, 1989), p. 257.

[25] BL, Lansd. MS 204, f. 223v.

labourers and domestic servants.[26] And to the south the people of Cumbria were firmly tied in to the rest of the country through the processes of government, through court sessions (when these were not prevented by war), through taxation (when not remitted for the same reason), by the activities of sheriffs, escheators, coroners and estate officers, and by all the apparatus of bureaucratic government.

There is always a danger of overestimating the effectiveness of central government anywhere in medieval England, let alone in the north-west. All the same, the evidence suggests that royal power in the latter region was real. The exercise of it fluctuated according to the policy and personality of the monarch wielding it, but potentially the king was the greatest lord in Cumberland, his power based not only upon the authority associated with his regality, but also upon his control of Carlisle, with its garrison, of Inglewood forest, a substantial block of land in the very centre of the county, and of the patronage placed at his disposal largely *through* his control of Carlisle and Inglewood – his ability to appoint sheriffs, justices of the peace, escheators, foresters, and other agents and officers. Only rarely are leading ecclesiastics found arbitrating in gentry disputes such as those between Heron and Maners in Northumberland,[27] because in the north-west, and especially in Cumberland, the king's peace was more often kept by the king's government. Of course much of his power had to be delegated – no English king came to Carlisle between 1335 and 1617 – and was commonly wielded in the king's name by one of the great lords of the region, which until 1471 usually meant a Neville or a Percy. To be warden of the west march, the officer chiefly responsible for the defence of the region against the Scots, in theory entailed the receipt of large sums of royal money, but in practice there tended to be long intervals between payments, and during those intervals the warden had to be able to pay garrisons and repair defences out of his own resources, something only a Neville or a Percy could easily do. There was in fact a large gap, in terms of wealth and power, a gap which their near-monopoly of the

[26] PRO, E179/90/27.
[27] See above, pp. 8–12.

march wardenship could only widen, between those two families and Cumberland's other noble families, the Dacres, Harringtons and Greystokes (the Cliffords were basically a Westmorland family, with little property in Cumberland). But although the warden of the march was a man of great authority in the north-west, his office came to him by royal grant, and could always – except, perhaps, for a very few months in 1483 – be revoked.

Turning from the general to the particular, to the ways in which individual kings actually exercised authority on the west march, it is easy to see that Henry VI's mismanagement of his position there was as complete as it was everywhere else. Having first allowed the Nevilles to build up a power-base in Cumberland, he then gave, or allowed to be given, a timid endorsement to the efforts made by the Percies after 1449 to challenge them.[28] The Carlisle fee-farm of £80 *per annum*, bestowed for life on Richard Neville, Earl of Salisbury, in 1439, was resumed by the crown in 1450, but in July 1452 granted to Henry Percy, Lord Poynings. Granted back to Salisbury in 1454, it was returned to Percy, now Earl of Northumberland, in 1459, along with a number of other royal rights and dues formerly held by Salisbury. Northumberland's brother, Thomas Percy, had been raised to the peerage by Henry VI in 1453 as Lord Egremont, in the expectation that he would devote himself to keeping the peace and suppressing the disorderly. There was little to warrant such optimism, as Egremont, operating from his family's base at Cockermouth, in the west of the county, where central authority was weakened by the fact that royal writs did not run there, had already inspired what the sheriff for the year 1451/2 described as 'divers dissensions, riots and debates moved within the shire', and in the following year promoted disorder so intense that the next sheriff reported that 'the one half of the Shire was divided from the other', and that the undersheriff and bailiffs had been beaten up by 'certain riotous people belonging to the Lord Egremont', who had sworn to have the sheriff's head. In this discouraging atmosphere it is hardly surprising that a year later no sheriff accounted for the issues of Cumberland at all. Without gaining any perceptible political benefit by

---

[28] For the events described in this paragraph see R.L. Storey, *The End of the House of Lancaster* (1966), pp. 124–6; Summerson, *Medieval Carlisle*, pp. 438–44.

doing so, Henry VI identified his own cause with that of the Percies, thereby earning the hostility of the Nevilles, and then, after Towton, ensured for himself a more general hostility through an alliance with the Scots, which led to the siege of Carlisle. By the end of 1461 it is probable that the cause of Lancaster, associated with civil strife and Scottish invasion, had been comprehensively discredited in the north-west.

At that time Edward IV is still likely to have been a largely unknown quantity, in both personal and dynastic terms, in Cumbria – hence the 'pedigree' of the new king's 'true and verray lineal descent' to the crowns of England and France which one Thomas Derwent, a Neville retainer who had twice been MP for Carlisle, was carrying on his journey 'to Karlileward' in 1461 or 1462, when he was captured by the Lancastrian Humphrey Dacre and imprisoned in Kirkoswald castle.[29] But he was apparently soon able to command a following in the region. Although Edward IV must have helped his own cause by the support he gave to the prolonged struggle to defeat the Scots and the Lancastrian rebels in the north-west, a struggle which seems to have lasted as long there as it did in the north-east, though there are no battles associated with it, this work was essentially done by the Nevilles, who were handsomely paid for it. Yet when the Nevilles rebelled in 1470, they found that the city of Carlisle, whose support they probably felt they could rely upon, was not just inactive but positively hostile. When Edward IV was at York in March of that year, he gave a verbal message to the bishop of Carlisle, to be conveyed to the mayor and citizens, 'for the reducing of the castle of our said city to our obeissance out of the possession of our rebels and enemies', and this operation the mayor and his men duly performed, perhaps by a surprise attack, at a cost of £20.[30]

The fact that in the aftermath of the siege of 1461 the citizens of Carlisle had successfully petitioned the new king for a reduction by half of their annual fee-

---

[29] PRO, SC8/107, no. 5322.

[30] PRO, E404/75/3, no. 56 – where the events recorded seem to be erroneously attributed to 1469 instead of 1470.

farm, from £80 to £40,[31] doubtless constituted an extra claim on the city's loyalty to Edward IV, but the king's command, and the citizens' response to it, are still striking evidence for the authority the crown could wield in the north west, when its wearer chose to speak over the heads of its magnate families. But a king had to be able to keep his crown on his head. Although the fact that Carlisle Castle remained in Edward's hands will have been an important reason why the Neville-inspired rising of July 1470, so energetically prosecuted in Yorkshire, was ineffective in Cumberland, by October 1470 Edward IV was in exile, and for several months documents public and private were dated by reference to the Readeption of Henry VI. Carlisle did not swim against this tide, on the evidence of a deed disposing of city property which is dated to the forty-ninth year of the reign of Henry VI and the first of his Readeption.[32] This need not be attributed to cowardice, or even to simple prudence. All the signs are that obedience to the *de facto* monarch was one of the principles traditionally guiding Carlisle's civic life. Allegiance was given to the king as such, rather than to the representative of a particular dynasty – such was the importance of his role in the direction of the region's defences. If royal power was effective in the north-west, an important reason was that the people there wanted and needed it to be.

Scottish attack, or the fear of it, was a constant factor in the life of fifteenth-century Cumbria. The fear extended throughout the region – as late as 1536 'the rulers of this country' could be plausibly denounced for their failure to keep the border effectively against the Scots[33] – and the reality was not far behind. In 1436 the Scots burnt Wigton, south-west of Carlisle and halfway to Cockermouth,[34] while in the 1450s they penetrated as far as Blencarn, east of Penrith at the southern end of Cumberland.[35] But inevitably it was the north of

---

[31] Ferguson, *Royal Charters*, pp. 53–8.

[32] Castle Howard, York, Dacre Deeds A1, no. 176.

[33] S.M. Harrison, *The Pilgrimage of Grace in the Lake Counties 1536–7*, Royal Historical Society, Studies in History, no. 27, London (1981), p. 83.

[34] CRO, D/Lec/29/1.

[35] PRO, C139/170, no. 28.

the latter county which suffered most. In 1474 a lease of Carlisle's mills included the proviso that if the mills were burnt by the king's enemies, then the rent should be reduced in proportion to the damage done,[36] and three years later Carlisle Priory, petitioning for the grant of the hospital of St Nicholas in the city suburbs, could refer to the 'great jeopardy' in which it and its goods stood from the Scots.[37] Shortly afterwards Bewcastle Castle was garrisoned,[38] and the bishop gave his little fort – *forcelletum* – at Linstock to his tenants there, 'for the safekeeping of their persons and goods'.[39] In 1480 Edward IV's charter to Armathwaite Nunnery, a few miles south of Carlisle, was granted because that house had been 'by our enemies of Scotland totally destroyed and wasted in house, enclosures and other buildings . . . .'.[40] By then open war was imminent. This everpresent danger of attack, even in peacetime, and the threat of war behind it, constitutes one of the most important dimensions to the career of Richard of Gloucester in the north-west. The heir to the Nevilles, he took over their retainers, and many of those of the Percies, but nevertheless he was the king's agent, and as such the defender of the border. He might have warlike aspirations of his own, but if they did not coincide with royal policy he would be called to order. Hence the instructions sent to Gloucester, in about 1475, to give 'due reformation . . . according to right and custom of our said marches' to the tenants of Sir John Carlill, Scots robbed by Englishmen on the west march,[41] and other orders for the giving of redress on the marches. When the defences of Carlisle needed repairing, it was the king's money that was spent on them, even though Gloucester might be the intermediary. An indenture of December 1480 records the duke as handing over to the mayor some of the £100 lately granted by the king for the repair of the city walls, and gunpowder, arrows and bows

---

[36] CRO, Ca5/1, no. 28.

[37] H. Barnes, 'Leprosy and Local Leper Hospitals', in *TCWAAS*, 1st Series, vol. 10 (1889), p. 109.

[38] H.M. Colvin, D.R. Ransome, J. Summerson, *The History of the King's Works*, vol. III, Part I (HMSO, 1975), pp. 233–4.

[39] CRO, DRC/2/13, m. 2.

[40] Sir William Dugdale, *Monasticon Anglicanum*, vol. III (1821), pp. 271–2.

[41] BL, Cottonian MS Vesp.C.XVI, f. 127.

from 'the king's stuff', as well as two guns and two crossbows from the duke's own stock.[42]

Even though he was sometimes constrained in his ambitions by the demands of royal policy, Gloucester was still a dynamic figure in the north-west, above all in the war with Scotland which broke out in the early 1480s. He burned Dumfries in 1482,[43] and was said to have subdued the Scottish west march to a depth of thirty miles. It was a war fought by sea as well as by land, and in western as well as eastern waters.[44] In 1481, for instance, payment was made for '300 men at arms retained by the King to serve him against the Scots by sea on the west side of Scotland'. The centre of these English naval operations appears to have been Chester, and one of their aims was the defence of English merchant-ships against attack on their way to Bordeaux, but as in the past, the protection of the Cumbrian coastline is also likely to have been an objective. This was an aspect of the Scottish war which may have had political repercussions, by giving the Stanleys cause for grievance. As lords – indeed, till 1505 kings[45] – of Man, the Stanleys may well have felt that the western seas were their preserve. In 1457, after all, they had singlehandedly launched a seaborne attack on the Scottish west march and burnt Kirkcudbright.[46] But although they brought 3,000 men to the campaign of 1482, the Stanleys do not appear to have had any control over the 'divers men about to set out to war in the western sea against the Scots at the duke's discretion', and as that phrase indicates, in all these operations Gloucester remained the man in charge.

In charge, but not the man in ultimate control. That continued to be the king, and the king's underlying control can be seen even in the celebrated grant made to the duke in the 1483 Parliament.[47] The substance of the grant is well

[42] PRO, E405/58, m. 5d; CRO, D/Lons/L C61.

[43] Pollard, *North-Eastern England*, pp. 239, 243.

[44] See PRO, E101/329/2; E405/70, m. 7; E405/71, m. 5d; E405/566, f. 58.

[45] M. Jones, 'Richard III and the Stanleys', in Horrox (ed.), *Richard III and the North*, p. 30.

[46] A.I. Dunlop, *The Life and Times of James Kennedy, bishop of St Andrews* (Edinburgh, 1950), p. 202.

[47] *Rot.Parl.*, VI, pp. 204–5.

known. Gloucester and his heirs male were given the wardenship of the west march, Carlisle, Bewcastle and Nicholforest, the shrievalty of Cumberland, and practically all the king's rights and revenues in the county, and he was also licensed to create for himself a palatinate in south-west Scotland which would be held in fee-simple, that is, without any restrictions upon its descent at all. As it stands, the grant presents some problems, in that the preamble to the grant relating to Cumberland, and the grant of the Scottish palatinate, contradict one another. For whereas the grant of the palatinate, which seems to have been inserted into the Cumbrian grant without regard to its context, speaks of the Scottish lands the duke will conquer as being ones 'whereof great part is now in the Scots' hands', the grant for Cumberland refers to the duke as having lately 'subdued great part of the West borders of Scotland, adjoining to England, by the space of 30 miles and more', a distance which, if true, would have taken the line of conquest to Hawick and Moffat, far beyond most, if not all, of the dales which the palatinate grant describes as being yet to be overrun. The likeliest explanation for this is that following the Treaty of Fotheringhay in June 1482, between Edward IV and the Scottish pretender the Duke of Albany, by which the latter promised to transfer to Edward lands in Scotland practically identical with those listed in the palatinate grant to Gloucester,[48] Edward then made his rights in those lands over to his brother, who subsequently chose to strengthen his title in them by having the king's earlier grant incorporated into the later one promulgated in Parliament, and thereby given the force of statute.

Be that as it may, the whole grant was certainly generous, but not unlimitedly so. Even as far as the palatinate was concerned, there were restrictions. The duke's rights were to be those of the Bishop of Durham in *his* palatinate, and both king and duke must have been perfectly well aware that whatever the bishop might claim, his actual independence of royal control in his own palatinate was far from boundless. Indeed, in one important respect the duke was given less than the bishop, in that forfeiture for treason – which in newly

---

[48] Rymer, *Foedera*, vol. V, Part III, pp. 120–1.

conquered territory were likely to be numerous – were reserved to the king. The mention of treason underlines the fact that the inhabitants of these Scottish dales were intended to be the subjects of the English king. In Cumberland, too, the king did not give everything away. Again, forfeitures for treason were reserved, as were wardships of heirs to lands not held of the duke, and so, too, were the wardships and marriages of the heirs of lords of Parliament. When a Lord Dacre or a Lord Greystoke, or even an Earl of Northumberland, died leaving an under-age heir, his lands in Cumberland would come under royal control during that heir's minority. The temporalities of the bishopric when the see was vacant were to remain at the disposal of the king, who also retained the power to appoint the bishop; the latter could be a valuable agent for royal power in the region, as the events of 1470 showed. Edward IV gave his brother a very great deal, but he did not make a complete surrender of his position in the north west, and he clearly expected his brother to continue to act on behalf of the crown. The clause licensing Gloucester to receive Scots into English allegiance – 'under the allegiance and obeisance of our said Sovereign Lord or of his heirs, Kings of England' – could hardly have been more specific on the point.

Gloucester's advance to almost princely status on the west march could have entailed a splendid role for Carlisle, which would inevitably have acquired something of the status of a regional capital, had the duke not become king shortly afterwards. Unfortunately, little is known about Gloucester's dealings with Carlisle before his accession. As warden of the west march he was probably a familiar figure in the city, and he was certainly well placed to make his presence felt and to have his wishes obeyed. His principal agent in Carlisle was probably Henry Denton, whom he retained 'to await and attend upon him, as well in time of peace as of war', in 1473.[49] Denton was several times mayor, and it was to him as mayor that Gloucester gave money and armaments in 1480. There were works in progress on the castle late in 1483, and it is very probable that they had begun some time earlier. Their connection with Gloucester is

[49] CRO, D/Lons/L D65.

attested by the stone carved with a boar which Camden reported seeing on the walls,[50] and it may be a sign of the duke's ambitions for Carlisle that they should have been carried out in brick – not a sign of work done on the cheap, but rather, as at Tattershall and Kirkby Muxloe, a material indicative of modernity and magnificence. The man who, in fifteenth-century England, built or rebuilt a castle in brick, was a man keen to advertise his wealth and status.

Perhaps it was a similar concern for appearance which later caused Richard III to give Carlisle Priory £5 'towards the making of the glass window within the same our Monastery'.[51] He was generous to the priory, and the expression 'our Monastery' is significant in this context, for it was a royal foundation, and Richard was doubtless anxious to be seen taking his due place in the ranks of its kingly benefactors. Even so, his gifts to it – two tuns of red wine yearly 'for using divine observance', £20 *per annum* from the lordship of Penrith, the reimbursement of fees paid for a charter of confirmation,[52] as well as money for a window – suggest a personal attachment as well as a connection acquired along with his office, the result, perhaps, of a devotion to the cult of the Virgin in the cathedral, or to one of the other saints whose relics the priory held. Indeed, Richard III seems to have had a higher regard for the priory than for the city of Carlisle, since he gave the former's canons the right to all tithes from 'all things within the City of Carlisle tithable', and when the citizens demurred, administered a stiff rebuke ordering them to pay the tithes 'without any manner a grudge, excuse or contradiction, so that we hear not of your contrary demeaning, as ye intend to avoid our grievous displeasure and the lawful peril that may ensue unto you in that part'.[53] The tone of royal displeasure is fully in keeping with the firm control which Richard as king exercised over the city and its region. He did not, after he became king, appoint a successor to himself as

---

[50] M. McCarthy, H. Summerson, R. Annis, *Carlisle Castle: a survey and documentary history*, English Heritage Archaeological Report, no. 18 (1990), p. 162.

[51] *British Library Harleian Manuscript 433*, eds R. Horrox and P.W. Hammond, vol. II (Richard III Society, 1980), p. 28.

[52] Ibid., I, pp. 145–6; II, pp. 118, 119.

[53] Ibid., II, p. 133.

warden, but rather remained the nominal warden, and appointed lieutenants to govern the march in his name, first Humphrey, Lord Dacre, and then no less a figure than Sir Richard Ratcliffe, one of his principal councillors. Thus it was Ratcliffe's name which, after the war with Scotland had been ended by a truce in September 1484, in the following April headed the list of commissioners appointed to meet the Scots near Lochmaben and negotiate redress for breaches of that truce.[54] The continued directness of Richard III's rule in the north-west is underlined by his referring to the Carlisle garrison as 'our household at our castle of Carlisle'.[55]

Did Carlisle grieve, as York is reported to have grieved, in August 1485? Regrettably, it is only possible to say that if tears were shed over the outcome of the battle of Bosworth, mourning did not prevent those who mourned from giving their allegiance to Richard III's successor. It is in fact hard to tell how many Cumbrians fought at Bosworth. The *Ballad of Bosworth Field* provides a list, often in garbled form, of 'their names . . . that came to king Richard'.[56] They include two peers, the young Thomas, Lord Dacre, who 'raysed the north contrye', and Lord Greystoke, who though well over seventy apparently 'browght a myghty many'; but otherwise only Sir William Musgrave, Sir Alexander Heighmore, Sir Thomas Broughton, Sir Thomas Strickland, Sir John Harrington, his brother Sir Robert, and Sir Ralph Dacre 'of the northe' (probably a younger brother of Lord Dacre) can be identified with confidence as Cumbrians. King Richard sent out letters of summons on 11 August, and the battle was fought eleven days later. The two peers, said to have brought forces with them, probably came with mounted retinues. But many who might have served were probably still assembling when battle was joined. Absence did not necessarily imply disloyalty, and one would have expected the men of Cumberland, a region where royal power was effective and the Nevilles had

[54] Rymer, *Foedera*, vol. V, Part III, p. 162. For the implications of Ratcliffe's appointment see below, pp. 143–5.

[55] *Harleian Manuscript 433*, II, p. 28.

[56] BL, Add. MS 27879, ff. 31–2. The reliability of the ballad is discussed by C. Ross, *Richard III* (London, 1981), pp. 235–7.

long been influential, to have been responsive, had time allowed, to an appeal
from the man representing both the crown and the Nevilles. But the fact that
they did not mount a serious rebellion *after* 1485 is irrelevant to the issue of their
allegiance *before* then. The needs of the border, which had been much ravaged
in the recent war, were such as always to incline the men of the west march to
give their allegiance to an anointed king, regardless of the dynasty he
represented. Civil strife was something they could ill afford, as its consequences
in 1461 made very clear. They would probably not have formulated their
outlook in such terms, but their loyalties were generally given to the crown
rather than to the man who wore it.

After 1485 King Henry VII was the man ultimately responsible for the
defence of the west march, and most of its inhabitants served him for that
reason. There were a few exceptions, especially from Furness (this seems to have
been largely the consequence of a quarrel between the Stanleys and the
Harringtons),[57] but there was a striking continuity in local office-holders, with
many of the same surnames, and sometimes the same people, acting as sheriffs
and JPs in the late 1480s and after as had acted under the Yorkist kings –
Salkeld, Moresby, Huddleston, Thornburgh, Bewley and others all recur. It is,
however, misleading to speak of continuity in terms so bald. Henry VII
probably felt that he had little choice but to employ men who had served his
immediate predecessors, but he did not have to trust them as well. He certainly
did not treat many of them as though he trusted them, and his reign provides
striking testimony to the coercive power an English monarch could wield, even
on the peripheries of his realm.

Henry VII had a two-pronged policy for the far north of England. He
wanted to make, and keep, peace with Scotland, and he wanted to control the
men who might break that peace. The former he achieved, not without
difficulty (notably the war of 1496/97), through a series of truces, culminating
in the so-called Perpetual Peace of 1502, as part of which Henry's daughter
Margaret married James IV of Scots. The latter he achieved by following his

[57] See Jones, 'Richard III and the Stanleys', in Horrox (ed.), *Richard III and the North*, n. 45 above.

predecessor in using members of his council along with, or even instead of, the leading men of the region, in tasks relating to the security of the border, while for the internal government of the region, he divided powers which had previously been held by one man, an Earl of Warwick or a Duke of Gloucester, among several.[58] Like Richard III, he retained the wardenship of the west march for himself and ruled through lieutenants, at first Sir Richard Salkeld, the hero of 1461. In 1486 the lieutenancy was transferred to Thomas, Lord Dacre of Gilsland, but Salkeld was moved sideways rather than down, becoming captain of Carlisle Castle and city. Dacre was thus effectively deprived of control of the centre of his wardenry. And he lost control of its peripheries as well, since Sir Christopher Moresby (another man with experience in government, who had been sheriff in 1471) was made responsible for Penrith, and, for some years, of Inglewood Forest, while in 1492 or 1493 (perhaps earlier), Dacre was given a rival in his own power-base of Gilsland, when Sir Thomas Musgrave was appointed captain of Bewcastle. Nor was that always the end of it, for in 1491 and again in 1494 the king appointed Sir Henry Wyatt, the keeper of the jewel house, to oversee the defences of Carlisle, and on both occasions Wyatt took over the castle, leaving Salkeld in command of the city alone.

The result of this division of authority among up to five people was a series of quarrels, especially between Dacre and Musgrave – the ill-will which this engendered lasted well into the sixteenth century – and between Dacre and Moresby, the latter dispute involving Lord Clifford, Moresby's neighbour in north Westmorland, as well. But the king was alert to the consequences of his own determination to divide and rule in the north west, and in 1487 Dacre, Moresby and Clifford were hauled before the royal council. One of the questions there put to Dacre perfectly illustrates Henry VII's concern for peace in the borders – 'Item, remembering the said Lord Dacre is the king's lieutenant in those marches, and remembering the unstableness of peace between both the realms, why and for what cause he would suffer any such riots and insurrections

---

[58] For what follows see Summerson, *Medieval Carlisle*, pp. 466–75.

to be had and made within the precinct of his office . . .?'[59] It seems unlikely
that Dacre had in fact been as lax in the performance of his office as the
question implied – at around this time he was recorded as going to Brougham
to try to settle the dispute between Moresby and Clifford.[60] But a further reason
for Lord Dacre's supposed ineffectiveness, and one which was also in large part
the king's responsibility, lay in the fact that Henry VII was keeping him very
short of money. Not long after Bosworth, Dacre abducted and married
Elizabeth Greystoke, a marriage which would eventually place his family among
the richest in the English peerage. But not only did several years pass before
Elizabeth was in actuality the heiress she was potentially when Dacre married
her, it was also considered royal policy to keep Dacre out of the Greystoke lands
even when they became nominally his in the right of his wife, and he had to pay
heavily to have possession of them. And as a final measure of restraint, whereas
a mid-fifteenth-century warden of the west march could hope to receive £1250
yearly in peacetime and double that sum in time of war, Lord Dacre's fees as
lieutenant amounted to a miserly £153 6s 8d per annum.[61] The emergence of the
so-called border tenures, lands held by peasant farmers who owed military
service as part of the terms on which they received their tenements, seems to
date from this time, and to have been largely the result of Henry VII's
reluctance to give his own lieutenant the money which would enable him to
perform his duties as previous wardens had done. They were energetically
promoted by Dacre on the king's demesnes around Carlisle when he gained
control of them at the end of the century, and he gave shares in them to many
of his own tenants.

As time passed and the borders stabilized, especially after the war of 1496/7,
as first Moresby and then Salkeld died, Dacre gathered in the offices earlier
wardens had held. Finally in about 1501 he gained the custody of Carlisle, in
effect buying it for £200, and also undertaking to keep the city walls and the
castle in repair at his own expense (a promise he never showed the slightest

[59] PRO, STAC/2/26/11.

[60] CRO, DRC/2/16, m. 1d.

[61] PRO, E101/72/3, no. 1062.

inclination to keep).[62] But that did not lead to any relaxation of the king's hold over either Dacre or the west march. The use of bonds and recognisances – obligations to do, or not to do, specified acts, with penalties for their breach – was not new to the reign of Henry VII, they were used by both Edward IV and Richard III, and by other kings before them. That they were applied to the English aristocracy with a new comprehensiveness by Henry VII has become well known.[63] But it was not only the aristocracy which suffered. How such recognisances worked can be seen, for instance, in the case of William Thornburgh, a member of a family of Neville followers who was arrested in 1486 on suspicion of residual Yorkism and imprisoned in Nottingham Castle. Thornburgh clearly had influential friends, and in February 1488 he was released, on condition that he himself was bound in the sum of £500, and that four sureties, headed by Sir Christopher Moresby, were bound in 500 marks each, for, in the words of the king's command, 'his good bearing unto us and all our subjects'.[64]

In this case the treatment worked, and Thornburgh became a JP and gaol delivery justice in Cumberland. In later cases, too, Cumbrian gentry had to find assurances for their future loyalty. In 1495, for instance, John Skelton of Cardurnock (near Bowness on the Solway) found four guarantors for his allegiance, bound in sums ranging from forty marks to £100.[65] In other cases men gave bonds for keeping the peace, and forfeited them when they failed to do so. In 1494 William Pennington, member of a family with Percy connections, forfeited no less than £1,000 on what was described as 'a security for keeping the king's peace towards the king's people', with disastrous consequences for his own sureties, one of whom proceeded to bring what seems likely to have proved a fruitless action against William in chancery for exposing him to financial ruin.[66] Such bonds could be used to punish, they

[62] PRO, E101/415/3, f. 292.

[63] See J.R. Lander, *Crown and Nobility, 1450–1509* (1976), pp. 267–300.

[64] PRO, C82/35 (unnumbered).

[65] PRO, E101/414/6, f. 125.

[66] PRO, E372/339, m. 6; C1/209, no. 33.

could be used to command obedience, they could be used to do both. Sir Thomas Curwen, another Percy follower, paid £400 for a pardon for 'intrusions and alienations', while another recognisance for 400 marks was 'to hang at the king's pleasure'.[67]

When a great man gave a bond for his own good behaviour, that of his followers might be comprehended within it. It was essential for the keeping of the peace, internally or across the border, that this should be so. Even if the kings of England and of Scots wanted peace, mere willpower was not likely to bring it about if lesser men could not be prevented from raiding over the frontier, with all the dangers of retaliation and escalation which this entailed. In about 1501 Sir John Saville and Edward Musgrave forfeited 500 marks each, and Lord Dacre forfeited £500, for failing to bring one Robert Skelton into Star Chamber. This arose from the quarrel between Dacre and the last Lord Greystoke over the Greystoke inheritance, for which Dacre and 'other his brethren and servants' gave bonds to appear in Star Chamber. They all came except Skelton, and the bonds were declared forfeit for the latter's non-appearance, even though he had the best possible excuse for not being there. Skelton, said Dacre, had been 'slain upon the borders by the Scots afore the day of appearance as all the country knows'.[68] The incident may illustrate the fragility of peace upon the borders. It would also appear to show plainly the opportunities for oppression which bonds and recognisances gave to the government which wielded them, and was the sole interpreter of their observance. Later evidence suggests that those opportunities were not missed. Lord Dacre gave a recognisance 'of his good obeying' for £2,000. According to Dacre himself, Henry VII's financial hatchet men, Empson and Dudley, converted the conditional recognisance into an outright debt on the king's own instructions. In 1506 Sir John Pennington gave a bond for 500 marks 'for the appearance of the same Sir John, and also that he should not depart without licence'. Pennington subsequently had to pay 200 marks for breach of

---

[67] PRO, E101/414/16, f. 136.
[68] BL, Add. MS 21480, f. 191v; PRO, SP1/1, ff. 71v–72.

this departure clause, even though, in Dudley's own words, 'for truth I was by when the king took him by the hand at his departure'.[69] Sir John Huddleston paid £300 'by recognisance for the king's most gracious favour to him to be had for the discharging of his intrusion in the lordship of Millom'.[70] Since Millom was Huddleston's own hereditary lordship, it is not easy to see how he could have intruded himself into it.

This last case was doubtless linked to another form of pressure which the king was able to exert upon north-west England, that connected with the exploitation of his feudal and prerogative rights. This was at its most intense in the closing years of Henry VII's reign, but it was not unknown earlier. In 1489, for instance, John Lord Greystoke and four others, headed by the Earl of Northumberland, bound themselves in the sum of 2,000 marks each to give the king the wardship and marriage of Greystoke's own son and heir, and undertook to place the boy in the king's keeping whenever Henry VII required them to do so.[71] In the light of Lord Dacre's recent abduction of Elizabeth Greystoke, the king's anxiety to secure his rights in a wardship valued at £1,000 are easily understandable. But later on in the reign the screw was tightened with less discrimination, largely through the agency of Bishop Senhouse of Carlisle (another example of the usefulness of the bishop as a royal officer), who in 1499 was appointed 'receiver and surveyor of all manner wards, marriages, all other debts belonging to his grace by the king's prerogative in Cumberland and Westmorland and York shires . . .'.[72] Probably it was through him that the election of Robert Chambre as abbot of Holmcultram cost him or his supporters £100,[73] that Sir John Pennington had to pay at least £200 for the marriage of his daughter to Walter Strickland,[74] that Sir Lancelot Thrilkeld, who had been sheriff in 1491, had to pay £146 for 'intrusion' into various

---

[69] C.J. Harrison, 'The Petition of Edmund Dudley', *EHR*, LXXXVII (1972), pp. 90, 98.

[70] BL, Lansd. MS 127, f. 47v.

[71] PRO, E368/262 Hilary *recognitiones*, rot. 2d.

[72] PRO, E101/414/16, f. 134v.

[73] Ibid., f. 106v.

[74] PRO, E101/691/41 (unfoliated).

properties.[75] Senhouse's successor had to pay £240 for the temporalities of his own see.[76] Perhaps it is not surprising to find Lord Dacre being subjected to a *Quo Warranto* challenge to his rights and franchises in his manor and lordship of Gilsland. But a similar challenge to Henry, Lord Clifford, is less to be expected.

Clifford was the son and heir of that John, Lord Clifford, who was alleged to have dispatched the young Earl of Rutland at the battle of Wakefield, and who was himself killed shortly before the battle of Towton, and subsequently attainted. He owed everything to Henry VII, whose accession led to his own reinstatement in his family lordship of Westmorland, and he and his descendants were unfailingly loyal to the Tudors. Nevertheless he was recorded as owing the king 4,000 marks 'as well for divers dangers that he stood in to the king's grace as touching the Quo Warranto of the sheriffwick of Westmorland, the misusing of the cornage of the same, and the forfeiture of an obligation of £1000, as for divers other offences . . .'.[77] The investigation of the Westmorland shrievalty is particularly noteworthy, in the light of the central government's concern in Henry VII's reign that sheriffs and other officials should perform their duties effectively and without corruption.[78] The hereditary sheriffdom of Westmorland held by the Cliffords was arguably the weakest link in the chain of administrative command in the whole of northern England, the border franchises in Northumberland possibly excepted, and seems to have helped to make the maintenance of law and order in that county very difficult to achieve. It is striking how often recorded acts of violence in north-west England in Henry VI's reign involved Westmorland men.[79] The *Quo Warranto* inquest held under Henry VII was a clear signal to Lord Clifford that his great lordship would not be permitted to stand outside the structure of judicial administration as that had developed elsewhere, and it also demonstrates that Henry's policy

---

[75] BL, Lansd. MS 127, f. 18.

[76] BL, Add. MS 21480, f. 102.

[77] BL, Lansd. MS 127, f. 22v.

[78] See above, p. 23–6.

[79] R.L. Storey, *The Fall of the House of Lancaster* (1966), pp. 117–22; *idem*, 'Disorder in Lancastrian Westmorland; some Early Chancery Proceedings', *TCWAAS*, 2nd Series, vol. 53 (1954), pp. 69–80.

for the region was not just, or at any rate only, a campaign of financial aggression. He wanted order in the north-west, and intended to constrain the freedom of manoeuvre of any who, by sins of omission *or* commission, might threaten the region's stability, away from the border as well as on it.

The same policy can be seen at work at the administrative centre of the west march, in Carlisle itself. In February 1498 he sent letters under the signet to the mayor and bailiffs whose preamble deserves quoting in full:

> Insomuch as ye know well that the same our city is one of the chief keys and fortresses to the defence of this our realm, and that the loss thereof by any sudden enterprise of the Scots should be not only your utter destruction but also a great and an universal hurt to all our said realm, which God defend, we therefore will and charge you in our straitest wise not to suffer any manner of person or persons dwelling within our said city to be from henceforth retained with any man, be he spiritual or temporal lord or other, by livery, badge, clothing, cognisance, or in any other wise, nor to ride or pass out of the same our city in harness to any field, skirmishing, affrays or riots with any gentleman or other, whatsoever estate or degree he be of, but to be abiding or attending at all seasons, both of war and of peace, in the same our city for the defence and surety thereof against the Scots if they would make any sudden attempt thereunto by siege or otherwise . . .

The bishop was therefore to take oaths of fealty from 'ye of the same our city'.[80] The king was determined to be master in that city. In the first instance there was the need to repel any danger from Scotland, which must have seemed a distinct possibility after the war of 1496/7. The destructive effects of that war in the north of Cumberland are attested in such sources as the inquisition *post mortem* in 1499 of Sir Christopher Moresby, recording devastation at such places as Scaleby, Houghton and Westlinton,[81] and Lord Dacre's account of 1,500 for the issues of the county's ancient cornage dues, making allowance for

---

[80] CRO, Ca2/105.

[81] *Calendar of Inquisitions post mortem, Henry VII*, vol. II, no. 292.

destruction at Liddell, Bewcastle and Kirklinton.[82] And there was also, judging by the ban on movement *out* of the city, the need to prevent attacks, either in retaliation or for simple plunder, being made north of the border.

Henry VII divided in order to rule. He split up powers of government among his officers, and then used financial restraints to keep them under control, and he further curtailed their freedom of action by employing his councillors as his agents in the north west. But it was a policy which could only succeed as long as peace was kept and the king did not have to free the hands of the great men of the marches for campaigns in Scotland. When in 1513 Henry VIII's irresponsibility, and James IV's equally lethal alliance with France, led to a renewal of hostilities, nothing that Henry VII had achieved could prevent the English border shires from collapsing into chaos. By the early 1520s there was no sheriff in Cumberland and not enough JPs to make a quorum. But in the short term Henry VII's handling of the borders worked.[83] The bishop's revenues rose, and so without much doubt did those of his cathedral city. After a gap of about eighty years, the sequence of Carlisle's mayor's court records begins again. On the face of it they are rather disappointing. The schoolmaster sues a pupil for a fee of 13s 4d. The barber-surgeon is owed 12d for healing a finger. A merchant sues for money owed for cloth, oil and wax. The Dominican prior has hired a horse and failed to pay for it.[84] It is all the sort of thing which could be happening in any English town in the years around 1500.

In the light of past experience, of events like the siege of 1461, the fact that the citizens of Carlisle were able to lead humdrum lives represented a notable success for royal policy, at least in the short term. But the fact that the King of England continued to claim sovereignty over the Scottish realm, and that the King of Scots inevitably continued to resist that claim, meant that war was always liable to break out again, especially by way of the French dimension to the foreign policy of both kingdoms, thereby to trouble the whole Anglo-Scottish border region, Carlisle with the rest. Henry VII did better than any

[82] CRO, D/Lec/148 *verso*.

[83] Summerson, *Medieval Carlisle*, pp. 476–9.

[84] CRO, Ca3/1/14, ff. 10, 12v, 14, 15v (court book of November 1504).

other fifteenth-century English ruler in his efforts to solve what, in the context of the period and the monarchic aspirations associated with it, was really an insoluble problem, but no more than anyone else could he square this particular circle. It was left to James I to do what Edward IV, Richard III and Henry VII had been unable to do, and he owed his success in the pacification of the borders to the happy circumstance – itself the consequence of what ultimately proved to be one of Henry VII's most effective strokes of policy – that he was also James VI.

6

RICHARD III AND SCOTLAND

Alexander Grant

In the January Parliament of 1483 Edward IV gave his brother Richard of Gloucester a hereditary grant of the wardenship of the west march, the city of Carlisle, all other royal possessions and rights in Cumberland together with the right to appoint its sheriff, all the lands Richard could conquer for himself across the western border in Scotland, in Liddesdale, Eskdale, Ewesdale, Annandale, Wauchopdale, Clydesdale and the Scottish West March, and 10,000 marks for his initial finance; the Scottish conquests, moreover, were to be held as a palatinate or quasi-independent principality.[1] That was the climax to a dozen years of aggrandizement by Richard in the north of England, which had brought him the lordships of Middleham, Sheriff Hutton, Penrith and Barnard Castle, and the offices of warden of the west march, steward of the duchy of Lancaster in the north and sheriff of Cumberland.[2] Even without the Scottish lands, Richard was the most powerful northern English magnate since the Norman Conquest; with them, he would have been a truly regional potentate – like the Norman barons of the Welsh marches, who had carved out their own

---

[1] *Rot. Parl.*, VI, pp. 204–5. The Scottish conquests were to be held in fee simple, the English lands and offices in tail male. Charles Ross caused some confusion by stating that Westmorland was included in the grant and that the palatinate rights covered the English lands as well as the Scottish conquests: C. Ross, *Edward IV* (1974), p. 202; C. Ross, *Richard III* (1981), pp. 25–6. In fact, Edward IV did *not* create a new palatinate in England – as R. Horrox, *Richard III: A Study in Service* (Cambridge, 1989), p. 71, correctly points out. Of the lands in Scotland, Eskdale, Ewesdale, Annandale and Wauchopdale nowadays make up the eastern part of Dumfries and Galloway region, lying roughly along and to the east of the modern A/M74; Liddesdale is to the east, forming the extreme south-west part of Borders region; and Clydesdale is the valley of the River Clyde, to the north, i.e. the southern part of Strathclyde region, lying either side of the modern A/M74 as far as Glasgow.

[2] A.J. Pollard, *North-Eastern England during the Wars of the Roses* (Oxford, 1990), ch. 13; Ross, *Richard III*, chs. 2–3.

principalities in Wales. But is there perhaps an even earlier parallel, in the old Anglian kingdom of Northumbria, which covered middle Britain from the Humber to the Forth? Had the northwards momentum of Richard's aggrandizement continued, his area of dominance would actually have been not too unlike that of the ancient Northumbrian kings.

Consider, moreover, his personal feelings, which are illustrated by his religious devotions. These appear to have focused largely on St Cuthbert, Northumbria's patron saint, and on the Scottish St Ninian. Richard belonged to the fraternity of St Cuthbert, and regularly visited the saint's shrine at Durham; while Cuthbert's banner was displayed on his Scottish campaign in 1482.[3] As for St Ninian, his shrine at Whithorn in Galloway is within ancient Northumbria; and Whithorn, alone among Scottish bishoprics, was in the archdiocese of York; that is one Northumbrian legacy. There was an important cult of St Ninian throughout the north-west. Richard invoked Ninian in each of his main religious foundations, and had a collect for the saint added on the first page of his *Book of Hours*.[4] Saints Ninian and Cuthbert (who, incidentally, came from Melrose) transcend the Anglo-Scottish border – just as in 1482–3 Richard's political career was doing. We all know of Richard as the great northerner, but should we not substitute 'Northumbrian', in its widest sense?

A more sober long-term context for Richard's dealings with Scotland, however, is that of the Anglo-Scottish conflict which, from 1296, dominates the history of late medieval Britain.[5] Five points about this conflict are relevant here. First, at its height during the earlier fourteenth century, despite the longest and most intense period of warfare in medieval English history, both Edward I and Edward III failed either to conquer Scotland or to install a puppet king on its throne. They failed largely because of the Scottish defensive strategy developed by Robert I

[3] A.J. Pollard, 'St Cuthbert and the Hog: Richard III and the County Palatine of Durham, 1471–85', in R.A. Griffiths and J. Sherborne (eds), *Kings and Nobles in the Later Middle Ages* (Gloucester, 1986), pp. 117–18.

[4] Pollard, *North-Eastern England*, pp. 192–3; *The Hours of Richard III*, A.F. Sutton and L. Visser-Fuchs (eds) (Gloucester, 1990), pp. 41–4.

[5] The main themes of the Anglo-Scottish warfare of the later Middle Ages are sketched in A. Grant, *Independence and Nationhood: Scotland 1306–1469* (1984), chs. 1–2.

(Robert Bruce): avoid battle, follow a scorched-earth policy, and deny the English any bases north of the border by dismantling the major Scottish castles. The effect was that English invading armies invariably ran out of momentum, supplies and money, and in the end (after only a few weeks, in many cases) had to retreat. That pattern was still to apply in the 1480s.

Second, from 1337 England was at war with France as well. But English royal resources were not enough to wage aggressive warfare effectively on two fronts, and the English kings generally gave priority to the French war – so the Anglo-Scottish conflict gradually slackened off. France and Scotland, however, naturally came together in the 'auld alliance' against England; that was vital to both countries' war efforts, and, as will be seen, it was in the end highly significant for Richard III.

Third, to protect the north of England against Scottish counter-attacks, Edward III created an English-occupied buffer-zone in southern Scotland. Throughout that zone and in the English border region, military responsibility was delegated to the great English border families, especially the Percies and Nevilles, who virtually monopolized the new offices of march warden. That made good sense; but it also produced a clash of interests between the crown and border lords. The crown wanted truces or limited fighting (no English campaigns in Scotland after the 1330s lasted much longer than a fortnight). But the border lords wanted much more active warfare, so that they could carry out lucrative plundering raids, and even conquer territory in southern Scotland. Also, the march wardenships helped them greatly to build up their local power.[6] Moreover, their followers were equally keen to plunder and raid in Scotland. Border society had come to terms with the Anglo-Scottish warfare, and indeed had come virtually to depend upon it, preferring the war to a state of peace.[7]

[6] R.L. Storey, 'The Wardens of the Marches towards England', *EHR*, LXXII (1957), pp. 593–615; J. Campbell, 'England, Scotland and the Hundred Years War', in J.R. Hale *et al.* (eds), *Europe in the Late Middle Ages* (1965), pp. 192–3, 207–9; Pollard, *North-Eastern England*, pp. 150–3.

[7] A. Goodman, 'Introduction', in A. Tuck and A. Goodman (eds), *War and Border Societies in the Middle Ages* (1992), pp. 1–29; A. Goodman, 'The Anglo-Scottish Marches in the fifteenth century: a frontier society?', in R.A. Mason (ed.), *Scotland and England, 1286–1815* (Edinburgh, 1987), pp. 18–33.

That, of course, was still the case in the lifetime of Richard of Gloucester, himself the greatest of all border magnates.

Fourth, as Richard's own career illustrates in various ways, the clash of interests between the crown and border magnates could have major political consequences. For example, Percy opposition to Richard II and Henry IV was largely caused by those kings' peace policies towards Scotland. And the immediate Neville reward for helping overthrow Richard II was a grant from Henry IV in 1399 of Annandale, with Lochmaben Castle. Since Annandale had been recaptured by the Scots in 1384, what the Nevilles actually wanted was Henry's commitment to occupy south-west Scotland once again.[8] That reminds us of the grant of Scottish conquests to Richard of Gloucester: Richard was the heir of the Nevilles – and, no doubt, to their ambitions for expansion into south-west Scotland.

Fifth, when Annandale was regained by the Scots, so was most of the rest of the English-occupied buffer zone. But some English outposts were left, and two of these, the heavily fortified Roxburgh and Berwick, stayed in English hands until the 1460s. Scottish attacks on them had been countered by relieving English armies, often under Neville leadership. But the Wars of the Roses changed the situation. Roxburgh was captured in 1460, Berwick was surrendered by Henry VI in 1461 – and so the Scottish Wars of Independence at last came to an end. At the same time, England had finally been defeated by France in the Hundred Years War. Thus while Richard of Gloucester was growing up, a new era appeared to be dawning in England's foreign relations.

The next issue to consider, therefore, is what, in this new era after 1461, were the English and Scottish diplomatic aims? For James III, King of Scots, the answer is simple: peace. Now that the English-held territory was recaptured, there was no need for war. Nor did Scotland have to help France in the 'auld alliance', for the Anglo-French war was also over. And since that left England

---

[8] *Cal(endar of) Doc(uments relating to) Scot(land)*, eds J. Bain *et al.* (5 vols, Edinburgh, 1881–1988), IV, no. 525; cf., more generally, A. Tuck, 'Richard II and the border magnates', *NH*, III (1968), pp. 27–52, at 48–52; P. McNiven, 'The Scottish policy of the Percies', *Bulletin of the John Rylands Library*, LXII (1979–80), pp. 498–530.

freer to attack Scotland than at any time since 1337, there was all the more reason not to provoke the English king. Peace with England was James III's most consistent policy.[9]

For Edward IV of England, things were more complex. Should not Berwick, lost at the beginning of his reign, be regained? And would not successful foreign war, in Scotland if not in France, help restore internal political harmony after the Wars of the Roses? On the other hand, all warfare, even in Scotland, was hugely expensive; and unsuccessful warfare was political suicide. For Edward IV, the latter points outweighed the former. In 1464 a fifteen-year truce was agreed, which was extended the following year to last until 1519; in 1474 this was reconfirmed, and it was also agreed that James III's son and heir should marry Cecily, Edward IV's second daughter.[10] That was, in effect, a peace treaty, the first since 1328. Peace with Scotland, of course, was a prerequisite for Edward's 1475 invasion of France. But he did maintain the peace thereafter, paying annual advances on Cecily's dowry, and in 1478 arranging a second marriage, between his brother-in-law, Earl Rivers, and James III's sister, Margaret.[11]

Anglo-Scottish peace, however, lasted for only six years; war broke out in 1480. Several forces were working against the two kings' peace policies. One was Louis XI of France: as the Crowland chronicler (providing the English 'Foreign Office' view)[12] stated, 'it was he who encouraged the Scots to break the

[9] Grant, *Independence and Nationhood*, pp. 50–4; N.A.T. Macdougall, 'Foreign relations: England and France', in J.M. Brown (ed.), *Scottish Society in the Fifteenth Century* (1977), pp. 101–11.

[10] Ibid., p. 109; N. Macdougall, *James III* (Edinburgh, 1982), pp. 116–17; Ross, *Edward IV*, pp. 212–13.

[11] Macdougall, *James III*, pp. 140–1; Ross, *Edward IV*, p. 279.

[12] In the Introduction to *Crowland Chronicle*, pp. 78–95, Nicholas Pronay argues convincingly that the author of the Continuation of the Crowland Chronicle was a Chancery clerk who specialized in diplomacy. This argument is perhaps supported by the formal documents of Anglo-Scottish relations during the first half of the 1480s, which strike me as corresponding remarkably closely with the Crowland chronicler's account. On the other hand, that account is ignorant of Richard's secret diplomacy in 1484, and mistaken over the date of the Nottingham conference (below, p. 137; and see also the comment in note 88).

truce and to spurn the offer of our Cecily in marriage'.[13] Louis XI did not care about the traditional Franco-Scottish alliance, and wanted Edward IV to be distracted by the war in the north. Earlier, he had proposed helping Edward to conquer Scotland; after 1475, he tried hard to persuade the Scots to break the peace.[14] He was successful, because many Scots agreed with him. During the Anglo-Scottish conflict, hatred of the English had understandably developed across most sections of Scottish society. And, of course, the Scottish borderers had acquired much the same taste for warfare as their English counterparts. Thus there was much Scottish hostility to the 1474 peace. The attitude of many southern lairds is reflected in a well-known line from Blind Hary's *Wallace*, the intensely anti-English poem about one of Scotland's past heroes, written in the mid-1470s: in these days, it says, 'Till [to] honour ennymis is our haile entent.'[15] But it was not simply the Scottish borderers who preferred war. So did Alexander, Duke of Albany, James III's youngest brother. He was the greatest magnate on the Scottish borders, with the earldom of March in the east and the lordship of Annandale in the west; and he was the Scottish march warden. Charles Ross described him 'as a kind of Scots Clarence',[16] and that is true enough. Medieval kings' younger brothers often caused trouble, probably because they normally found themselves in the very difficult situation of having the highest social status in the land yet lacking any inherited power bases – and so being entirely dependent on royal goodwill for their actual political positions. Little wonder that they tended to quarrel with the kings and became focal points for opposition. That certainly happened in Scotland, where Albany led those who opposed the peace with England. He encouraged it to be broken,

---

[13] *Crowland Chronicle*, p. 151.

[14] Ross, *Edward IV*, pp. 56, 278–9; Macdougall, *James III*, pp. 143–4.

[15] ['Blind Hary'], *Hary's Wallace: Vita Nobilissimi Defensoris Scotie Wilelmi Wallace Militis*, ed. M.P. McDiarmid (2 vols, Edinburgh, Scottish Text Society, 1968–9), I, Book I, line 5. But for Scottish poems of the same date which seem to argue for peace with England, see E. Walsh, '*Golagros and Gawane*: a word for peace', in J.D. McClure and M.R.G. Spiller (eds), *Brycht Lanternis: Essays on the Language and Literature of Medieval and Renaissance Scotland* (Aberdeen, 1989), pp. 97–100.

[16] Ross, *Edward IV*, p. 287. Details of Albany's career are to be found in Macdougall, *James III* (see index, at 'Stewart, Alexander, Earl of March, Duke of Albany').

most shockingly during a wardens' 'Truce Day' (court), when one English gentleman was killed and several others were imprisoned, 'in the presence and by auctoritee of the wardeynes lieutenaunt of Scotland'.[17] As a consequence, in 1479 James III indicted him for 'the tresonable . . . violacioun . . . of the trewis . . . be slauchteris and hereschippis [ravagings] tresonably committit contrar to the kingis hienes And to the comoun goud of his Realme the said alexander being wardain in the sammyn [same] boundis.'[18] Scottish historians have considered the treason charge excessive;[19] but if Albany's actions had destroyed James III's peace policy, then surely it was justified? And where Albany led, other Scottish borderers followed, especially the Earl of Angus, who in 1480 led a three-day raid which burned Bamburgh in Northumberland.[20]

Thus, by 1480, what Crowland called the 'shameless' Scottish provocation had made Edward IV's patience snap (probably the Woodvilles' patience, too: the Scots were reneging on Earl Rivers's royal marriage).[21] And in the English borders, all the old local pressures for war came to a head. There, as in Scotland, the lead was given by the king's younger brother – Richard of Gloucester. He was the greatest borderer, and he had his personal interests in Scotland; whether he was another Albany or Clarence is a matter for debate, but he does appear to have taken an aggressive attitude over the Anglo-Scottish peace. Admittedly he was not directly to blame for its breakdown, but it is unlikely that he regretted it. As Pollard has emphasized, Richard 'had for long wished to mount a war against Scotland', and by 1480 Edward IV was no longer able or willing to resist his wishes.[22]

---

[17] According to Edward IV's bitter complaint in early 1480: *Cal. Doc. Scot.*, IV, Appendix, no. 28, at p. 414 (wrongly dated there to before February 1476).

[18] *(The) Act(s of the) Parl(iaments of) Scot(land)*, T. Thomson and C. Innes (eds) (12 vols, Edinburgh, 1814–75), II, p. 126.

[19] e.g. A.A.M. Duncan, in his revised version of W.C. Dickinson, *Scotland from the Earliest Times to 1603* (Oxford, 3rd edn, 1977), p. 241; and N. Macdougall, 'Richard III and James III: contemporary monarchs, parallel mythologies', in P.W. Hammond (ed.), *Richard III: Loyalty, Lordship and Law* (1986), pp. 159–60 (cf. Macdougall, *James III*, p. 129).

[20] Macdougall, *James III*, pp. 129, 144–5; Pollard, *North-Eastern England*, pp. 236–7.

[21] *Crowland Chronicle*, p. 147; Macdougall, *James III*, p. 142.

[22] Pollard, *North-Eastern England*, pp. 232–7, 242–4.

What did Edward – and Richard, who was forthwith appointed Edward's lieutenant-general – hope to gain from the war, apart from punishing the Scots? Edward's ultimatum of 1480 made various demands, including the old claim of homage from the Scottish king, but it is clear that the chief demand was the surrender of the town and castle of Berwick.[23] Richard and the Earl of Northumberland besieged Berwick in 1481, but it seems that a Scottish counter-attack on Northumberland's territories made them withdraw.[24] In late July 1482, however, Richard led some 20,000 men across the border. A smallish detachment besieged Berwick again, but the main army carried on north, finishing up in Edinburgh. This time the scale of the English invasion prevented any Scottish counter-attack, and the town of Berwick was soon surrendered. The castle held out – but when Richard returned south a few weeks later with his main army he was able to take it by storm.[25] Edward IV was delighted, telling the Pope that, 'The chief advantage of the whole expedition is the reconquest of the town and castle of Berwick.' Berwick had been lost shortly before his coronation, and since it had belonged to his forefathers, 'we are bound to recover what was ours'.[26] And if Berwick had been the main object of the campaign (and so Richard's massive invasion of Lothian had been an essential diversion), then the whole operation had gone like clockwork.

But Edward's delight was only temporary, according to the Crowland chronicler:

This trifling gain, or perhaps more accurately loss (for the maintenance of Berwick costs 10,000 marks a year) diminished the substance of the king and the kingdom by more than £100,000 at the time. King Edward was grieved

---

[23] *Cal. Doc. Scot.*, IV, App., no. 28, at p. 413.

[24] Pollard, *North-Eastern England*, p. 238.

[25] For details, see Macdougall, *James III*, pp. 153–5, 168–9; Ross, *Edward IV*, pp. 287–90; Pollard, *North-Eastern England*, pp. 239–40.

[26] *Calendar of State Papers . . . relating to English Affairs . . . in the Archives . . . of Venice*, vol. I: *1202–1509*, R. Brown (ed.) (1864), p. 146.

at the frivolous expenditure of so much money although the recapture of Berwick alleviated his grief for a time.[27]

For the chronicler, here giving a 'Treasury' opinion, so to speak, the campaign should have achieved much more; and he believed that Edward thought the same. Crowland was perhaps correct. Earlier in 1482 the Scottish Duke of Albany, who had fled to France, was brought to England, and in June made a treaty with Edward. Edward would help to make him King of Scots; in return, 'Alexander IV' (as Albany was styled) promised to do homage, break off Scottish relations with France, marry Princess Cecily, and cede not only Berwick but also Liddesdale, Eskdale, Ewesdale and Annandale in south-west Scotland.[28] So here on the agenda, along with Berwick, are the ideas of installing a Scottish puppet king and annexing several Scottish lordships. Is that what Edward *really* hoped for?

Albany was not the only exiled Scottish magnate in England: James, Earl of Douglas, once the head of Scotland's most powerful noble house, had been there since 1455.[29] One of Albany's undertakings to Edward IV was the restoration of Douglas; so it seems likely that Edward meant to use this 'Scottish fifth column'[30] to his advantage. But how? The army with which Richard of Gloucester (and Albany) invaded Scotland in 1482 was one of the largest English armies of the fifteenth century, and on a par with those of Edward I and Edward III. But those kings' campaigns had lasted much longer than anything Edward IV could have afforded – and even so had failed. In fact Richard's army was only financed for a single month:[31] what good was that? Did Edward expect the Scots to support Albany? If so, he was badly mistaken. Or, since his only experience of fighting was in the Wars of the Roses, when short campaigns

---

[27] *Crowland Chronicle*, p. 149. The wording of this passage seems to tally closely with that of Edward IV's letter to the Pope; did the Crowland chronicler perhaps draft that letter?

[28] T. Rymer, *Foedera, Conventiones, Literae . . . et Acta Publica* (20 vols, original edn, 1704–35), XII, pp. 156–7; *Cal. Doc. Scot.*, IV, nos 1475–6.

[29] *Cal. Doc. Scot.*, IV, pp. 258–300, *passim*.

[30] Macdougall, *James III*, p. 211.

and quick battles were essential, did he think that warfare in Scotland would be the same? That conclusion might well have been correct, for James III, apparently thinking along the same lines, almost certainly meant to lead his Scottish army in an immediate, and surely disastrous, attack on the English invaders (perhaps fury with Albany was a factor there). The Scots nobles, however, remembering the traditional way of coping with English invasions, refused to fight, and, instead, arrested James, withdrew the army, made a deal with Albany, and left Richard to besiege the virtually impregnable Edinburgh castle. He was still there when his men's wages ran short, and he had to return to Berwick.[32]

Thus any more grandiose plans which Edward IV might have had for the 1482 invasion came to nothing. Also, as Ross pointed out, the Scottish war tied his hands with respect to France. By the end of 1482 he had been outmanoeuvred diplomatically by Louis XI and probably wanted to go to war against France – but could not, because of the Scottish entanglement.[33] Edward might well, on reflection, have been disappointed, even angry, over how the Scottish invasion had gone.

Richard of Gloucester, on the other hand, probably viewed things very differently. From a borderer's standpoint, as Pollard has argued, it was a most spectacular and profitable raid – just what the borderers wanted.[34] It should be noted, however, that Richard was not simply raiding: to the Crowland chronicler's disgust, he did not sack Edinburgh.[35] So, was Berwick his main aim, with the invasion being an essential diversion? Berwick's capture, which greatly strengthened the defences of north-east England, was certainly important to the borderers. But surely the main beneficiary of that was not so much Richard as the Earl of Northumberland, the dominant power on the eastern border? It was, after all, Northumberland who became captain of Berwick.[36]

[31] Ibid., p. 154.

[32] Ibid., pp. 155, 168–9.

[33] Ross, *Edward IV*, pp. 290–5.

[34] Pollard, *North-Eastern England*, pp. 243–4.

[35] *Crowland Chronicle*, p. 149.

[36] C.L. Scofield, *The Life and Reign of Edward the Fourth* (2 vols, 1923), ii, p. 349.

Richard, it may be suggested, perhaps had something else in mind. In England, his career so far shows he was highly acquisitive:[37] understandably, for he was in the king's-younger-brother situation. Thus it is fair to assume that he had territorial hopes in Scotland. But where? Berwick, and beyond it Lothian, were really in the Percy sphere of influence. The west, where the Nevilles had had earlier ambitions, was a different matter. In May 1482 Richard had raided across the west march as far as Dumfries, and had apparently occupied territory there.[38] In June, Albany had agreed to cede four south-west Scottish lordships. And in January 1483, those same lordships were at the centre of the territory which Richard was authorized to conquer for himself.[39] That all makes a consistent pattern, indicating that what Richard had always wanted from Anglo-Scottish warfare was the opportunity to create his own principality in south-west Scotland – the region of St Ninian; in other words he was a true marcher baron. And support for Albany would have been a means to that end; Richard might realistically have hoped that Albany's return to Scotland would spark off a Scottish civil war, which would have greatly facilitated his own ambitions in the western borders.[40] That, at any rate, is my conjecture about Richard and Scotland in 1482–3.

What Edward IV would have made of those ambitions is impossible to say; it depends on how the grant in the January 1483 Parliament is interpreted. There are probably two scenarios. One, the confrontational, is that if, in their post-mortems on the 1482 campaign, Edward and Richard had fallen out – Edward complaining, say, about under-achievement, Richard about under-financing – then letting Richard do his own thing in Scotland, financed out of

---

[37] M. Hicks, 'Richard III as duke of Gloucester: a study in character', in M. Hicks, *Richard III and his Rivals* (1981), pp. 247–80, esp. 268–71.

[38] Pollard, *North-Eastern England*, p. 239; *The Cely Letters, 1472–1488*, ed. A. Hanham (Oxford, 1975), p. 164; *York Civic Records*, ed. A. Raine (2 vols, Yorkshire Archaeological Society, 1939–41), I, pp. 54–5; *Rot. Parl.*, VI, p. 204.

[39] See above, at notes 1 and 28.

[40] Although Albany had come to terms with the Scots in August 1482, he may have made a secret promise to Richard to stand by the treaty with Edward IV: Ross, *Edward IV*, p. 289, note 1.

his own resources, could have been a compromise. The other scenario is of 'privatization' – giving Richard *carte blanche* in Scotland was the best way to continue the war. A long campaign of piecemeal local conquest was more likely to gain results than spectacular *chevauchées*, as Henry V's war in Normandy had proved. It would not cost the crown very much (the 10,000 marks for Richard was a lump sum pay-off in lieu of future warden's salaries), and would release Edward from the Scottish entanglement, leaving him free to deal with France. If that is the way men were thinking in January 1483, then the idea probably came from Richard, who was surely a more innovative thinker than his brother; but both royal brothers would have been happy. Admittedly, those scenarios are purely speculative; but there must have been some policy behind the January 1483 grant, and those seem to be the best possibilities.

Yet what would have happened – in the *Scottish* context – if Edward IV had survived for several more years? Letting Richard fight his own Scottish war may have made sense in 1482–3, but, judging by past Anglo-Scottish history, it seems safe to conclude that eventually he would have got bogged down, that his own resources would have proved inadequate, and that he would have to have sought help from his brother. So, ultimately, Edward IV would have been sucked into unwinnable and fiscally horrifying Scottish warfare – with potentially disastrous political consequences in England. In his Scottish ambitions of 1482–3, Richard, it would appear, was proposing to bite off more than he could chew.

In the event, of course, none of that happened. Instead, Edward IV died in April 1483, and Richard did bite off more than he could chew – but in England, not Scotland. Once he had become king, how did Richard's relations with Scotland develop? It is sometimes implied that Richard III was too busy elsewhere to bother much with Scotland.[41] In a sense that is correct – but it would be wrong to conclude that during his reign Scotland was only a side-show. In recent years it has been strikingly demonstrated that, as king, Richard

---

[41] E.g., Ross, *Richard III*, pp. 192–4; Macdougall, *James III*, pp. 208–10. In Pollard, *North-Eastern England*, ch. 9, 'Anglo-Scottish relations, 1448–1485', effectively ends in 1482.

retained his strong personal interest in the north of England.[42] In that case, would his attitude towards Scotland have changed? Probably not; Scotland actually seems to have been high on Richard's agenda for most of his brief reign.

But, of course, his foreign policy could not be devoted to Scotland alone. In the first three months of his reign he had diplomatic contacts not only with Scotland but also with France, Castile, Burgundy and Brittany.[43] To all, except Scotland, he was conciliatory and pacific. Castilian and Burgundian requests for military aid against France were politely turned down, and he made the right noises about the recent devastating outbreak of piracy at sea. The piracy had probably resulted from the growth of tension between Edward IV and Louis XI in the early 1480s – it was a good way of damaging a foreign enemy without actually going to war – but it had escalated out of control, involving ships from England, France, Brittany, the Low Countries, and Castile.[44] In a letter to Duke Francis of Brittany, Richard condemned the English piracy, and blamed it on 'diverse folkes of simple disposicione, peraventure supposing that the peas had be [sic] expired by the dethe' of Edward IV.[45] That might seem disingenuous, but probably indicates how Richard was thinking. It tallies with his instructions to restore captured ships, even French ones seized at Calais, and to arrange conferences to tackle the piracy problem.[46]

So far as Scotland was concerned, however, he was tougher. With the capture of Berwick, the basis of Anglo-Scottish relations had reverted to the pre-1461 situation: James III wanted to regain his lost town.[47] And the Duke of Albany provided an extra complication: as James reasserted his authority, Albany changed sides again in April 1483, let an English garrison into his strong castle

[42] Pollard, *North-Eastern England*, ch. 14; R. Horrox (ed.), *Richard III and the North* (Hull, 1986); R.B. Dobson, 'Richard III and the church of York', in Griffiths and Sherborne (eds), *Kings and Nobles*, pp. 130–54.

[43] *Harley MS 433*, III, pp. 23–8, 32–5, 45–8.

[44] Ibid., pp. 1–2, 8, 28, 32–41; *CPR, 1476–1485*, pp. 355–6, 376, 425.

[45] *Harley MS 433*, III, p. 34.

[46] Ibid., II, pp. 14–15; III, pp. 32–4.

[47] Macdougall, *James III*, p. 209.

at Dunbar, north of Berwick, and fled to England, where he joined the exiled Earl of Douglas.[48] Thanks to Albany, Richard now had two outposts on the Scottish coast. The Scots might be expected to have attacked these before Richard had a firm grip on the throne. But in August James III actually wrote in friendly terms, blaming the Anglo-Scottish war on 'the werkyngis and menys of evil disposed persones' (Louix XI? Albany?), and stressing his own permanent desire for 'luff pece concorde and amyte'. He proposed an Anglo-Scottish peace conference, and, while the arrangements for this were being made, that there should be an eight-month truce until the following May.[49]

That would have given Richard eight months' breathing-space for dealing with other matters – but he was not interested. He simply replied on 16 September that he too wanted peace, and therefore would issue safe-conducts for the Scottish embassy as soon as James III named its members.[50] That was disingenuous, for James's herald had already provided a list of the proposed Scottish ambassadors. And Richard did not mention an interim truce at all. About a week later, however, he did make a truce with Scotland; but this was only to last for two months, until the end of November.[51] That may be connected with his order of 23 September to seize the temporalities of Bishop Lionel Woodville:[52] news of a Woodville conspiracy, which that implies, perhaps made him agree the Scottish truce – but even so it was for a far shorter period than James III had suggested.

In those two months, Richard dealt triumphantly with the so-called 'Buckingham' rebellion; not surprisingly, foreign affairs were put to one side. But on 6 November James III wrote again, reiterating his general desire for peace and his request for a conference – but adding that he was 'Marveland in a part that it liked not youre Cousinage to sende youre saufconduit with ouer said pursewant', and asking now for a truce to last until the end of March next

---

[48] Ibid., pp. 187–9.

[49] *Harley MS 433*, III, pp. 47–8.

[50] Ibid., p. 48.

[51] Ibid., II, p. 26; this can be dated to the week before Sunday 28 September.

[52] Ibid., pp. 23–4; cf. Horrox, *Richard III*, p. 131; J.A.F. Thomson, 'Bishop Lionel Woodville and Richard III', *BIHR*, LIX (1986), pp. 132–3.

year.[53] Richard answered, on 2 December (after his two-month truce had expired) that he had now issued the safe-conducts, but otherwise the reply was even less satisfactory for the Scots. He stated that no truce could be made, because no Scot had been authorized by James to agree it; the march wardens were unable to conclude truces on their own behalf; and anyway they could not inform the border population quickly enough; so the Scots would have to wait for a truce until their embassy arrived.[54] None of the excuses holds water; in fact Richard privately authorized Lord Dacre and Sir Thomas Percy to make local truces on the borders.[55] That makes his letter to James III all the more off-hand; he clearly had no intention of conciliating the Scottish king.

At the same time, in December 1483, Richard got tough with Brittany: the piracy he had earlier condemned now became all-out naval warfare. On 20 December he warned the inhabitants of the south coast to be ready for a sea battle which he was anticipating would soon be fought against a Breton fleet.[56] It is unclear whether that sea battle ever took place, but Breton shipping was now being attacked, arrested and confiscated.[57] The reason for the Anglo-Breton war appears to stem from a remarkable ducal message the previous August, in which Richard was told that Brittany was under severe pressure to hand Henry Tudor over to Louis XI of France, and that unless Richard supplied 4,000 archers for six months, as Edward IV had promised, the duke might not be able to resist.[58] Earlier in his reign, the fugitive in Brittany about whom Richard had worried had been Sir Edward Woodville, not Henry Tudor;[59] now Duke Francis had thrust Tudor into the limelight. But in the

[53] *Harley MS 433*, III, pp. 50–1.

[54] Ibid., p. 51.

[55] *Rotuli Scotiae in Turri Londiniensi . . . asservati* (2 vols, 1814–19), II, p. 461.

[56] *Harley MS 433*, II, p. 65.

[57] Ibid., pp. 53, 66, 72, 79, 84, 89; *CPR, 1476–1485*, p. 411.

[58] *Harley MS 433*, II, pp. 49–50; translated in *Letters and Papers Illustrative of the Reigns of Richard III and Henry VII*, ed. J. Gairdner (2 vols, Rolls Series, 1861–3), pp. 37–43.

[59] *Harley MS 433*, II, p. 34. Note, however, that the men executed in early August 1483 for conspiring to rescue the Princes in the Tower were apparently also accused of writing to the earls of Richmond and Pembroke in Brittany: Horrox, *Richard III*, pp. 149–50.

autumn of 1483 (by which time Louis XI was dead) Richard ignored the Breton blackmail. As a result, the duke supported Henry's attempt to join the 'Buckingham' rebellion and subsequently sheltered its refugees.[60] So Richard ordered the war at sea to punish 'our enemies the Bretons'.[61]

Simultaneously, English hostility was increasing towards France as well. The speech which Bishop Russell wrote for Richard's Parliament has a long implicit attack on the folly of a peace policy with Louis XI, which concluded, 'What have we gotten by that blind bargain?'[62] The truce with France was supposed to last until April 1484, but it is clear that by February French shipping, like Breton, was under authorized English attack. And the sea war also extended to Scotland: on 12 February Richard was making arrangements 'to victual certain of our ships of war to resist our enemies the Frenchmen, Bretons and Scots'.[63] In early 1484, therefore, Richard, flushed with success after crushing the 'Buckingham' rebellion, and (with hindsight) probably at the peak of his power, had committed England to a naval war against Brittany *and* France *and* Scotland!

Of these three enemies, Scotland probably took priority. In Richard's Parliament, although Russell's opening speech brought up relations with France, foreign policy debate seems to have focused on Scotland. Polydore Vergil stated that Parliament decided on peace with Scotland;[64] but if so, that peace was to

[60] R.A. Griffiths and R.S. Thomas, *The Making of the Tudor Dynasty* (Gloucester, 1985), pp. 102–5.

[61] *Harley MS 433*, II, p. 65. And see, in general, C.S.L. Davies, 'Richard III, Brittany, and Henry Tudor', *Nottingham Medieval Studies*, XXXVII (1993), pp. 110–26.

[62] 'Speeches prepared for the opening of parliament', in *Grants etc. from the Crown during the Reign of Edward the Fifth*, J.G. Nichols (ed.) (Camden Society, 1854), p. liii. This passage actually comes from the speech originally prepared for November 1483, but the February 1484 speech appears to have been much the same.

[63] *Harley MS 433*, II, p. 92. In late January John Goyse was commanded 'to doo us service upon the see with his shippe or shippes and to make werre upon oure Enemyes of Fraunce & Britteyn': ibid., II, p. 79.

[64] *Three Books of Polydore Vergil's English History*, ed. H. Ellis (Camden Society, 1844), pp. 204–5. The theme is Scottish aggression: 'Also by authorytie of the same parlyament a peace was made with the Scottis, who a lyttle before had run forrows about the borders.' On the other hand, since Polydore's chronology is very confused here, he may have had the Nottingham treaty of September 1484 in mind.

be achieved through military action. On 18 February Richard sent letters to country gentry, declaring that:

> by the advice of the lords spiritual and temporal . . . we be fully determined, by God's grace, to address us in person with host royal toward the party of our enemies and rebels of Scotland, at the beginning of this next summer. . . . We . . . charge you that . . . you dispose you to serve us personally in the said voyage, accompanied and apparelled for the war, according to your degree.[65]

The campaign was planned to start on 1 May, but the recipients of the letters were told to join Richard in Newcastle at the end of the month. Thus, early in 1484, Richard was planning a full-scale summer invasion of Scotland.

North of the border, James III's response was to give up his vain hopes of a truce. By 24 February the Scottish Parliament was preparing for war against 'oure Souuerane lordis Inymyis of ingland'. All able-bodied men were to be put on eight days' stand-by 'to cum to the king or his lieutennant . . . for the defens of the Realme'. At the same time, preparations were made for raising an army to besiege Dunbar in May; and, indeed, some siege of Dunbar was already under way in March (by which time Richard had ordered its refortification).[66]

In France, meanwhile, the states-general held in January heard its chancellor accuse Richard of killing his nephews, and went on to consider the danger of an English invasion.[67] At the time, Richard was more concerned with Scotland. But given his opposition to Edward IV's French treaty in 1475, and the current escalation in channel piracy, it is not surprising that Charles VIII's minority government feared Richard. It would probably have agreed with Maximilian of Austria: 'Also, it is likewise to be considered that the king of France is young, and the kingdom governed by a number of princes who agree ill, so that the

---

[65] J.O. Halliwell, *Letters of the Kings of England* (1848), pp. 156–7; cited in Pollard, *North-Eastern England*, p. 240.

[66] *Act. Parl. Scot.*, II, pp. 164–5; Macdougall, *James III*, pp. 209–10; *Harley MS 433*, II, pp. 101–2.

[67] Ross, *Richard III*, pp. 100, 200.

king of England will never have so good an opportunity as he has at present.'[68] That is one of the arguments Maximilian used early in 1485 when he tried to persuade Richard to attack France; no doubt the French government was worrying along similar lines.

In the past, when France and Scotland had both faced English hostility, they allied together. That was their response in 1484, too. By 13 March a French embassy had arrived in Scotland, and James III had reconfirmed the 'auld alliance', which had been vital to both countries during the Hundred Years War. The treaty reconfirmed the old agreement for mutual assistance if either country was attacked by England; Franco-Scottish relations had been restored to their Hundred Years War footing, back to before the time of Louis XI when Scotland was treated as a pawn. Moreover, the main French Ambassador, Bernard Stuart d'Aubigny, a cadet of the Scottish Lennox Stewarts and commander of the French king's Scots guard, apparently recruited a sizeable number of Scottish soldiers, presumably with James III's blessing.[69] The Franco-Scottish alliance, in abeyance for several decades, had been revivified; that was one effect of Richard's policy during the winter of 1483/4.

In March Richard probably continued in the same direction. He did authorize Bishop Langton as special messenger to Charles VIII, 'to treat . . . concerning truces'; but Langton did not reach Paris for several months.[70] Similarly, although a routine safe-conduct was issued for Scottish ambassadors, nothing came of it.[71] More illuminating is Richard's commission in late March or early April of four ships 'to doo service of werre upon the see in the north parties'; and in a letter to the Pope of 31 March he mentioned 'this most serious war which we are waging with the very cruel and fierce people of the Scots'.[72]

---

[68] Gairdner, *Letters and Papers*, II, pp. 40–1.

[69] Macdougall, *James III*, p. 210.

[70] *Harley MS 433*, III, p. 62; Griffiths and Thomas, *Making of Tudor Dynasty*, p. 110.

[71] *Rotuli Scotiae*, II, p. 461.

[72] *Harley MS 433*, II, p. 123; III, p. 68.

In April, however, there *are* signs of a change in Richard's policy. On 13 April he agreed £150 compensation for piracy against a Rouen merchant. More significantly, on the same day he told a herald to wait at Berwick for Scottish ambassadors until 15 May; if they arrived, and were in agreement, the herald was to proclaim a truce throughout the borders until 31 October. And it was also presumably in late April or in May that Richard began the negotiations with Brittany which led to a truce in the summer.[73]

The proposed truce with Scotland did not, of course, imply the surrender of Dunbar and Berwick; far from it. On the other hand, the land invasion of Scotland envisaged for the summer had been cancelled; Richard, for the first time, seems on the defensive towards Scotland. He may have realized that he could not continue tackling three enemies at a time indefinitely, and he probably could not finance a land campaign. News of the Franco-Scottish alliance may also have influenced him. More poignantly, his son and heir died in April, and that possibly sapped his confidence.[74] Also in April, we find him having his title to the throne publicly explained in London;[75] that suggests that his defeat of the 'Buckingham' rebellion had not brought him so much security as he had initially thought. And, indeed, the *Crowland Chronicle* states that 'at that time [just after his son's death] there was a rumour that the . . . exiles . . . would shortly land in England together with their leader, the earl of Richmond'.[76] In that case, Richard certainly could not risk a Scottish campaign – and, of course, many of his northern followers, who would form the core of his army, were now needed to run, and perhaps defend, southern

---

[73] Ibid., II, p. 126; III, p. 71; Rymer, *Foedera*, XII, pp. 226–7. Note the statement by the Flemish chronicler Adrien de But that 'Richard concluded a treaty with Brittany to resist the Scots, then sought a truce with France': Davies, 'Richard III, Brittany, and Henry Tudor', p. 115, note 26, citing *Chronique d'Adrien de But*, K. de Lettenhove (ed.), in *Chroniques de l'histoire de la Belgique* (3 vols, Brussels, 1870–6), I, p. 600.

[74] Cf. *Crowland Chronicle*, p. 171: 'The father and mother . . . [were] almost out of their minds for a long time when faced with the sudden grief.'

[75] A. Sutton, 'Richard III's "Tytylle and Right": A New Discovery', *The Ricardian*, IV (1977), pp. 2–7.

[76] *Crowland Chronicle*, p. 171. An invasion from Brittany was indeed planned for April 1484, but it came to nothing: Griffiths and Thomas, *Making of Tudor Dynasty*, p. 105.

England.[77] Thus domestic political worries probably told most heavily against the projected invasion of Scotland, and stimulated the change in his foreign policy.

So, by the summer of 1484, we find Richard pursuing a new, scaled-down, foreign policy. Its most striking aspect is the truce with Brittany, proclaimed on 8 June, which was to last until the following April.[78] Now, at last, Richard was trying to re-establish good relations with Brittany – no doubt in order to get hold of Henry Tudor. Alas for Richard, it was too late: Tudor was now established as the rival king (which had not been the case the previous August), and with the English refugees in his following it was much harder now for the Bretons to arrest him. In the event, Henry avoided Breton arrest, and in September or October 1484 he found asylum with Charles VIII of France. Richard's Breton policy might be described as 'too little too late' – disastrously so, as it turned out.[79]

But we are more concerned here with Scotland. In the summer of 1484, Richard's Scottish policy was two-edged. He may have been more conciliatory than in late 1483; but the war at sea went on, and indeed was Richard's main concern during June and July. From a base at Scarborough, he supervised the activities of 'our army now being upon the sea', which was combating both Scottish and French shipping.[80] The efforts paid off, at least with respect to Scotland. In early July, 'near the town and castle of Scarborough', stated the Crowland chronicler, 'in the same maritime theatre

[77] A.J. Pollard, 'The tyranny of Richard III', *Journal of Medieval History*, III (1977), pp. 147–65; Horrox, *Richard III*, pp. 188–205 – but note her qualifications on pp. 191–2.

[78] Rymer, *Foedera*, XII, pp. 226–7. For detailed examination of the new Anglo-Breton relationship, see Davies, 'Richard III, Brittany, and Henry Tudor', pp. 113–16. But, as Davies demonstrates convincingly in this article, the agreement by Richard to send 1,000 archers to Brittany, dated 26 June 1484 in *CPR, 1476–85*, pp. 517, 547, should actually be dated a year later: 26 June 1485.

[79] See Davies, 'Richard III, Brittany, and Henry Tudor'; Griffiths and Thomas, *Making of Tudor Dynasty*, chs 8, 9; A.V. Antonovics, 'Henry VII, King of England, "By the Grace of Charles VII of France"', in Griffiths and Sherborne (eds), *Kings and Nobles*, pp. 169–84.

[80] *Harley MS 433*, II, p. 146; cf. pp. 134, 136, 145. He was at Scarborough from 27 June until 11 July: R. Edwards, *The Itinerary of King Richard III* (London, 1983), p. 21.

he had remarkable success against the Scots'.[81] No details of this are known, but it was surely a significant naval victory for Richard's 'army upon the sea'.

The battle, according to Crowland, forced the Scots to the conference table. 'So considerable was this [success] that they sent the most noble petitioners who could be found in the kingdom as ambassadors to the king at Nottingham town and castle on 7 September.' James's siege of Dunbar had clearly failed, probably because Richard had kept it supplied by sea,[82] and since he could not keep an army in the field for much longer than a month, he, even more than Richard, needed a truce. But Crowland also links the sea battle with a Scottish victory on land: 'in that same summer . . . they inflicted no less destruction upon us, for the Scottish fugitives, Lord James Douglas and many others . . . besides many Englishmen . . . fell into their hands'.[83] What Crowland is describing is the fate of a raid launched by the two exiles, the Duke of Albany and the Earl of Douglas, into south-west Scotland; they were defeated at Lochmaben by a local force on 22 July.

Historians who have studied this episode conclude that in summer 1484 Richard was trying 'to resurrect the Scottish fifth column'; that he supported Albany and Douglas; and that when their raid turned out a fiasco, he decided to negotiate a truce.[84] But the dates do not fit. The battle at Lochmaben took place on 22 July; but a day earlier, James III had dated a letter to Richard stating that: 'we ar nowe advertisit be . . . oure . . . Counsaillor Robert lord Lile [and] oure . . . Squiere Duncan of Dundas And also by . . . youre familiere squier Edward Gower', that Richard now wished for an Anglo-Scottish truce and marriage alliance. That is certainly the Nottingham agenda, and in the letter James named his embassy. He also said that since Richard had given instructions for a truce with Scotland until after the conference, he would do

[81] *Crowland Chronicle*, p. 173.

[82] *Harley MS 433*, II, pp. 134, 145, 149–50.

[83] *Crowland Chronicle*, p. 173.

[84] Macdougall, *James III*, pp. 211–12; Ross, *Richard III*, p. 193; R. Nicholson, *Scotland: The Later Middle Ages* (Edinburgh, 1974), pp. 516–17; Pollard, *North-Eastern England*, p. 240.

the same.[85] (The difference in Richard's behaviour, compared to the second half of 1483, should be noted.)

Thus on 21 July the preliminaries for the Nottingham conference were already well advanced – before Albany's defeat at Lochmaben – as a result of messages carried by Lord Lyle and by Edward Gower. In that case, far from supporting Albany and Douglas, Richard must have been abandoning them. They were with Richard at York on 25 June,[86] and they must have learned of the about-face in Richard's Scottish policy either around then or when the news of the naval victory came through, and as a desperate last fling tried invading Scotland on their own, without official English backing. (Those Englishmen with them were probably borderers along for the raid.) That interpretation is confirmed by the fact that after the battle Albany, who escaped capture, fled to France, not to England.[87] He had had a bad time in England, being ignored by Richard after 1482, but he hardly deserves any sympathy.

One other point should be made about the preliminaries of the Nottingham conference. James III's letter apart, there is no surviving evidence for the contacts between Lyle and Gower and their sovereigns. This was secret diplomacy, not the subject of written record. And that may be why the *Crowland Chronicle* gives a rather false impression of what was happening; its account seems to be based only on official documents – which the chronicler may well have had a hand in writing.[88] It is particularly significant that he gives 7

---

[85] *Harley MS 433*, II, pp. 105–6. Gower was an usher of the king's Chamber: *CPR, 1476–1486*, p. 381.

[86] Rymer, *Foedera*, XII, p. 228.

[87] Macdougall, *James III*, pp. 211–12.

[88] I follow Nicholas Pronay's argument that the Crowland chronicler was at or near the head of Chancery's diplomatic section: *Crowland Chronicle*, pp. 78–98. To me, the impression of Anglo-Scottish relations which comes from the formal documents (printed in Rymer, *Foedera*, and in *Rotuli Scotiae*) seems to tally very closely with the *Crowland Chronicle's* account. It is, however, worth adding that the minutes of the initial stages of the Nottingham conference (printed in Gairdner, *Letters and Papers*, I, p. 63) list 'Maister Thomas Utton, doctor of canon' among those participating; that might tell against Pronay's argument that the author of the Continuation could not have described himself as 'Doctor in Jure Canonico' because such terminology was not used in that period (*Crowland Chronicle*, pp. 94–5). Hutton was a Doctor of Civil Law (1474–5) and also of Canon Law (1477): A.B. Emden, *Biographical Register of the University of Cambridge to 1500* (Cambridge, 1963), pp. 323–4.

September as the date of the Nottingham conference. That was the date originally agreed between James and Richard, and specified in all the preliminary documents, but, in fact, the Scottish ambassadors did not reach Nottingham until 11 September.[89] So it looks as if the Crowland chronicler remembered the date in the preliminary documents rather than when the conference actually took place; the implication is that he may not have been present in Nottingham at that time.

Whatever the case, Crowland's account of the Nottingham conference does highlight its two most striking features: that the Scots 'earnestly ask[ed] for peace in a long and eloquent address'; and that 'agreements . . . were drawn up, as the king desired, between the commissioners of each kingdom on those matters which seemed to require particular attention'.[90]

Let us first take the long and eloquent address; although generally dismissed as verbiage, it well deserves serious consideration (a translation by David Shotter is published below, pp. 194–202).[91] It was delivered by Master Archibald Whitelaw, secretary to James III, in the presence of King Richard himself.[92] It was not too long, probably taking about half an hour to deliver; it is in competent Ciceronian Latin, with carefully chosen quotations from Virgil and other classical authors; and in places it is certainly extremely eloquent.

[89] Gairdner, *Letters and Papers*, I, p. 63.

[90] *Crowland Chronicle*, p. 173.

[91] The text is printed, from British Library MS. Vespasian C. xvi, as 'Oratio Scotorum ad regem Ricardum tertium pro pace firmanda inter Anglos et Scotos. XII Sept. M.CCC.LXXXIV', in *The Bannatyne Miscellany*, II, ed. D. Laing (Bannatyne Club, Edinburgh, 1836), pp. 41–8. Modern political historians have paid it little attention, apparently agreeing with Gairdner's remarks in *Letters and Papers*, I, p. 63: '. . . the speech of Archibald Whitelaw . . . is scarcely necessary to print, as Bucke has given some extracts (Kennet's Complete Hist., I. 572), that pretty tolerably indicate its general character. The only fact of interest that it contains is a statement that the speaker had been sent as ambassador by James II, about twenty-five years before, to the king's father (Richard Duke of York), in Ireland, and concluded a treaty with him.'

[92] Judging by the evidence of Richard's books, and of course the prayer specially written for him, it is reasonable to assume that he himself understood Latin. Cf. A.F. Sutton, 'The court and its culture in the reign of Richard III', in J. Gillingham (ed.), *Richard III: A Medieval Kingship* (London, 1993), pp. 75–92, at 83–4, and the references on p. 92. See also below, pp. 153ff.

Whitelaw himself is a very interesting figure, a master at St Andrews and Cologne Universities and collector of an elegant Renaissance library.[93] James II made him tutor to the young heir to the throne in the 1450s; in 1462, early in James III's minority, he became royal secretary, and he continued in that office for thirty-one years, until 1493, through a whole sequence of Scottish political upheavals.[94] He is exactly the kind of fifteenth-century university-educated civil service career bureaucrat who, Nicholas Pronay has shown, was taking over the central administration in England.[95]

Whitelaw's oration is worth dwelling on, because it ties in well with the main drift of Scottish foreign policy at the time (of course, as secretary, Whitelaw presumably was intimately concerned with foreign affairs). He starts with normal protestations of his own unworthiness, and continues with the most elaborate praise of Richard's famous kingly qualities, especially his magnificent military reputation. The flattery is remarkably skilful. For instance, he quotes Statius's *Thebaid* to the effect that 'Never before has nature dared to encase in a smaller body such spirit and such strength', and 'In his small body the greatest valour held sway' – clearly passages carefully chosen to reflect Richard's slight build.[96]

[93] J. MacQueen, 'The literature of fifteenth-century Scotland', in J.M. Brown (ed.), *Scottish Society in the Fifteenth Century* (London, 1977), p. 194; J. MacQueen, *Robert Henryson* (Oxford, 1967), pp. 13–15. Professor MacQueen describes Whitelaw's Latin as 'that of a Christian humanist, modelled on Cicero' ('Literature of fifteenth-century Scotland', p. 194); for a classical scholar's analysis of the style, see David Shotter's remarks, below, pp. 203–4. The contents of Whitelaw's library are listed in J. Durkan and A. Ross, 'Early Scottish Libraries', *Innes Review*, ix (1958), pp. 3–167, at p. 159.

[94] See, e.g., Macdougall, *James III*, pp. 53, 64, 66, 71, 76, 79–81, 85, 92, 116, 149, 165–6, 173, 185, 200, 213–14, 217, 254; N. Macdougall, *James IV* (Edinburgh, 1989), pp. 51, 73, 105. As Dr Macdougall remarks, Whitelaw was 'the ubiquitous royal secretary', but his oration at Nottingham 'is the only example of his emergence from the relative obscurity, routine, and drudgery of his position' (Macdougall, *James III*, pp. 116, 213); his political significance, however, was probably greater than that implies.

[95] N. Pronay, 'The Chancellor, Chancery and Council at the end of the fifteenth century', in H. Hearder and H.R. Loyn (eds), *British Government and Administration: Studies presented to S.B. Chrimes* (Cardiff, 1974), pp. 96–103.

[96] Whitelaw thus gives us disinterested confirmation that Richard had a small body; this was noticed by J. Gairdner, *History of the Life and Reign of Richard III* (Cambridge, new edn, 1898), p. 180, but seems to have been missed in more recent accounts of Richard III.

Also, he combines two lines from Virgil's *Aeneid* with three from the *Eclogues* in order to state that 'So long as rivers flow into the sea . . . so long as the wild boar delights in the mountains . . . your honour, your name and your glory will survive for ever' – a composite verse obviously constructed to highlight Richard's boar symbol. But this is not simply diplomatic sycophancy: the implication is that Richard has already won all possible laurels (beyond the praise even of Cicero), and therefore has no need to win any more. Then there is a switch to the theme of peace – peace which was reigning at the time of Our Lord's incarnation, thanks to the victories of Augustus Caesar (so the main achievement of a great warrior is to bring peace). 'Truly, it was in peace that Christ was born; in peace that he was buried; in peace that he fell asleep; in peace that he went to his rest.' And just as God requires peace, so did the great Romans exalt it. Also, recently, Richard's own subjects, who formerly 'in their arrogance preferred war to peace', now 'praise peace and condemn war and battles', and 'call you to brotherly love with our most noble Prince', the king of Scots. 'Satis enim pugnatum est', Whitelaw continues poignantly: 'For there has been enough fighting, enough wrongdoing; enough Christian bloodshed in this most recent conflict . . .'. Next he turns to war, which was instilled into men's minds by Satan: there is a long exposition on war's evils, on which thrive every kind of cruelty and sin. Peace, on the other hand, promotes divine worship, justice, virtue, and the flourishing of the goods of the earth; during peace, 'princes, nobles, merchants and the common people enjoy an abundance of gold, silver and jewels' (nowadays we would call that 'the peace dividend'). But one of the things preventing peace is 'the lust for power and domination', which has caused terrible wars. Therefore, 'let every prince be content with the limits, bounds and confines of his own kingdom, so that he would rather retreat than advance; lest, contrary to the commandment of our Lord and Saviour, he steals other people's property . . .'. When kings 'become overbearing' and their insolence cannot be checked, disputes and warfare – 'devised by God, as Livy says, for the humiliation of mighty potentates' – are bound to follow, resulting in their destruction. That, surely, is Whitelaw's key point. Moreover, he adds, 'it is an unnatural thing that war should be fought between us – we who are bound together within a small island in the western sea, and who are linked by living in the same climate and neighbouring lands, sharing similarity of physique, language, appearance, colouring and complexion'. He emphasizes the absence of any need for hostility between English and Scots: instead they should be 'joined together in one chain of love and goodwill'. Hence he concludes by looking forward to 'the joining of your people and ours in love, in sweet marriage, matrimony and kinship' – following the negotiations on which God was obviously smiling, as witnessed by 'the kind, mild weather and the balmy conditions'.

Thus, underneath all the hyperbole, what Whitelaw was arguing very firmly was that there was no point to war, that finances were much better in peacetime, and, especially, that kings should not take over other countries' lands – in other words that Berwick and Dunbar should be restored to Scotland. And that, surely, was the policy of James III and his ambassadors. During his reign, James appears to have been obsessed with being a European peace-maker:[97] an effect, perhaps, of being tutored by Archibald Whitelaw. But, on the other hand, to achieve peace Berwick and Dunbar had to be restored. What James and the Scots wanted was to return to the pre-1482 *status quo*. The Scottish desire for peace does not, therefore, indicate any capitulation; the embassy would take a tough bargaining stance.[98]

Crowland's other remark about the conference is that 'agreements . . . were drawn up, as the king desired, between the commissioners of each kingdom on those matters which seemed to require particular attention'. The credence, or authorization, for the English commissioners indicates, I think, that the words 'as the king desired' can be taken literally. Whereas the Scottish ambassadors' credence was issued by James III some time in advance, as was normal practice, the English commissioners' credence is dated 20 September, the day before the conference ended.[99] That is most unusual. The explanation is probably that no

[97] See, e.g. Macdougall, *James III*, pp. 92–6, 113–19.

[98] Whether or not Whitelaw's final passages were calling for eventual Anglo-Scottish Union – as a generation later John Mair was to do in his *A History of Greater Britain, as well England as Scotland . . . by John Major . . . 1521*, A. Constable (ed. and trans.) (Scottish History Society, Edinburgh, 1892) – brought about through the proposed marriage alliance is unclear; personally I doubt it, but the question has to remain open.

[99] *Rotuli Scotiae*, II, pp. 465–6; cf. *Cal. Doc. Scot.*, IV, nos 1,501–2.

earlier English credence was needed, because Richard himself headed the negotiators; he probably conducted most of the negotiations, and then at the end authorized the experts to draw up the agreed treaty. This would be one more example of personal, hands-on government by Richard III.

But that does not necessarily mean that Richard dictated his own terms. Analysis of the treaty suggests that the negotiations were more complex than that.[100] At first sight it seems an anticlimax, given the build-up to the conference: for although it provided that James III's son and heir should now marry Anne de la Pole, Richard's niece and closest eligible female relative, that was accompanied only by a three-year truce. By comparison, in 1465 and 1474 an armistice until 1519 had been agreed. But in the 1460s and 1470s the Scots had held Berwick and Dunbar. In 1484, the Scottish delegation could hardly consent to their long-term loss. Later, James III and the Scottish Parliament are to be found stipulating, in preparation for similar negotiations with Henry VII, that unless Berwick was either surrendered or had its fortifications dismantled, no long-term agreement could be reached.[101] The same no doubt tacitly applied to the Nottingham negotiations of 1484: the Scots would not have accepted a long truce unless they had managed to talk Richard into surrendering Berwick and Dunbar. Despite Whitelaw's eloquence, that was hardly likely. Or was it? With respect to Dunbar, at least, it might have been. Whereas Berwick was specifically included in the general truce, Dunbar was only covered for six months at a time, and James III could refuse even that; if he did refuse, however, any fighting over Dunbar was to be localized, and was not to affect the main truce.[102] That proviso surely suited the Scots more than the English – in other words it was a concession by Richard. Dunbar seems to have been dispensable; but Berwick was not.

There follow a dozen clauses dealing with the truce's practical operation, mostly modifying and tightening up existing procedures. They contain detailed

---

[100] Rymer, *Foedera*, XII, pp. 235–43.

[101] *Act. Parl. Scot.*, II, p. 182 (1488); cf. Macdougall, *James III*, pp. 217–21.

[102] Rymer, *Foedera*, XII, pp. 236–7.

regulations about marginal cases, such as over-staying safe-conducts because of illness; and several deal with maritime problems, especially shipwrecks.[103] In most cases, these are reworkings of truce provisions made in the 1450s,[104] and, since the 1484 truce was only to last three years, they may look like overkill; but the intention may have been to lay down new rules for the future, since previous practices had obviously proved inadequate. At least some of the clauses probably had the one clause that is entirely new – that any march warden or his lieutenant making war on the other side during the truce should immediately be denounced as a traitor and rebel – which clearly relates to the behaviour of the Duke of Albany in 1479.[105]

On the other hand that clause, severely limiting the march wardens' activities, would probably have had full approval from Richard: Richard the king, that is, not Richard the pre-1483 warden. As Pollard has taught us, one of the most important aspects of Richard's kingship is his maintenance of his *own* authority in the north, at the expense of the border magnates who had, hitherto, effectively run the region.[106] The treason clause is entirely consistent with that. There is a sharp contrast with a previous Anglo-Scottish truce made in 1473 (which developed into the 1474 armistice); the earlier truce had almost as many provisions, but in nearly every one the initiative was left for the wardens' 'Days of Truce'.[107] That, in 1484, was no longer the case. The 1484 truce provisions were mostly to be upheld in ordinary law courts; nothing was

[103] Ibid., pp. 237–40.

[104] See the general analysis of Anglo-Scottish truce provisions, 1453–1502, in A.A. Cardew, 'A Study of Society in the Anglo-Scottish Borders, 1455–1502' (University of St Andrews Ph.D. Thesis, 1974), pp. 258–75. Interestingly, these provisions are not to be found in Edward IV's reign; but the text of the 1464 truce, which was the basis for the Anglo Scottish truce under Edward IV, is illegible (ibid., p. 258).

[105] Rymer, *Foedera*, XII, p. 237: '. . . quod si . . . aliquam Gardianum Locumvetenentum alicujus Regum praedictorum sine Mandato vel Jussu sui Principis Exercitum ducere, aut alias hostiliter intrare . . .; in eo Casu Princeps . . . ipsum Gardianum aut Locumtenentem sic Intrantem . . . declarabit aut declarari faciet Rebellem et Proditorem . . .'

[106] Pollard, *North-Eastern England*, pp. 355–63.

[107] Rymer, *Foedera*, XI, pp. 788–91.

left to the wardens' initiative, and indeed the wardens seem irrelevant. Here, surely, Richard's hand can be seen; though given that James III and his civil servants also had a highly exalted sense of royal authority, some credit is probably due to the Scots as well.

One other clause – the sixteenth – must also be considered.[108] It states that, 'because both the most excellent and invincible prince the king of England and his cousin the most excellent and illustrious prince the king of Scots' believe that, without good judicial machinery, many breaches of the truce are inevitable, therefore, whenever either king learns of such breaches, he must notify the other one, who shall immediately – and once or twice a year on a regular basis – send two or three members of his council to the borders to meet royal councillors from the opposite side; both sets of councillors are to have sufficient power to settle all problems concerning the truce, and check on negligence by the truce conservators or their lieutenants. This very striking provision has no Yorkist antecedents; but it can be found almost verbatim in truces made during the reign of Henry VI.[109] Thus, unlike the clause threatening the wardens with treason, it was not a novel idea in 1484. On the other hand, it is highly likely that Richard III would have taken the provision very much more seriously than Henry VI did. As Leslie Macfarlane has pointed out, it dovetails closely with the machinery of the Council of the North, which Richard had established in July 1484.[110] In that case, it is hard to believe that Richard would not have viewed the idea of using royal councillors to supervise justice on the borders as an extension of, or adjunct to, that council; it is worth pointing out that the list of English conservators of the 1484 truce starts with John de la Pole, Earl of Lincoln,[111] the Council of the North's head. Thus it may be suggested that, under Richard III, royal conciliar jurisdiction was intended

---

[108] Ibid., XII, p. 240, 2nd item.

[109] E.g., ibid., XI, pp. 252 (1449), 298 (1451), 395 (1457). It might also have been included in the 1464 truce; see note 104, above.

[110] L.J. Macfarlane, *William Elphinstone and the Kingdom of Scotland, 1431–1514* (Aberdeen, 1985), p. 134. See Pollard, *North-Eastern England*, pp. 346–7, for the Council of the North.

[111] Rymer, *Foedera*, XII, p. 243.

to take over supervision of the borders from the wardens' courts: that, in effect, a joint Anglo-Scottish Council for the Marches was probably being established.

If that is the case, then in this machinery, as in Richard's Council of the North, there was little room for border magnates. These had gained their power largely through the march wardenships – but what happened to those offices? On the west march, Richard himself kept the office when he became king, and employed a lesser peer, Lord Dacre, as his deputy: thus the former Neville wardenship had come under direct royal control.[112] In the east, Henry Percy, Earl of Northumberland was warden of the east and middle marches and captain of Berwick – but his last known period of office expired on 8 December 1484, and there is no evidence that he was reappointed by Richard.[113] Moreover, when Richard authorized commissions on 30 January and 18 April 1485 to consider, with their Scottish counterparts, the implementation of the Nottingham treaty and any breaches of the truce – which used to be the march wardens' jobs – both commissions were headed by that most prominent royal councillor and household man Sir Richard Ratcliffe;[114] these commissions perhaps represent the conciliar machinery described in the sixteenth clause of the Nottingham treaty. Thus it seems as if, by early 1485, Richard had effectively abolished the wardenships of the marches. If we are to look for grievances which Henry Percy may have had against Richard by the time of Bosworth,[115] then this, I think, might well have been the most serious of them all.

But that analysis also suggests that Richard viewed the Nottingham treaty as a mechanism for governing the north of England, rather than as a settlement with Scotland. During his prolonged stay in the north in mid-1484, he appears to have been thinking hard about how to run the region – and the Nottingham

[112] Storey, 'Wardens of the Marches', p. 615.

[113] See ibid., p. 615, note 7. Northumberland's last-recorded reappointment as warden was on 24 July 1484, but only until 8 December: *Rotuli Scotiae*, II, 463–4.

[114] Ibid., II, pp. 466–7; *Cal. Doc. Scot.*, IV, no. 1513.

[115] Cf. Pollard, *North-Eastern England*, pp. 358–60; M. Hicks, 'Dynastic change and northern society: the fourth earl of Northumberland, 1470–89', in Hicks, *Richard III and his Rivals*, pp. 365–94, at 376–9.

treaty, albeit with Scottish help, looks like one of the consequences. Moreover, there was probably a commercial aspect. One of the reasons for the fact that north-east merchants lost out to Londoners during the fifteenth century[116] may well have been that the north-eastern sea-route to the Continent was extremely vulnerable to the endemic North Sea piracy. If Richard, in mid-1484, asked the York merchants what they wanted from him as king, one answer would surely have been, 'tackle North Sea piracy' – as he did, both in the naval war and in the Nottingham treaty.

If those points are valid, however, then it is surely inconceivable that Richard intended to let the truce lapse after three years. He must have regarded the Nottingham treaty as an end in itself, to be prolonged as necessary in the future. The Scots, on the other hand, probably saw things differently. For James III, Berwick must still have been a major goal – and an obstacle to any long-term truce. What James may have hoped was to use his heir's marriage to Anne de la Pole as a way of getting Berwick back. In later, similar, marriage negotiations with Henry VII, the return of Berwick was made the condition for the royal marriage;[117] it could have been the dowry of the English princess. That is probably what James's ambassadors were to ask of Richard III, at a second conference which (it was arranged in May 1485) was to be held in York later in the year.[118] For the Scots, therefore, if not for Richard, the Nottingham treaty was part of an ongoing diplomatic process.

The York conference never took place, for the battle of Bosworth intervened. But the Scots continued to negotiate – the York embassy went to Westminster for Henry VII's coronation instead.[119] In late 1485, James III may have preferred Henry VII on the throne to Richard III – though James did have strange judgement: within two years he had agreed to marry Elizabeth Woodville![120] Actually, on this issue the change of monarch probably made little

---

[116] Cf. Pollard, *North-Eastern England*, pp. 72–80.

[117] *Rotuli Scotiae*, II, p. 480; *Act. Parl. Scot.*, II, p. 182.

[118] *Act. Parl. Scot.*, II, p. 170.

[119] *Rotuli Scotiae*, II, p. 469.

[120] Ibid., II, p. 480.

difference. Henry VII did let Dunbar go in 1486, but kept Berwick;[121] Richard would doubtless have done the same.

Be that as it may, were the Scots actually hoping for Richard's overthrow? The answer must depend on how they assessed Richard's long-term intentions. Did they think he had come to want a long-term peace, or not? One wonders what impression he made on Whitelaw and the others at Nottingham – and whether they felt they could trust him. But for James III, Richard's attitude to Berwick would have been the acid test; on that, it may be suggested that he would have anticipated getting more joy out of Henry Tudor.

In addition, it should be noted that the Scottish Parliament of May 1485, which discussed the York conference, decided also to ask the Pope for 'a confirmacioun in the best forme of the aliance and confederacioun maid betwix the king of france and our souverane lord and ther Realmez'.[122] The Franco-Scottish alliance was thus on the Scots' minds in May 1485. This takes us back to March 1484, when that alliance was reconfirmed. Then, Richard had been threatening Brittany, Scotland and France. While his relations with Brittany and Scotland subsequently improved, those with France did not. Throughout 1484, in fact, he maintained the naval war with France,[123] and even gave the impression of gearing up for an invasion of France. That is what the French government consistently feared – which is why it helped Henry Tudor when he fled from Brittany – which made Richard all the more hostile towards France.[124] Charles VIII's government certainly had a vested interest in Richard's overthrow; from its point of view Tudor would be a much better king. And, on 22 August 1485, it was probably the professional French soldiers who had accompanied Henry

---

[121] Macdougall, *James III*, pp. 217, 220–1.

[122] *Act. Parl. Scot.*, II, p. 171.

[123] E.g. *CPR, 1476–1486*, pp. 492–4, 518, 520, 529; *Crowland Chronicle*, p. 173; C.S.L. Davies, 'The alleged "Sack of Bristol": international ramifications of Breton privateering, 1484–5', *Historical Research*, lxiv (1994), pp. 230–9, at 233–4.

[124] Davies, 'Richard III, Brittany, and Henry Tudor', pp. 114–22; Antonovics, 'Henry VII, King of England', in Griffiths and Sherborne (eds), *Kings and Nobles*, pp. 172–4; Ross, *Richard III*, pp. 200–1.

Tudor from Normandy who were chiefly responsible for his victory in the battle of Bosworth.[125]

There were also Scottish soldiers at Bosworth. As Norman Macdougall has shown, Henry's army in 1485 is likely to have contained some 500–1,000 Scots[126] – perhaps the archers mentioned in Polydore Vergil's account of Bosworth, for Scottish troops in France tended to be archers.[127] They were led by Sir Alexander Bruce of Earlshall, who within six months had received not only a £20 annuity from Henry VII 'in gracious remuneration . . . of his great labours . . . lately done in person', but also lands in Berwickshire from James III, 'for his faithful . . . service to the king both within and beyond the realm';[128] does that show James III's true feelings about Richard? Moreover when, much later, Bernard Stuart d'Aubigny visited England, Henry VII personally greeted and entertained him at Greenwich.[129] Bernard Stuart, as has been seen, had negotiated the confirmation of the Franco-Scottish alliance in March 1484 and had recruited troops in Scotland – probably the Scots who fought at Bosworth. His Scottish mission took place when Richard was seriously threatening both Scotland and France. So Stuart stood for the Franco-Scottish alliance against Richard III's England; and he would surely have promoted Henry Tudor's cause in France – hence Henry's subsequent gratitude. Thus there probably was, albeit indirectly, a Scottish diplomatic dimension to the vital French support for Henry Tudor. But it is a dimension deriving from the circumstances of March 1484, which were before the Nottingham treaty, and indeed take us back to the Franco-Scottish alignments of the Scottish Wars of Independence and the Hundred Years War. The clock had been turned back.

[125] Suggested in R.A. Griffiths, 'Henry VII: the training of a king', in R.A. Griffiths, *King and Country: England and Wales in the 15th Century* (1993), pp. 115–36, at 128, 134; and by A. Grant, 'Foreign affairs under Richard III', in Gillingham (ed.), *Richard III*, pp. 113–32, at 128–30.

[126] Macdougall, *James III*, pp. 215–16.

[127] P. Contamine, 'Scottish soldiers in France in the second half of the fifteenth century', in G.G. Simpson (ed.), *The Scottish Soldier Abroad* (Edinburgh, 1992), pp. 16–30.

[128] *Cal. Doc. Scot.*, IV, no. 1,518; *Registrum Magni Sigilli Regum Scotorum*, J.M. Thomson *et al.* (eds) (Edinburgh, 1888–1914), II, no. 1,638.

[129] Griffiths and Thomas, *Making of Tudor Dynasty*, p. 174.

But that was done, too, by Richard himself. In his anti-Tudor proclamations he used Hundred Years War rhetoric, claiming to defend the realm against England's ancient enemy.[130] And, with respect to Scotland, it was Richard as much as anybody who turned the clock back, in his warfare of 1480–2 and in his dreams of Scottish conquests. At the beginning of this essay, it was remarked that by the 1460s Anglo-Scottish relations, like Anglo-French ones, had entered a new era. But in 1485 we are back in the world of the earlier fifteenth century.[131] Responsibility for the changed circumstances surely rests most of all with Richard III. Despite his new ideas for governing the north and the borders, his main effect on both Anglo-French and Anglo-Scottish relations was to take them back to the era of the Hundred Years War and the Scottish Wars of Independence – and he met his death in battle against an essentially Franco-Scottish army. In our present context, the point is typified by his capture and retention of Berwick. That is his one permanent achievement: it should be remembered that Berwick – 'that standis in Scotlande the qwhilke toune yhe call yhouris', as one Scots noble told an English king[132] – was never liberated from English possession after Richard took it. But, tragically, in Richard's capture of Berwick were sown some, at least, of the seeds of his own downfall.

---

[130] E.g. *Harley MS 433*, II, pp. 124–5, 127–8, 228, 230.

[131] As argued in Grant, 'Foreign affairs under Richard III', in Gillingham (ed.), *Richard III*, pp. 130–1.

[132] Letter of James Douglas of Balvenie (brother of the 4th Earl of Douglas) to Henry IV, 26 July 1405: *Facsimiles of the National Manuscripts of Scotland* (2 vols, 1867–71), II, no. 54.

7

'True Ornaments to Know a Holy Man': Northern Religious Life and the Piety of Richard III

Jonathan Hughes

In the fourteenth and early fifteenth centuries the north of England was the centre of profound religious changes. Standards of education among clergy and laymen were raised through the administration of confession and through the production of such works as the *Epistle on the Mixed Life, The Mirror of the Life of Christ* and the Corpus Christi plays. The mystical and eremitic teachings of Richard Rolle of Hampole were adapted and controlled and the foundations were laid for the growth of lay piety and participation in a religious life that had formerly been the preserve of the clergy.[1] By the mid-fifteenth century this had taken the form of the translation, copying and dissemination among secular clergy, barons, gentry and merchants throughout the country of works of devotion that had been written in the north of England. When we consider the development of the religious culture of the north in the second half of the century two strands are of particular importance. One is the continuing role of the clergy of the diocese of York who were educated at the university of Cambridge in following the traditions established at the turn of the fifteenth century. The other is the emphasis placed by them on private prayer in the pursuit of the mixed life of spiritual devotion and public activity which was practised by many of the laity. Of all the northern laity of the late fifteenth century Richard III, as duke and king, stands out as the most influential patron of the church and exemplar of personal piety. This paper explores the impact of

---

[1] J. Hughes, *Pastors and Visionaries: Religion and Secular Life in Late Medieval Yorkshire* (Woodbridge, 1988), *passim*.

the late-medieval religious culture of the north on its most famous son. It considers his links with and patronage of Cambridge-educated clergy, their influence on his practice of the mixed life, and the manner in which his 'personal' prayer and early surviving portraits reveal his perceptions of himself in the world.

The changes in religious sensibility associated with the concept of the mixed life had been pioneered by Cambridge-educated clergy under the patronage of Thomas Arundel, Archbishop of York in 1388–96. The careers of the intellectual leaders of the church in the second half of the fifteenth century followed similar patterns to their predecessors, the protégés of Thomas Arundel, with Cambridge as the focus of their lives. The churchman most reminiscent of Arundel himself was John Alcock, 1430–1500, the son of a burgess of Kingston-on-Hull. Alcock, like Arundel, was closely connected with Peterhouse, where he was a fellow, and he too was Bishop of Ely. He was an influential figure in Edward IV's government who took on the role of keeper of the Great Seal and president of the king's council in 1475 during the king's absence in France.[2] Thomas Rotherham, from Rotherham in Yorkshire, a fellow of King's Hall, 1446–60, chancellor of the university of Cambridge, 1469–71, and Archbishop of York, 1480–1500, was also a prominent servant of Edward IV in the 1470s and chancellor of England from 1474.[3] William Melton of Yorkshire was a prominent fellow at Michaelhouse from 1485 and a chancellor of York Cathedral in 1495.[4] His pupil at Michaelhouse was John Fisher, a mercer's son from Beverley who was ordained by Archbishop Rotherham. Fisher was a pensioner fellow of Michaelhouse and vice-chancellor of Cambridge at the end of the century.[5] He moved in court circles and was chaplain to Margaret Beaufort.[6]

---

[2] *BRUC*, p. 6.

[3] *CPR, 1467–77*, p. 450; *BRUC*, p. 489.

[4] *BRUC*, pp. 229–30.

[5] *BRUC*, pp. 229–30.

[6] D. Leader, *A History of the University of Cambridge*, I, *The University to 1546* (Cambridge, 1988), pp. 264–75. See also, M.K. Jones and M.G. Underwood, *The King's Mother* (Cambridge, 1992).

Apart from sharing in common close links with Cambridge, these northerners were all distinguished scholars and preachers. Alcock wrote four collections of sermons in English, all printed by de Worde, and a Latin sermon printed by Pynson.[7] He showed a personal interest in the printing of his works and supervised the designs of the accompanying woodcuts. Rotherham preached a 'noble sermon' at the re-interment of Richard, Duke of York in Fotheringhay in 1476[8] and bequeathed a large library to Cambridge University.[9] Melton was the author of the *Continuation of the Lives of the Archbishops of York from Alexander Neville to Thomas Wolsey* and an exhortative sermon to those who seek to be promoted to holy orders;[10] he also taught Fisher Greek and Hebrew.[11] Fisher was the most prominent preacher and controversialist of his age and the author of letters of spiritual consolation. These men were the intellectual, spiritual heirs of the northern Cambridge writers of the end of the fourteenth century. But they faced different challenges. Thomas Arundel and his clerks, John Newton, Richard Scrope and Walter Hilton, had established a pastorally acceptable structure for the piety of clergy and laymen in the face of heresy and devotional novelties.[12] By 1470 the increasing sophistication and independence of the laity in religious matters and their increasingly secular outlook posed an indirect threat to the prestige and sanctity of secular clergy and the religious orders. The northern Cambridge-educated clergy responded with the same energy as their predecessors had shown and endeavoured to meet the challenge of lay piety and to restore the reputation of clergy by infusing

[7] *Mons perfeccionis, the hyll of perfeccion; In die innocencium sermo pro episcopo puerorum;* an English sermon on Luke viii *Qui habet aures audiendi: audiat;* and *Desponsacio virginis Christo, Sponsage of a virgin to cryste; Gallicantus ad confrates suos curatos in sinodo apud Barnwell* (Wynkyn de Worde, Westminster, 1496–7).

[8] C.L. Scofield, *The Life and Reign of Edward IV*, 2 vols (1929), II, p. 168.

[9] *BRUC*, pp. 490–1.

[10] Ibid., p. 401; *Historians of the Church of York and its Archbishops*, ed. J. Raine Jr, II, Rolls Series (1879–94), p. xxv.

[11] *Test. Ebor.*, V, pp. 251–2.

[12] Hughes, *Pastors and Visionaries*, p. 197ff. See also R.B. Dobson, *'Preserving the Perishable': Contrasting Communities in Medieval England* (Cambridge, 1991) for recent comment on the link between the university and northern clergy.

greater spirituality into the lives of priest and monks. One way this was attempted was through educational reform: the provision of education in grammar in new schools for young men training to be priests; and the foundation of colleges in Cambridge with a new emphasis on Theology rather than Canon Law, that would provide a training for pastoral service and encourage greater spirituality. Alcock's career pattern was so similar to Arundel's because he was consciously working within the same tradition, and no doubt taking Arundel as the model of a successful bishop who combined spirituality with a strong orthodoxy that was manifested in service with a sense of pastoral duty. In 1479 he founded in Hull a free school teaching grammar and song.[13] Rotherham founded a grammar school in Rotherham called Jesus College; its purpose was to preach the word of God in the parish and diocese of York and to raise the standards of the clergy by teaching the rules of grammar and song to scholars from all parts of England but especially the diocese of York.[14]

However, it was in the universities, especially Cambridge, that they directed most of their efforts: between 1496 and 1525 six new colleges were founded in Oxford and Cambridge; five of them were northern foundations. Between 1470 and 1473 Thomas Rotherham built the eastern front of the Cambridge library, to which he contributed over two hundred volumes.[15] During this period Michaelhouse became a centre for the study of Theology under William Melton and his pupil John Fisher who recounted his teacher's exacting standards.[16] In 1496 John Alcock founded the college of Jesus; its first master was a Yorkshireman, William Chubbes.[17] Alcock took a close interest in the architecture of his educational institutions (like the Roman pontiffs of this period) and he supervised the design of Jesus College, placing various images of

---

[13] *VCH Yorks, East Riding: City of Hull*, ed. K.S. Allison (1969), pp. 449–50.

[14] *Test. Ebor.*, III, pp. 140–1; A.F. Leach, *The Schools of Medieval England* (1915), pp. 275–6.

[15] R. Willis and J.W. Clark, *The Architectural History of the University and of the Colleges of Cambridge and Eton*, 4 vols (Cambridge, 1886), III, pp. 14–15.

[16] M. Underwood, 'John Fisher and the Promotion of Learning', in J. Bradshaw and E. Duffy (eds), *Humanism, Reform and the Reformation* (Cambridge, 1989), p. 128.

[17] *VCH, Yorks., East Riding*, ed. W. Page (1907), I, p. 449; Leader, *Cambridge*, I, pp. 270–5.

cocks and globes to symbolize his name. The senior proctor was John Fisher who wrote the foundation charter in 1496. The college was committed to the spiritual life: among its fellows was William Atkynson of Pembroke who, at Lady Margaret Beaufort's request, translated the *Imitatio Christi* from French into English.[18] Fisher went on to establish Christ's College and St John's, both of which specialized in the study of theology and showed a preference for admitting northerners.[19] These northern clergy, in their activities as founders of educational institutions and as patrons of Cambridge, in their preferential patronage of northerners, and in their dedication to the ideals of clerical education and to the study of theology and devotional literature, were continuing the traditions of those northerners who had established Cambridge's identity as a bastion of orthodoxy, pastoral reform and correct religious enthusiasm at the outset of the century.

Richard III as a patron and protector of the church shared the same attitudes as these clergy. In some respects Richard was a man of clerical temperament and outlook. As he was the youngest son it is possible that his mother (or his uncle, George Neville, the Archbishop of York) originally intended him for the church. This would explain his knowledge of Latin, which is implied in the large proportion of Latin books in his possession, including those readily available in English such as *De regimine principum*; the high quality of his handwriting;[20] and the Crowland chronicler's admiration for the legal knowledge Richard displayed in his dispute with his brother George over the Warwick inheritance: 'So much disputation arose between brothers and so many keen arguments performed on either side with greatest acuteness – that all, even those learned in law, marvelled at the profusion of their arguments'.[21] Most suggestive of the possibility of early clerical training is his decision to purchase a second-hand book of hours which was originally put together for a

---

[18] Ibid., pp. 275–85.

[19] *BRUC*, p. 238; Leader, *Cambridge*, I, pp. 284–91.

[20] A.F. Sutton and L. Visser-Fuchs, 'Richard III's Books Observed', *The Ricardian*, IX, no. 120 (March 1993), p. 385.

[21] *Crowland Chronicle*, p. 133.

clergyman (the *confiteor* includes the admission of having administered the holy office with an impure heart).[22]

Richard surrounded himself with northern graduates from Cambridge, many of whom were interested in the new humanist learning of Italy. Dr Thomas Langton from Appleby in Westmorland, a student of Pembroke Hall, Cambridge, was chosen by Richard when he was protector for the bishopric of St David's.[23] He provided to the bishopric of Durham John Shirwood, son of the town clerk of York; Shirwood was a protégé of George Neville, Archbishop of York and he owned one of the largest collections of classical literature in England.[24] Richard recommended Shirwood to the Pope in 1484 as one 'whose integrity of life, exceptional gentle manners, together with the unparalleled virtue with which he is endowed draw and attract our love to him'.[25] Other northerners in Richard's clerical circle were: his confessor, John Roby, who was licensed to hear confessions in the diocese of York;[26] John Gunthorpe, dean of Wells and keeper of the Privy Seal in 1484, a noted Cambridge Greek scholar who left a large collection of classical literature to Jesus College;[27] Dr Thomas Barowe of King's Hall, keeper of the Privy Seal in August 1483;[28] and Richard's private chaplain, John Doket, a scholar of King's Hall who had studied in Padua and was the author of a commentary on Plato's *Phaedo*.[29] It was natural that Richard's patronage was weighted towards Cambridge University. In 1477 he made provision for the education of four priests and fellows at Queens' College, Cambridge; and the foundation statutes of Richard's college at Middleham a year later required that if no suitable dean could be found among the six priests in the foundation then he should be selected from one of the Queens' men.[30] Richard

[22] Lambeth Palace, MS 274, ff. 124–6. See also below, pp. 159, 175.

[23] *BRUC*, pp. 352–3.

[24] Ibid., pp. 524–5.

[25] *Harley MS 433*, III, p. 58.

[26] Borthwick Institute, Reg. Neville, xxii, f. 316; *CCR, 1476–85*, p. 380; *BRUC*, p. 483.

[27] *BRUC*, pp. 275–6.

[28] Ibid., pp. 40–1.

[29] Ibid., pp. 190–1.

[30] J. Raine, 'Statutes for the College of Middleham, dated July 4 1478', *Archaeological Journal*, 14 (1857), pp. 160–70.

and his wife Anne gave to the college £329 3s 8d.[31] Richard also gave King's Hall £300 for its building programme.[32] Richard and Anne visited the university on 9–11 March, 1484.[33] The only Oxford graduates in Richard's circle were his chancellor, John Russel, Bishop of Lincoln, who was described by More as 'one of the best learned men undoubtedly that England had in this time'[34] and Robert Stillington, Bishop of Bath and Wells and Bishop of Ely in 1479.[35] It is significant that these clergy, and others noted for piety and learning, made no objection to Richard's assumption of the throne. John Alcock made no recorded protest, and he must have been in a position to know about Richard's intention to invalidate his nephew's claim to the throne: he was Edward, Prince of Wales' principal tutor at Ludlow and a pupil of Stillington. According to the Crowland chronicler, Stillington (who had revealed to Richard the story of Edward IV's pre-contracted marriage) did nothing without consulting Alcock.[36] His relationship with Richard was ambiguous for he was removed from his post as tutor to Edward V in 1483,[37] but he was a royal commissioner in diplomatic negotiations with the Scots in 1484. Likewise John Shirwood did nothing and he knew the princes' physician, John Argentine, who gave a grave report of their fate in the Tower.[38]

Given Richard's closeness to the clergy who were at the forefront of reform of the church it is not surprising that he was austerely religious and a practitioner of the mixed life. In this, northern and family influences were undoubtedly important. Among the Yorkshiremen in his service were the descendants of the Richmondshire families who had been patrons of Richard Rolle and his followers and with whom Richard as a Neville had close links. The FitzHughs'

---

[31] C.D. Ross, *Richard III* (1974), p. 135; *CPR, 1476–85*, p. 477.

[32] Ross, *Richard III*, p. 135.

[33] C.H. Cooper, *Annals of Cambridge*, Vol. I (Cambridge, 1842), pp. 288–9.

[34] *BRUO*, III, pp. 1,609–10; *The Conclusion of the History of King Richard III as given in the continuation of Hardyng's chronicle, London, 1563*, ed. J.R. Lumby (Cambridge, 1883), p. 23.

[35] *BRUO*, III, pp. 1,777–9.

[36] *Crowland Chronicle*, p. 133.

[37] *CPR, 1476–77*, p. 401.

[38] D. Mancini, *The Usurpation of Richard III*, C.A.J. Armstrong (ed.) (2nd ed. Oxford, 1969), p. 93.

manor at Tanfield was ten miles from Middleham Castle and Richard, Lord
FitzHugh was a member of the ducal council. The Scropes of Bolton and
Masham (both close to Middleham) had been involved in the suppression of
Buckingham's rebellion. John Scrope, the fifth lord of Bolton was a member of
Gloucester's council in 1475; his widow, Ann, a member of the confraternity of
Syon left a white rose to her son, Henry.[39] Gloucester's links with the Scropes of
Masham were even closer: on the death of the fifth lord of Masham his widow,
Elizabeth, arranged for the Duke of Gloucester to retain her sixteen-year-old
son, Thomas, 'to guide him and be a good and loving lord to Thomas and his
servants'.[40] Thomas became a devoted follower of Richard III and was involved
in the Lambert Simnel rebellion. The most likely vehicle for the transmission of
the religious influences of the north however was Richard's mother, Cecily
Neville, whose daily routine of prayer, celebration of mass, confession and the
reading of the devotional literature of Hilton, Nicholas Love and St Bridget is
fully described elsewhere.[41] There is no reason to doubt the closeness of Cecily
and her youngest child, the last of her three children to survive infancy, and
who was only eight when her husband died. In one letter he addressed her in
the following manner: 'Beseeching you in my most humble and effectuouse wise
of youre daly blissing to my synguler comfort and defense in my nede. And
madam I hertely beseech you that I may often hear from you to my comfort –
and I pray God send you the accomplishment of your noble desires. Your most
humble son.'[42]

It is surprising that Richard's familial connection with an equally famous
devout laywoman Margaret of York, his eldest sister, has been ignored. Her
friendship with the reforming clergy of the Low Countries (who like Alcock

[39] *Test. Ebor.*, IV, p. 149.

[40] L.C. Attreed, 'An Indenture between Richard, duke of Gloucester, and the Scrope family of
Masham and Upsall', *Speculum*, 58 (1983), p. 1,018.

[41] C.A.J. Armstrong, 'The Piety of Cecily Neville, Duchesse of York', in C.A.J. Armstrong,
England, France and Burgundy in the Fifteenth Century (1983), p. 138; *Wills from Doctors' Commons*, eds J.G.
Nichols and J. Bruce, Camden Society, LXXXIII (1863), p. 5.

[42] Printed in J. Gairdner, *Richard III* (1898), pp. 189–90.

and Fisher were trying to restore the purity of the religious life of the monastic orders) and her devotion to a mixed life of reading books of devotion and hours and works of charity in her adopted Burgundy are equally well attested.[43] The influence of Burgundian piety can be seen in illuminations in her books of hours showing her living a mixed life of prayer and performing the deeds of mercy;[44] Hans Memlinc's triptych (now in the National Gallery) possibly shows Margaret as St Barbara affirming the values of charity and family life.[45] Richard was brought up with his elder sister in early childhood (Margaret, unlike her older sisters, remained in the family household with her two younger brothers at Fotheringhay and in London) and Richard continued to maintain contact with her after her marriage to Charles, Duke of Burgundy in 1468, visiting her on a number of occasions in Burgundy.[46]

Richard's devotion to daily mass at his chapel at Middleham would have pleased Cecily. He was a strict enforcer of daily worship in his own chapel: an ordinance made by the king for those in the north in his household stipulated that 'the hour of goddes service, diet and rising be at a reasonable time and convenient hours'. Anyone breaking this ordinance was to be punished.[47] Music played an important part in the daily celebration of hours in his chapel: in 1484 he gave a licence 'to his well beloved servant, John Melyonek, one gentleman of our chapel, knowing his expertise in the science of music to license him and give him authority in all chantries, chapels, religious houses, and colleges to take and seize for us in our name all singing men and children who are experienced in

---

[43] W. Prevenier and W. Blackmans, *The Burgundian Netherlands, 1380–1530* (1986), p. 249; M.J. Hughes, 'Margaret of York', *The Private Library*, 3rd ser., 7, nos 1 and 2, Spring and Summer 1984; W. Blackmans, 'The Devotion of a Lonely Duchess', in T. Kren (ed.), *Margaret of York, Simon Marmion and the Visions of Tondal* (Malibu, 1992), pp. 29–44; N. Morgan, 'Some Remarks on the Character and Content of the Library of Margaret of York', in Kren (ed.), *Margaret of York*, p. 63.

[44] Bod. Lib., MS Douce, f. 365.

[45] K.B. McFarlane, *Hans Memlinc* (Oxford, 1971), pp. 28–45. See also below, p. 167.

[46] C. Weightman, *Margaret of York, Duchess of Burgundy, 1446–1503* (Gloucester, 1989), pp. 7, 16–17, 91–2.

[47] *Harley MS 433*, III, p. 112.

the science of music'.[48] The elaboration of Richard's daily mass at Middleham in May 1484 and the beauty of the music was admired by Nicolas von Poppelau, the Silesian diplomat.[49] This was more than mere show: Richard's knowledge of and interest in the liturgy was unusual for a layman. In his foundation statutes for Middleham, after long deliberation with his ecclesiastical counsellors including the first dean, William Beverley, he reserved the sole power to amend to himself, stipulated the use of Salisbury and spelt out in detail the daily round of divine service, instructing the anthem of St Ninian, confessor, to be daily sung after matins. These statutes indicate the importance of the Divine Office in Richard's life. He requested a daily mass of Our Lady, a mass of Jesus on Fridays and on every Wednesday a Requiem mass.[50]

There was also a literary dimension to Richard's piety. From early childhood Richard was surrounded by religious books. One of his earliest was a metrical paraphrase of the Old Testament which was written *c.* 1400–10 in north-east England and influenced by the York Corpus Christi plays.[51] Richard's interest in the stories of the Old Testament and in the cycle plays that dramatized them is attested by his membership of the York Corpus Christi Guild and his attendance at a performance of the Creed Play in York on 7 September 1483; and performances of the Corpus Christi plays in York on 17 June 1484 and in Coventry on 2 June 1485.[52] He was also, apart from Henry VI, the only English king to have owned an English New Testament.[53] The influence of his mother,

---

[48] *Harley MS 433*, III, p. 163.

[49] Mancini, *Usurpation*, pp. 97, 137.

[50] Raine, *Archaeological Journal*, 14, p. 169.

[51] Longleat MS 257; 'A ME Metrical Paraphrase of the Old Testament, I', ed. H. Kalen, *Gotebergs Hogskolas Arsskritt*, 28 (1992), clvii; 'A ME Metrical Paraphrase of the Old Testament, II', ed. U. Ohlander, *Gotebergs Universitets Arsskritt*, LXI (1955); *A ME Metrical Paraphrase of the Old Testament*, III, ed. U. Ohlander (Gothenburg, 1960); *A ME Metrical Paraphrase of the Old Testament*, IV, ed. U. Ohlander, Gothenburg Studies in English, 16 (1963); A.F. Sutton and L. Visser-Fuchs, 'Richard III's Books: II', 'A Collection of Romances and Old Testament Stories', *The Ricardian*, VII, no. 96 (1987), pp. 371–5.

[52] *The Itinerary of King Richard III 1483–1485*, ed. Rhoda Edwards, Richard III Society (1983), pp. 7, 20, 37. F.B. Burbridge, *Old Coventry and Lady Godiva* (1952), p. 222.

[53] P.W. Hammond, 'Richard III's Books: III. Vegetius *De Re militari*, *The Siege of Thebes* and the New English Bible', *The Ricardian*, VII (1987), pp. 479–85.

Cecily, can be seen in the joint ownership by Richard and his wife, Anne, of *The Booke of Gostlye Grace* by Mechtild of Hackeborn.[54] This work gives useful precepts for the living of the mixed life and especially significant is a meditation on the different fingers of the hand: the last finger signified doing service for others as Christ had done; whenever the reader was tempted by pride he was advised to put finger to that finger and think of the subjection and meekness of God.[55] Such a meditation would have been appropriate for Richard who, like his sister, Margaret, had strong notions of public duty. His own book of hours, modestly illuminated and decorated, was presumably for private reading rather than display. Originally produced around 1420 for a cleric, it probably came into his possession while he was king, for the calendar entry giving his date of birth describes him as *Ricardus Rex*.[56] Richard's taste in books, with his preference for religious literature and works in Latin and English, suggests an introspective piety that is in marked contrast to some of his predecessors as kings of England such as Edward III, whose religion was ceremonial and dynastically oriented and unaffected by the trends for private devotion based on books of hours,[57] or Richard II who was interested in French romances;[58] and while it accords with the tastes of fellow northerners from the families of FitzHugh or Scrope, it contrasts with the more secular tastes of the literary circles of the south-east such as that of Sir John Fastolf where there is a marked preference for classical literature in French translations, or of Sir John Howard who had a travelling library composed entirely of historical tales and light

[54] The text owned by Anne Neville and Richard of Gloucester is BL, Egerton MS 2006 and their names occur on the fly leaf. This copy of the English translation of Mechtild's revelations has been edited by Theresa A. Halligan, *The Booke of Gostlye Grace of Mechtild of Hakeborn* (Pontifical Institute of Medieval Studies, Toronto, 1979). The other surviving copy of the English translation is Bodley MS 2200. See also A.F. Sutton and L. Visser-Fuchs, 'Richard III's Books: I, The Book of Gostlye Grace of Mechtild of Hackeborn', *The Ricardian*, VII (1985–7), pp. 278–92.

[55] BL, Egerton MS 2006, ff. 185b–186b.

[56] BL, Lambeth MS 474; *The Hours of Richard III*, A.F. Sutton and L. Visser-Fuchs (eds) (Stroud, 1990), p. 39. See also above, pp. 153–4, and below, p. 175.

[57] W.M. Ormrod, 'The Private Religion of Edward III', *Speculum*, 64 (1989), pp. 849–77.

[58] E.F. Rickert, 'King Richard II's Books', *The Library*, 4th ser., XIII (1933), pp. 144–7.

romances, mainly in French.[59]

The most important manifestation of lay piety in the second half of the fifteenth century was the growth of private prayer. Members of the Yorkshire nobility projected an image of themselves as people who devoted an important part of their lives to solitary, devout communion with God. Funeral monuments usually depicted the departed with hands clasped in prayer, and owners of books of hours frequently had illuminations of themselves on bent knees praying to a patron saint or God. Private prayer was facilitated among the nobility in this period by family chapels, of which there are examples in Middleham Castle and the manor houses of Leconfield, Wressle (Percy) and in the gentry manors of Thorp Perrow (Danby) and Sedbury (Boynton). Even more personalized were the oratories which could be reserved for masses in times of sickness and mourning (a concession allowed Joan Boynton in 1455 when she was mourning her first husband) but which were almost exclusively associated with private prayer. The licence of Joan (the mother-in-law of Richard III's servant and friend Sir Richard Ratcliffe) was extended in 1474 when she was granted the privilege to have service in an oratory whenever she chose. Licences for the use of oratories were issued between 1480 and 1481 to Edward and Elizabeth Saltmarsh, Henry Percy the Earl of Northumberland, his wife Maud and Robert Haldyngby esq. and his wife Elizabeth in the parish of Howden.[60] These oratories were also increasingly associated with books of hours: in the household book printed by Wynkin de Worde the chamberlain of Lady Margaret Beaufort's oratory at Christ College was instructed to lay carpets and cushions and her book of prayers in the morning and then to draw curtains which opened on to the interior of the chapel.

However it is the increasing ownership of the primers themselves that indicates the growing significance of private prayer in the lives of laymen and women in the north of England and the rest of the kingdom. The book of hours was a layman's abbreviated version of the psalter consisting of the gradual

---

[59] *Household Books of John, duke of Norfolk*, J. Payne (ed.) (Collier, Roxburgh Club, 1844), p. 277.

[60] A.H. Thompson, 'Registers of Archdeacons of Richmond', *Yorkshire Archaeological Journal*, 30 (1931), pp. 116–18, 131; 32 (1936), p. 119; *Test. Ebor.*, III, pp. 345, 348–9.

psalms, Marian antiphons, lessons and collects celebrating the beauty and mercy of the Virgin, the penitential psalms, the litany of the saints, the office of the dead, and the psalms of commendation and the psalms of the passion; all the above offered laymen the opportunity to share in the monastic round of prayer over the seven monastic hours of the day.[61] These primers were produced in increasing numbers in the Low Countries and England in the early fifteenth century and were owned by most members of the Yorkshire nobility, who handed them down to their children. Richard III himself, his son and his servants and friends all owned their personal books of hours. Elizabeth, widow of Henry, Lord FitzHugh, patron of the Brigittines and owner of an autograph of Rolle's writings, left primers to her son, Robert, her daughters Margaret and Maud Eure, and her god-daughter, Elizabeth FitzHugh. One book, written around 1410, and illuminated by Herman Scheere and containing an office of Richard Scrope, may have been specially written for the Scrope family.[62] Thomas Cumberworth, who owned Hilton's *Letter on the Mixed Life*, bequeathed his red primer and a roll of prayers;[63] William Catesby, one of Richard III's inner circle, owned a 'great and a little primer';[64] Sir Brian Roucliffe, one of Richard Duke of Gloucester's servants, left a primer once owned by his wife to his son, John;[65] and Lady Elizabeth FitzWilliam, wife of Sir Richard FitzWilliam, a servant of Richard, Duke of Gloucester, left her best primer to her daughter Katherine Skipton.[66]

These prayer books were often described as precious, personal items to be used daily and often continually carried around. Sir Brian's kinsman, Peter Arderne, baron of the Exchequer, left his 'daily' primer to his wife in 1467;

[61] For English texts of the book of hours see H. Littlehales, *The Prymer of Lay Folk's Prayer Book*, EETS, OS, vols 104, 109 (1895, 1897), *passim*.

[62] Bod. Lib., MS Lat. Liturg. 12: N.J. Rogers, 'Books of Hours Produced in the Low Countries for the English Market in the Fifteenth Century', 2 vols (unpublished M.Litt. thesis, Cambridge University, 1982), pp. 136–42.

[63] *The Academy*, 16 (1876), pp. 230–2.

[64] Daniel Williams, 'The Hastily Drawn up Will of William Catesby', *Leicester Archaeological and Historical Soc. Trans.*, 51 (1975–6), pp. 45–51.

[65] *Test. Ebor.*, IV, p. 210.

[66] Ibid., p. 106.

Robert Constable esq. of Barnby-by-Bossall, bequeathed to his son, Robert, 'my Portative which I say to myself'; and to his friend and executor, Thomas Witham, who lived at Cornburgh, a mile from Gloucester's castle at Sheriff Hutton, he bequeathed his diurnal (a shortened form of the breviary written for the convenience of laymen) which 'I bear in my sleeve daily'.[67] Primers suitable for such daily use naturally do not survive in such numbers as the de luxe editions displaying wealth and position. One that is extant and of northern origin is small enough to fit into the palm of the hand and could be read while riding a horse.[68] John of Lancaster, Duke of Bedford, besides owning a large illuminated Horae, had a small prayer book which he carried with him daily on campaigns.[69] One contemporary witness to the daily reading of the Psalter was John Rous, the antiquary of the Earls of Warwick, who claimed that Henry Beauchamp, Duke of Warwick (d. 1446), recited the entire Psalter daily: 'he wolde dayle sey the hole daved sawter with owt he had the gretter besiness he cowd hyt will owt the boke *perfyzzle* (perfectly)'.[70] This was probably an abridged version of the Psalter ascribed to St Jerome which consists of a few lines from each of the psalms that are found in most primers.[71] Thomas Arundel's legislation restricting the circulation of vernacular religious works meant that English versions of the primer were rare in the fifteenth century. However through constant repetition and familiarity with the Latin primers of the church those with little formal Latin, such as Margaret Beaufort, could use these prayers intelligently. In fact Latin primers (as the name implies) were an important part of basic learning for many people even before they acquired a knowledge of written English.[72] Christine de Pisan advised daughters to learn to

---

[67] *Test. Ebor.*, II, p. 175; *CPR, 1461–7*, p. 447.

[68] Bod. Lib., MS Rawl. Liturg., f. 6.

[69] E.F. Bosanquet, 'The Personal Prayer Book of John of Lancaster, duke of Bedford K.G.', *The Library*, 4th ser., XIII (1933), pp. 148–54.

[70] *The Rous Roll*, C. Ross (ed.) (Gloucester, 1980), item 54.

[71] E.g. Lambeth Palace, MS 274, ff. 112–122v; Sutton and Visser-Fuchs, *Hours of Richard III*, p. 97, n. 135.

[72] E.A. Duffy, *The Stripping of the Altars: Traditional Religion in England, 1400–1580* (New Haven, 1992), p. 223.

read from books of hours; and indeed Sir Brian Roucliffe once wrote to Sir William Plumpton to tell him that his daughter, Mary Plumpton, had just learned her psalter.[73]

The popularity of these books makes them important sources for the study of lay piety in the fifteenth century. It is therefore necessary to examine the standardized contents of the books of hours, and Richard III's primer will be cited for this purpose. Later, when we consider how Richard conformed to and deviated from these patterns of religious behaviour, we shall look more closely at the king's personal additions to his prayer book and his own individualistic and idiosyncratic attitudes towards some of the prayers in the books of hours. While the works of Hilton and Nicholas Love circulated widely in the fifteenth century and gave general and practical advice to laymen who wished to live a mixed life, it was the book of hours, the most widely read religious text in this period, that enabled laymen to come closest to living a fully religious life.[74] Eamon Duffy's recent analysis of primers assumes that individual prayers were merely part of an enclosed catholic tradition which, like the law, had its own common language, and such points of reference as the liturgy, the seven deadly sins and the ten commandments. Laymen, he assumes, could use the primer to associate themselves with the more specifically liturgical routines of the clergy.[75] But it is arguable that late medieval prayer was a more emotional, individualistic and amateur activity that allowed worshippers to apply the prayers in their primers to their own secular worlds of family, and career; their individual personalities and situations, and above all their own self images.

The arrangement of the psalms according to the monastic hours enabled owners to pray in ways appropriate to the changes in the day, stages in their

---

[73] Christine de Pisan, *Le Livre des trois vertus*, M.P. Cosman (ed.), Bk I, pt. 15; *The Plumpton Correspondence*, T. Stapleton (ed.), Camden Society, Old Series (1839), p. 8.

[74] R. Wieck, 'Texts and Prayers of the Book of Hours', in Wieck (ed.), *The Book of Hours in Medieval Art and Life* (1988).

[75] Duffy, *Stripping of the Altars*, pp. 209–98.

lives and swings in individual moods. In early morning the psalms for *matins* and *lauds* praised God's creation and the birth of Christ the redeemer: 'I will praise thy name, O Lord; for it is good'. For *nones*, in mid-afternoon, the psalms emphasize achievements culminating in the birth of the saviour; by *compline* the emphasis is on the longing and disquiet of the soul: 'Hail Mary, we sigh groaning in this valley of tears, turn to us your merciful eye' – 'out of the depths have I cried to thee O Lord. My soul watcheth for the Lord more than they that watch for the morning'. Apart from expressing moods, these psalms and other prayers could help reconcile laymen and women to the crises and sufferings of life and these could be applied to people with vastly different horizons. A meditation on the seven blood lettings of Christ, known as the Revelation of the Hundred Pater Nosters, was owned by a monk of Mount Grace and copied by a Yorkshire parish priest for a local husbandman who 'used hit dayly as devoutly as he coude' and turned to the prayer in desperation to revive his oxen which one of his farm labourers had beaten senseless.[76] A moving instance of the turning to the psalms to come to terms with the suffering caused by violence occurs in the funeral of Sir Henry Vavasour in 1499. Vavasour, when making his will, had to come to terms with fratricide within his own family (in 1488 his son William had killed another of his sons, Richard). Sir Henry asked William and the other surviving son, Henry, to stand with chantry priests around their father's grave singing the psalm about the departure of Israel from Egypt (psalm 114): 'when Israel went out of Egypt, Judah was his sanctuary – tremble thou earth, at the presence of the Lord, at the presence of the God of Jacob'.[77] Archbishop Rotherham (who had handed over Richard Vavasour to the rural dean for purging) quoted from the Book of Job in his will asserting his belief that he would see the face of his redeemer.[78]

The penitential psalms were also used to enable supplicants to face their own sins: 'I acknowledged my sin unto thee, and mine incapacity have I not hid – the sacrifices of God are a broken spirit, a broken and contrite heart'. The

---

[76] *The Book of Margery Kempe*, S.B. Meech and H.E. Allen (eds), EETS (1940), pp. 164–202.
[77] *Test. Ebor.*, IV, pp. 164–7.
[78] Ibid., p. 139.

Office of the Dead, with readings from the Book of Job, emphasizes God's support and power, and provides comfort and guidance for those in trouble and prayers for those in exile or facing death or betrayal. It delivers the worshipper from feelings of guilt, self-loathing, hatred of the world and even of the Lord and enables him to praise God's creation. The Office of the Dead also encouraged in a worshipper an acceptance of the inevitability of the deaths of members of the family, friends and the self: 'Man that is born of woman is of few days, and full of trouble. He cometh forth like a flower, and is cut down; he fleeth also as a shadow, and continueth not'.[79] The resignation and pathos of the Office of the Dead made its mark on the wills and funeral monuments of the north. William FitzWilliam esq. of Sprotbrough prefaced his will in 1474 by a long Latin preamble in which he considered the 'lacrimose and ever-mutable human condition – in this vale of tears where nothing is stable or permanent and all mankind is bound to the preordained end in darkness and invisibility' and quoted from psalm 144: 'man is like to vanity: his days are as a shadow that passeth away'.[80] A key figure in Richard III's northern affinity, Sir Marmaduke Constable of Flamborough, a knight of the body who was at Bosworth,[81] willed in 1518 that his body be buried quickly as soon as God called him out of this transitory life,[82] and left a brass epitaph on his tomb (which contains the remains of an effigy of a skeleton) in the high altar of Flamborough church in which he reviewed his military past, including the French campaigns of Edward IV and the Scottish wars, and reflected on the transitoriness of life:

> But now all these tryumphs ar passed and set on syde,
> ffor all worldly joyes they wull not long endure.
> They are sonne passed, and away dothe glyde,
> And who that puttith his trust in them I call hym most unsure;
> ffor when deth strikith he sparith no creature,

---

[79] Lambeth Palace, MS 274, ff. 72–90.

[80] *Test. Ebor.*, III, p. 212.

[81] *Bishop Percy's Folio Manuscript*, eds J.W. Hales and F.J. Furnivall, vol. 3 (1868), p. 246.

[82] *Test. Ebor.*, V, pp. 88–91.

Nor geuith no warnyng but takith them by one and one,
And now he abydyth Godis mercy, and hath no other socure
ffor, as ye se hym here, he lieth under this stone.[83]

Above all the epitaph expresses the sense that this old Yorkshire soldier and servant of the king depended not so much on the intercession of priests but on the consolation of the prayers of those with whom he was most intimate: 'I pray you my kinsmen louers and frendis all to pray to oure lord Jhesu to have mercy on my sowl'.[84] The usual recipient of these world-weary prayers was Jesus. William FitzWilliam left his soul to Christ, who redeemed him from the Cross, with as much devotion as he could muster,[85] Thomas Witham Snr of Cornburgh had a perpetual chantry in the church of Sheriff Hutton (where Edward of Middleham was said to be buried) and a marble slab with the inscription 'Christ pity Thomas Witham and his wife Agnes';[86] she prefaced her will in 1490 with a prayer 'knowing I am to pass from the prison of this world of nature, I give my soul to Christ and his blessed mother'.[87]

If the psalms helped owners of primers to emerge from crisis and face rites of passage, they were also important in affirming the ties and responsibilities of the household. Christ and the Virgin, guardian angels and patron saints offered the sort of protection available from leaders of families and households.[88] God and Christ were addressed as feudal lords and the Virgin was addressed as a patron; they provided power, patronage and protection that could be tapped through prayers that used the language employed throughout society by those seeking the patronage of the great: 'O glorious Lady Virgin Mary think me worthy my unworthy petition which I pour forth from the heart to your sweetest son'.[89] The patron saint and patrons were linked in paintings and illuminations. In the

[83] *The Buildings of England, Yorkshire; York and the East Riding*, N. Pevsner (ed.) (1972), p. 230.
[84] *Test. Ebor.*, V, pp. 88–91.
[85] *Test. Ebor.*, III, p. 212.
[86] Ibid., pp. 264–8.
[87] Ibid., p. 265.
[88] William Christian, *Reason and God in a Spanish Valley* (New York, 1972), p. 132.
[89] Lambeth Palace, MS 274, f. 169.

Donne altar-piece, executed *c.* 1480 by Hans Memlinc for Sir John Donne, servant of Edward IV, and his wife, Elizabeth Hastings, sister of William, Lord Hastings, saints and supplicants share the same courtly world: St Barbara bears a resemblance to Margaret of York (Richard III's sister) as she stands behind Elizabeth Hastings. Service was an important part of the social, economic and political lives of all the nobility. Service given to a lord in return for protection, employment, financial rewards, and grants of local influence contributed to a person's self-esteem, and service to God was conceived in similar terms. There was therefore a close link between prayer and the language of household and service. God, like the lord of the manor, was a source of power to be tapped. Many prayers in primers include the phrase 'your servant N', and Richard, Duke of Gloucester, after years of dispensing and receiving patronage, expressed himself in his private prayers to God as a servant seeking the patronage and protection of a feudal lord. In the prayer added especially for him in his book of hours he describes himself to God as 'your servant',[90] a phrase that is echoed in his own warrants to his household servants as 'your well beloved squire'. The language of prayer was also used in appeals to kings. Subjects asking for help appealed to the king's grace; if they had served him, they appealed to his lordship.

More important however was the way prayer helped affirm the duties and joys of family life. Many prayers were addressed to God the father and the Virgin Mother as parents to be revered and loved, and guardian angels and patron saints offered similar protection. The psalms, the brief hours of the Cross, the hours of the Compassion of the Virgin, individual prayers to the Virgin and illuminations depicting the Annunciation, affirmed the need for wives and mothers to accept the fate of childbearing, and gave a religious dimension to such feelings as the happiness experienced at pregnancy, and to anxiety and bereavement. The close identification of female owners of books of hours with the Virgin was emphasized in illustrations which show the Virgin at the moment of the Annunciation reading her book of hours which would be identified with the owner's.[91] Some of the most popular prayers to the Virgin

---

[90] Ibid., ff. 182–3.
[91] Ushaw, St Cuthbert's College MS. 10, f. 25; Bod. Lib., MS Laud Lat. 15, f. 30v.

celebrate the beauty and goodness of womanhood. In *Obsecro te homina* the supplicant appeals to Mary as the 'mother of orphans' to provide comfort by showing her face at the hour of death 'through that inestimable humility in which you respond to the archangel Gabriel'.[92] This contemplation, near death, of the Virgin's fatalism during the Annunciation was presumably practised in 1488 by Joan Boynton of Yarm, the mother-in-law of Sir Richard Ratcliffe, who paid for an image of the Salutation of Our Lady and St Gabriel on her gravestone.[93] The prayer *Obsecro te homina* reaches a climax with a breathless appeal to a mother who is full of joy at the Annunciation, sorrow at the sufferings of her son, and pity for the supplicant. The prayer on the Five Joys of the Virgin evokes the happiness of the divine family: 'Hail to you who gave milk to the son of God. Hail to you who cradled and swaddled the son of God';[94] the prayer on the Five Sorrows of the Virgin encouraged the supplicant to face painful emotions because Christ too had felt them.[95] Prayers on the joys and sorrows of the Virgin celebrated the human body and the warmth and sorrow of life in the same manner as the Corpus Christi plays. The most important emotion from the supplicant's point of view was the love of the mother Mary for Christ; this appreciation of an indulgent and unqualified love expressed in a prayer such as *O intemerata* gave worshippers confidence that the Virgin would intercede on their behalf and secure the forgiveness of her son. 'I Believe he who wants to be yours will belong to God, for you can obtain whatever you ask from God without delay – I beseech you to offer your glorious prayers so that my heart would be made worthy of being captured, entered, and inhabited by the holy spirit'.[96] This assertion of the religious significance of emotions within the family, the serene affirmation of the values of family life, contrasts markedly with the indifference shown towards the family in confession manuals of the fourteenth century which stress integration into the

---

[92] Wieck, *Book of Hours*, pp. 163–4; *Horae Eboracenses*, C. Wordsworth (ed.), SS, cxxii (1920), pp. 66–7; Lambeth Palace, MS 274, ff. 158–60.

[93] *Test. Ebor.*, IV, 15.

[94] Lambeth Palace, MS 274, ff. 167–8; *Devotional Pieces in Verse and Prose from MS Arundel and MS Harleian*, J.A.W. Bennett (ed.), *6919*, Scottish Text Soc., 3rd ser., 23, Edinburgh (1955), p. 287.

[95] Lambeth Palace, MS 274, ff. 168–9.

[96] Ibid., ff. 156v–8; Wieck, *Book of Hours*, p. 164; *Horae Eboracenses*, pp. 67–8.

parish, and the hostility shown towards the same emotions in some of the penitential handbooks written in the north of England such as the *Prick of Conscience*, which anticipates a Last Judgment where saved mothers willingly separate from their children if they are sentenced to damnation.[97]

Affective prayers in books of hours encouraged worshippers to empathize closely with the sufferings of the Virgin and Christ. Illustrations in prayer books identified female owners (especially expectant mothers) with the Virgin Mary. Illustrations of the Annunciation usually showed the Virgin at the moment of Gabriel's appearance praying from the book of hours. In the Donne altar-piece Donne's wife, Elizabeth Hastings, prays holding an open book of hours before the Virgin who is also reading a book of hours. A prayer such as *Stabat mater dolorosa* takes the worshipper into the sufferings of the mother of Christ: 'Can the human heart refrain from partaking in her pain – make my heart with thine accord. Make me feel as thou has felt – let me share with thee this pain. Let me mingle tears with thee.'[98] The Fifteen Oes, a prayer ascribed to St Bridget, shows how sharing the pain of the Virgin and Christ was a way of convincing oneself of God's love, 'sweet Jesu, for your great pains that your innocence suffered Lord heartfully I require you to defend me from my foes both soul and body and grant me to find in high order your shield defence of hell and always to dwell with you in'.[99] The supplicant in this prayer is encouraged to confront his/her limitations, especially the inability to feel another's pain, and to try to escape the prison of the self and give and live for others by meditating on the mysterious and unfathomable well of mercy within the Virgin and Christ, and their selfless generosity and love; through intense prayer the supplicant can feel Christ's pain and follow his example and feel the pain of others.

[97] J. Hughes, 'The Administration of Confession in the Diocese of York in the Fourteenth Century', in *Studies in Clergy and Ministry in England*, ed. D. Smith, Borthwick Studies in History, York (1991), 3, p. 117; *The Prick of Conscience*, R. Morris (ed.) (Berlin, 1863), II, pp. 380–3.

[98] Lambeth Palace, MS 274, ff. 173–4; YML, Add. MS 2, ff. 171v–2; Wieck, 'The Book of Hours and Medieval Art', in *Book of Hours*, pp. 104–5; *Horae Eboracenses*, pp. 134–5.

[99] Lambeth Palace Library, MS 274, ff. 145v–151v; Bennett, *Devotional Pieces*, pp. 170–80; *Horae Eboracenses*, pp. 76–80.

Such affective meditating had been advocated by two northern writers, Walter Hilton and Nicholas Love, but it was the teachings of St Bridget that made an impact on prayer books in the region, possibly because of early popularity among such northerners as Henry, Lord FitzHugh of Tanfield. In a northern book of hours illuminated between 1405 and 1413 by Herman Scheere, which was possibly owned by Henry, Lord FitzHugh, or his son William, there are several lengthy readings from the *Revelations of St Bridget*.[100] A series of prayers to the saint occur in a book of hours of Flemish origin commissioned between 1420 and 1450 which bears the arms of de la Pole of Hull together with a miniature showing St Bridget dictating her revelations to a scribe.[101] William Scargill of Leeds gave two chaplains at his chantry chapel in the parish church of Whitkirk in 1448 a psalter and a *Life of St Bridget*.[102] The inclusion of extracts from devotional writers in prayer books is appropriate when the mystical potential of the psalms is appreciated. The rhythm of psalm and antiphon maintained when saying these hours aloud, especially if a friend provided the responses, would have recalled the alternation of voices in the monastic recitation of the Divine Office, and it was while listening to the chanting of the psalms in the Daltons' private chapel that Richard Rolle first felt the fire of God's love. Walter Hilton said in *The Scale of Perfection* that the prayers people generally found most helpful were the Our Father and the psalms; the Our Father for simple people and the psalms, hymns and other devotions of the church for the educated. Those engaged in active works, he observed, pray with a loud or normal tone, and their prayers are worthy and commendable even though, preoccupied as they are with worldly matters, they often have one thing on their mind while the words of the psalm express another; the devout, touched by grace, will utter their prayers in a very low voice and deep feeling because their minds are not troubled or distracted by outward things.[103] Fifteenth-century illuminations of books of hours, especially

---

[100] Bod. Lib., Lat. Liturg., f. 2, ff. 10v, 124–40, 147v, 171v.

[101] Rogers, 'Books of Hours', p. 54.

[102] *Test. Ebor.*, III, p. 256.

[103] W. Hilton, *The Scale of Perfection*, E. Underhill (ed.) (1923), Bk 11, ch. 22.

the Annunciation, convey the numinous atmosphere that could accompany private prayer: the portrait of Mary of Burgundy (the step-daughter of Richard III's sister, Margaret of York) at prayer in her oratory around 1490 opens into a vision of the Virgin and child in the holy and peaceful atmosphere of a cathedral.[104]

However, the most socially significant parallel between books of hours and the contemplative literature written in the fourteenth century was in the challenge they posed to institutional parish-oriented religion. Richard Rolle's first works were commentaries on the psalms and the Book of Job; he saw in them an affirmation of a close relationship with God expressed in terms of alienation from society, and he went on to expound to his followers a way of life that involved rejection of the world in pursuit of God. The pastoral reformers of the church of York in Arundel's circle, especially Walter Hilton and Nicholas Love, tried to moderate the extreme individuality of Rolle's message in their writings and to reconcile their own reservations about the communal pressures of the parish with their individualistic, introspective piety and their public pastoral duties which included strengthening the bonds within the family and parish.[105] However, by the late fifteenth century the widespread use of books of hours exposed these individualistic prayers to a far wider number of laymen than the devout minority who were reading the works of Rolle and Suso. While public prayers could strengthen such communities as families, institutions and even a realm in times of war, prayers in the primer reinforced individuality, emphasizing the close relationship that exists between the worshipper and God, who provides a source of strength against the hostility of neighbours, the frustrations of dealing with people: 'thou preparest a table before me in the midst of my enemies – though a host should encamp against me, my heart shall not fear: in time of trouble he shall hide me in his pavilion'. In the psalms of the Passion, David's isolation and his dependence on prayer anticipates that of Christ and echoes the image of Christ the rejected, isolated man of sorrows that occurs in Nicholas Love's *Mirror of the Blessed Life of Jesus Christ*: 'Into thine hand

---

[104] V. Reinburg, 'Prayer and the Book of Hours', in Wieck, *Book of Hours*, pp. 39–44.

[105] Hughes, *Pastors and Visionaries*, p. 208ff.

I commit my spirit for you have redeemed me O Lord. Mine enemies daily swallow me up: for they be many that fight against me'. Furthermore the penitential psalms convey a highly individualistic, intuitive conviction that sin was a private matter between the individual worshipper and God, and that salvation could be achieved through intimate prayer: 'Against thee, thee only have I sinned and done this evil in thy sight'. This conviction of the efficacy of private prayer lies behind the many rubrics to individual prayers which promised the supplicant forgiveness of deadly sins, and deliverance from Hell or Purgatory. A prayer found in the book of hours of the Bolton family, fifteenth-century merchants of York, is accompanied by the promise that 'He who says this prayer daily with bent knees will never die in mortal sin.'[106] One rubric to a prayer to Christ on the cross in a northern primer instructs the owner 'wane ye rise on morn of youre bed say this orisonys after' and concludes with the words 'Cross of Christ protect me, Cross of Christ defend me from all insinuations and temptations of the devil'. Another prayer in the same manuscript requests release of the soul of a friend from Purgatory: 'I pray omnipotent and eternal God. I pray to you that you raise the soul of your servant'.[107] In a northern book of hours in York Minster library a rubric accompanying a prayer to Christ explains: 'To each saying this prayer it is considered that if he be in a state of eternal damnation God transfers punishment to punishment in Purgatory. If he would be in Purgatory for a maximum time, God changes this punishment of Purgatory and reduces or delivers you outside Purgatory to eternal bliss.'[108] In another northern prayer book the owner, Sir Brian Roucliffe, baron of the Exchequer, who signed himself with the rebus of the chess rook, wrote 'if ya be in dedely syn or in tribulaccon or in any deses goy to the kerke and fall on thy knes'.[109]

Because reconciliation between God and man was seen to be such a private matter, there was in the primer no acceptance of the social ideology

[106] YML, Add MS, 2m ff. 166v–7.

[107] Bod. Lib., MS Laud Lat. 15 do. 114v; ff. 113v–14.

[108] YML, MS XVI. K.6, ff. 83–4.

[109] Ushaw, St Cuthbert's College MS 10, ff. 12v–13; Rogers, 'Books of Hours', p. 168.

propounded in confession manuals of the fourteenth century which defined sin as a form of social hostility and stressed the need to reintegrate penitents into the community. Sin was seen instead as a private matter between the supplicant and God, and the penitential psalms are the egotistic confessions of a worshipper who confesses to God to feeling a sense of isolation and being at odds with the world, persecuted by his enemies: 'They also that seek after my life lay snares for me and they that seek my heart speak mischievous things, and imagine deceits all day long. For I am ready to halt, and my sorrow is continually before me. I will declare mine iniquity; I will be sorry for my sin. But mine enemies are lively and they are strong and they that hate me wrongfully are multiplied.' This egocentric and abrasive expression of social hostility lacks the pathos and humility of the mystic's sense of rejection which had been communicated by Hilton and Nicholas Love, and as the pslams were more widely known and used in private prayer in the fifteenth century the possibility of others apart from Rolle reacting to them in an individualistic and unorthodox way was increased.

The Cambridge-educated clergy of Yorkshire enthusiastically endorsed the power of private prayer, seeing its individualistic potential. Their fourteenth-century forebears had seen in contemplative literature an opportunity to escape the communal pressures of the parish. Now in the late fifteenth century such literature and the increasing availability of prayers in the primers offered the devout man a refuge from the secular pressures of the state. Like his mentor, Arundel, Alcock was interested in the contemplative life and took a close interest in the Carthusian order: he addressed his first sermon to the Carthusians of St Anne of Coventry. In his capacity as Bishop of Ely he repeatedly endorsed the power of private prayer (although it is significant that Alcock in the process of describing such a private activity used imagery from the court, and compared those who frequently prayed to the most valued servants of the king, who would defend those whose names were on his check roll) and he granted a perpetual indulgence to all those who said the Lord's prayer three times with an angelic salutation before the image of St Ethelred in Holy Trinity chapel of Snaith parish church, indulgences to all who visited in prayer the chapel of St Mary at the Cross in Great Horkesley, Essex, and indulgences to those who said the entire office of the Virgin. He also issued indulgences to all those who said an entire psalter of the B.V.M. and a twenty day indulgence to all who attended divine offices.[110] In his *Mons Perfeccionis* (or 'the hyl of perfeccion'), a sermon delivered to the Carthusians of St Anne in Coventry in 1496, Alcock endorsed the power of prayer, 'A man never ceaseth to pray but when he ceaseth to have the name of a just man', neglecting to mention fasting and only discussing prayer, obedience and chastity (of which only the two former would be applicable to laymen). By recounting the benefits of prayer in a resounding repetition of *ora, ora*, he emphasized its function of stabilizing the thoughts and emotions, bringing peace of mind. And he claimed that the Holy Ghost would be served with no other thing but psalms and prayers.[111]

Psalms and private prayers in the book of hours could thus facilitate the same sort of mystical individualism that was encouraged by such religious writers of the diocese as Richard Rolle and Nicholas Love; but Richard III responded to them in a way that was as idiosyncratic as Rolle's but which had more profound social and historical consequences than the withdrawal from society advocated by the hermit of Hampole and his followers. The significance of prayer was probably impressed on Richard when as an eight-year-old at his brother's coronation he was made a Knight of the Bath and conducted to the chapel of St John in the Tower where he remained in prayer with his fellow knights before a lighted taper until dawn. At day break he made a confession and attended mass.[112] As a layman Richard would have been expected to make his prayers vocally on bent knees; but given his piety it is probable that he acquired the habit of what Hilton defined as a mixed mental and vocal prayer suitable for the devout layman, and it is even possible, if he had received some clerical training early in his life, that he prayed silently to himself, the type of prayer that Hilton labelled mental that

---

[110] Ely Diocesan Remembrancer, 1909, f. 11 ff.

[111] John Alcock, *Mons Perfectionis* (Wynkyn de Worde, Westminster, 1497), in *The English Experience, no. 706, its record in early printed books published in facsimile* (Amsterdam, 1974), no pagination.

[112] *The Coronation of Richard III*, A.F. Sutton and P.W. Hammond (eds) (Gloucester, 1993), pp. 28–9.

required the total concentration pertaining more to a contemplative person.[113]

There was nothing ostentatious about Richard's prayer book. It was not lavishly illustrated like the Duke of Bedford's and contains only three illuminations. The book was part of the booty of Richard's tent at Bosworth and went to Richmond's mother, Margaret Beaufort, who may have given it to Elizabeth, Lady Scrope of Upsall.[114] Incorporated into it were a number of unusual prayers found nowhere else, a prayer copied for the king and a litany composed for him. The prayer which was copied for him and which incorporates his name and title, Richard, King of England, gives revealing indications of his private religion. The supplicant in the prayer appeals to Christ to deliver him from sin, captivity, grief, temptation and immediate danger. Above all the prayer appeals for deliverance from, victory over, or reconciliation with, one's enemies in accordance with the militaristic spirit of many of the psalms.[115]

Such prayers were popular towards the end of the fifteenth century. The king's sister, Anne, Duchess of Exeter, owned a prayer book containing the same prayer and John, Duke of Bedford, owned a small prayer book that he carried on campaigns for daily use that contained a prayer of St Augustine to be said in times of trouble for thirty days.[116] The prayer and others like it was used throughout all sections of society. It was copied into the primer of Alexander, Prince of Poland, in 1491. John Alcock, when he was recounting to the Carthusians of St Anne the power of prayer to protect men from sin and to deliver them from danger, cited similar examples of deliverance or comfort including the stories of Moses, Joshua, Ezekiel, Jeremiah, Daniel, Job and the three children cast in the furnace and he recommended his audience to occupy

[113] Hilton, *Scale of Perfection*, Bk II, ch. 22.

[114] Sutton and Visser-Fuchs, *Hours of Richard III*, p. 39; M.K. Jones, 'Sir William Stanley of Holt: Politics and Family in the Late Fifteenth Century', *Welsh History Review*, 14 (1988).

[115] Lambeth Palace, MS 274, ff. 181–3v. In another prayer in this manuscript Richard prays to his good angel for protection against all enemies, visible and invisible (f. 179v).

[116] Bosanquet, *The Library*, 4th Ser. XIII, pp. 148–55.

their minds continually with the prayer 'Lord stretch out and help me Lord, hurry to my aid'.[117] Robert Thornton, who belonged to the lower ranks of the gentry and owned an estate in East Newton in the North Riding of Yorkshire, copied into his collection of devotional writings and romances between 1422 and 1453 a number of prayers including a prayer to the Trinity for patience, courage and 'victory over all my enemies, that they be not able to oppose me nor harm me, nor to speak against me'; in this prayer Thornton also begs Christ to deliver him as he freed Susannah from a false accusation, Daniel from the lion's den, Jacob from the hands of his brother Esau and Joseph from the hands of his brothers.[118]

The editors of Richard's book of hours conclude that the popularity of this prayer throughout Europe precludes its being used to make deductions about Richard's, or anyone else's piety.[119] Duffy, although acknowledging that a London grocer, Richard Hill, in a similar prayer beseeching Jesus to keep his unworthy servant 'from the malicious foe and all who hate me', had earthly enemies in mind, suggests that the enemies Richard III and Robert Thornton faced were primarily spiritual: the devil and his demons exorcised by the priest at the commendation of the departing soul, the original source of this prayer.[120] Behind such reluctance to apply these related prayers to the individual's personal life lies a view of prayer that is institutional and self-referential, which ignores the vastly different mental horizons that praying could encompass. For an ambitious judge like William Paston, who used his position to acquire land for himself and his clients, the social inferiors who obstructed his sharp practices became the focus of his prayers. In 1426 he wrote to three monks of Bromholm: 'I prey the Holy Trinite, lord of yowr cherche and of all the werld, delyvere me of my iii adversaries, of this cursed bysshop for Bromholm, Aslak for Sprouston, and Julian Herberd for Thornham'. Although Paston was primarily the aggressor, he expressed in his prayer to the Trinity the same sense

[117] John Alcock, *Mons Perfectionis*.

[118] *Yorkshire Writers*, C. Horstmann (ed.) (1895), pp. 376–7.

[119] Sutton and Visser-Fuchs, *Hours of Richard III*, pp. 83–5.

[120] Duffy, *Stripping of the Altars*, p. 268.

of persecution (which included the bishop's excommunication) that is communicated in Richard III's prayer: 'I have nought trespassed a-geyn noon of these iii, God knowith, and yet I am foule and noysyngly vexed with hem to my gret unease, and al for my lordes and frendes matieres and nought for myn own.'[121] Daily use of psalms and prayers that referred to one's enemies could have a worldly relevance.

It is thus quite possible that Richard III did indeed identify with his version of this prayer, and the others in his primer, in a personal way and applied to the plea for deliverance from his enemies his perception of his situation. There can be no doubting the personal importance of this prayer for him. The rubric to Richard's prayer is missing but was probably the same as the one accompanying the same prayer in the primer of Alexander, the Prince of Poland, which was copied in 1491: 'Whoever is in distress, anxiety or infirmity or has incurred the wrath of God, or is held in prison, or has experienced any kind of calamity, let him say this prayer on thirty successive days and he must be without mortal sin. It is certain that God will hear him completely, that his trouble turn to joy and comfort – and this is proven by many persons.'[122] The supplicant in the prayer appeals to Christ to deliver him from sin, captivity, desolation, grief, temptation, illness and immediate danger. The appeal of such a prayer to a king who was faced with the rebellion of his subjects in south-east England in 1483 and the subsequent deaths of his son and wife and the Tudor rebellion of 1485 is obvious. It is likely that Richard began to rely more on such prayers at this time of his life when the normal sequences were broken by bereavements and he was forced to stop and reflect.[123] Nearly all the rubrics to this prayer stress the need to say it over thirty days on bent knees, and biblical examples are used to point to the effectiveness of prayer. Although the prayer was copied after he became king, it is likely that Richard knew the prayer before he acquired the

[121] *The Paston Letters and Papers of the Fifteenth Century*, N. Davis (ed.), I (1970), p. 7; C. Richmond, *The Paston Family in the Fifteenth Century* (Cambridge, 1990), pp. 36, 169.

[122] BL, Add. MS 38603, ff. 57v–58; Sutton and Visser-Fuchs, *Hours of Richard III*, p. 105.

[123] See Christian, *Reason and God*, p. 131, for comparative observations among twentieth-century Catholics in rural Spain.

manuscript, for at one point it closely resembles part of his 1478 foundation for Middleham College. The prayer concludes:

> What am I Lord and what is my family that thou has brought me thus far? O Lord God it was thy purpose to spread thy servants fame and so thou hast raised me to this. I give and return thanks, and for all the gifts and goods granted to me because you made me from nothing and redeemed me out of your beauteous love and pity from eternal damnation by promising eternal life.[124]

The foundation charter for Middleham reads:

> Know yet it pleased God creator and redeemer of his manifold graces to enhabile, exhaunce and exalte me his most simple creature, nakedly born into this wretched world, destitute of possessions and enhereatments, to the grete estate, honor and dignite that he hath called me now unto, to be named, knowed, reputed and called Richard Duc of Gloucester – bot also to preserve, kep and deliver me of manyfold benyfets of His bounteous grace and godnesse to me, without any desert or cause.[125]

The conviction that he is chosen by God takes the form in the prayer of a close identification with the heroes of the Old Testament who are delivered from peril through prayer.[126] The potential for identification is particularly noticeable in the story of Joseph, the child of his mother's old age (Richard was Cecily's last of twelve children and her previous three children died in infancy). Joseph too was the youngest son who usurped his eldest brother's birthright. In Richard's prayer book there is a rare prayer to Joseph, son of Jacob, which was especially added for the original owner, and it begins: 'O God who gave wisdom to the blessed Joseph in the house of his Lord and in the presence of Pharaoh

---

[124] Lambeth Palace, MS 274, f. 183v.

[125] Raine, *Archaeological Journal*, 14, pp. 160–70.

[126] Lambeth Palace, MS 274, f. 179v.

and freed him from envy and hatred of his brothers but also raised in honour I pray to you Lord God Omnipotent that similarly you deliver over your servant Richard from the plots of my enemies and to find grace and favour in the eyes of my adversaries and all Christians'.[127] Here again there is a strong suggestion that Richard was identifying with the youngest brother, the man of prayer, who was raised by God to high honour. In Richard's Old Testament there is a similar sanctioning of the usurpation of a younger brother when Jacob blesses Joseph's younger son Ephraim, saying, 'his younger brother shall be greater than he and his descendants shall be a whole nation'.

The most important Old Testament figure with whom Richard might have identified himself was King David, who figures prominently in Richard's prayer. The youngest of seven sons of Jesse of Bethlehem, David was chosen by God's prophet, Samuel, to be King of the Jews instead of his eldest brother, the tall and beautiful Elijah, who was rejected by the Lord who judges the heart. Once more, the parallel with Richard and his handsome brother, Edward, who was six foot three inches tall, is striking. The depiction in the Middle-English version of The Book of Kings of the civil war among the Hebrews between Ishbosheth, son of Saul, and his duke Abner, and David and his duke Joab during the royal minority occasioned by the death of Saul provides more potential parallels with the power struggle of Richard's own time and his own rise to power. David's claim during this royal minority was not lineal but based on divine inspiration.

However he is likely to have identified most strongly with David as a man of God betrayed by those closest to him. He expressed his sense of betrayal and persecution in a letter to the Pope informing him of his assumption of rule and explaining why he had not done so sooner: 'had not the unexpected perfidy and evil conspiracy of certain people hostile to us, to loyalty and their oath prevented us'.[128] Richard reacted to the news of Buckingham's betrayal by writing in his own hand a postscript to a letter to the chancellor requesting him to send the great seal which he needed urgently in dealing with the rebellion

[127] *Metrical Old Testament*, II, pp. 7,325–7,440.
[128] *Harley MS 433*, III, p. 58.

that says:

'Her love be God ys as well and trewly determyned and for to resyste the malysse of hym that hadde best cause to be trewe the duc of Bokyngham the most untrewe creature lyvyng whom with Godes grace we shall not be long tyll we wyll be in that partyes and subdewe hys malys. We assure you was never fals traytor better purvayde for as berrer Gloucestre, shall shewe you.[129]

This is strikingly similar to the outbursts of David to the treachery of Achitophel who counselled David's son, Absolom, to rebel. In Psalm 41 which is in Richard's hours, David says 'Yea, mine own familiar friend, in whom I trusted, which did eat out of my bread, hath lifted up his heel against me. But thou, O lord, be merciful unto me, and raise me up, that I may requite them'. From Psalm 55 Richard would find a similar reaction to betrayal: 'for it was not an enemy that reproached me; then I would have borne it; neither was it he hated me that did magnify himself against me; then I would have hid myself from him: but it was thou, a man mine equal my guide and mine acquaintance.'[130] Something of the extremity of Richard's reaction to Buckingham's rebellion echoes the same psalm: 'we took sweet counsel together, and walked unto the house of God in company. Let death seize upon them quick unto hell: for wickedness is in their dwelling; and among them. As for me I will call upon God; and the Lord shall save me.'

Many of David's psalms communicate a sense of the hostility of enemies and the need to defeat them through prayer, and while Rolle and other mystics turned to the psalms to reinforce a sense of their separation from society, for Richard the psalms of David and the daily round of prayer might have served a more directly political purpose, strengthening his resolve to act ruthlessly against the enemies he regarded as traitors. Richard would have found on almost every page of his prayer book a sense of persecution and an affirmation

[129] P.W. Hammond and A.F. Sutton, *The Road to Bosworth Field* (Stroud, 1985), p. 145; PRO, C81/139/6.
[130] Lambeth Palace, MS 274, ff. 72–90.

of the power of prayer to defeat one's enemies: 'strangers are risen up against me, and oppressors seek after my soul: they have not set God before them. He shall reward unto mine enemies: cut them off in thy truth. I will freely sacrifice unto thee. I will praise thy name – for he hath delivered me out of all trouble; and mine eye hath seen his desire upon mine enemies.'[131] The self-righteous sense of mission and of persecution in these psalms: 'But many are my enemies, all without cause, and many are those who hate me wrongfully, those who repay good with evil oppose me because my purpose is good'[132] suggests, therefore, that, while he was neither unique in his identification with Biblical figures, nor unusual in the way he saw his political world in religious terms, Richard may well have identified closely with the persecuted and misunderstood David.

He may well also have identified with David the man of sorrows, punished and tested by God for his sins. There are indications that Richard had a disturbed conscience and experienced moments of doubt as early as 1478. After publicly proclaiming in the opening preamble to the foundation statutes of his college at Middleham the sinful state of his soul and how he has nevertheless been favoured and elevated by God, Richard instructed the dean of his college to say the *De Profundis* and asked the local people to pray for his soul and to say a *De Profundis*, either secretly to themselves or with companions when it pleases them. The significance of this psalm of David, which occurred among the penitential psalms in his book of hours, would have increased after July 1483: 'Out of the depths have I called to thee, O Lord; Lord hear my cry. / If thou Lord shouldst keep account of sins/who O Lord could hold up his head/But in thee is forgiveness.' His doubts and anxieties may well have increased after July 1483 when rumours concerning the disappearance of the princes spread and his unpopularity increased.

Richard seems also to have expressed his anxieties in his investiture of his only legitimate son, Edward of Middleham, as Prince of Wales: 'We have turned the gaze of our inward eye to the greatness of this noble state and of its members, having great care that, in the great anxieties that press upon us, those

---

[131] Psalm 54 (prime).

[132] Psalm 37 (penitential psalms).

who are necessary to support us should not now seem to be lacking.' An indication that Richard's public persona was that of an embattled anxious monarch can be seen in Caxton's dedication of Lull's *Order of Chivalry* to the king: 'I pray almighty God for his long life and prosperous welfare and that he may have victory of all his enemies and after this short transitory life to have everlasting life in heaven where as in joy and bliss without end.'[133] Richard's addiction to the regular performance of divine hours at his collegiate chapel at Middleham and his own private chapel at Middleham Castle perhaps reflects his need for a regular reassuring routine. His dependence on prayer and his identification with David may have increased after the death of his son, Edward, in April 1484. He had the opportunity to read in his Old Testament that David was punished with the death of his son for his adultery with Bathsheba and for arranging the murder of Uriah, and that Nathan prophesied that David would henceforth never be free from fighting by the sword. David's reaction was to pray all the harder. According to the Middle English version of the story owned by Richard, David composed *miserere mei Deus* in response to the death of his son 'to god that gouerans all/forgyfnes forto geyte/yf we in care be cast'.[134] This penitential psalm must have had a poignant significance to the bereaved king: 'My iniquities are gone over mine head; as a heavy burden they are too heavy to me. My wounds stink and are corrupt because of my falseness I am troubled; I am bowed down greatly.' Such psalms may also have enforced in Richard the feeling that, like David, he was only answerable to God: 'Against thee, thee only have I sinned and done this evil in thy sight.'

If this is how Richard saw himself, the question arises as to whether he attempted to project a public image of himself as a man of prayer who was patiently suffering the blows of fortune and the hostility and misunderstanding of others, while he was intent on serving his people and his God. Something of this, it has been suggested, lay behind the public justification of his actions and condemnation of his enemies. But what of the visual representation of himself?

[133] *Harley MS 433*, II, p. 42; *The Book of the Order of Chivalry printed by William Caxton*, ed. A.T.B. Byles, EETS, Old Series, CLXVIII (1926), pp. 121–5.
[134] *Metrical Old Testament*, II, 223–32.

Richard's sister, Margaret of York, became the first Burgundian duchess to develop a distinctive portrait image that shows the diverse aspects of her religious character, especially her devotion to daily prayer.[135] There are nine portraits in the thirty books she owned or patronized, including books of advice on how to approach prayer and contemplation. Sometimes she is shown providing a clear example to her court, as in the miniature accompanying a book of nine moral and religious texts, which shows her under a canopy, kneeling at a prayer bench before a book of hours and a painting of Christ, accompanied by her ladies-in-waiting and watched by a vain but curious young man.[136] At others she is shown in private prayer; for example, in a compendium of moral treatises in Brussels she is depicted in a side chapel before an altar showing the Trinity.[137] In a miniature accompanying a text of the seven acts of mercy, written for her by her almoner, she is shown at her devotions at a prayer bench in the robes of the duchess of Burgundy to emphasize her spiritual duties as head of state and the public importance of her prayers. Did she and the illuminators in her household, especially the Master of Mary of Burgundy, influence the way Richard III had himself painted as a man of prayer?

Two almost contemporary panel portraits of Richard III survive in the Netherlandish style. One, the source of all the later copies, in the Royal Collection, Windsor, with the subject facing to the viewer's right, was copied *c.* 1518 to 1523 from an original dating from probably the last year of Richard's reign. Copies were made at the same time of contemporary portraits of Henry V and Henry VI which adorned Henry VIII's new palace at Bridewell. They were all given a red brocade background (which was probably only original to the portrait of Richard) and they comprise a natural trio of three pious kings. The original portrait of Richard III was probably intended to have a close relationship with that of Henry VI. Both kings wear similar heraldic collars: Henry VI the Lancastrian SS and Richard the white and red roses. In 1484,

---

[135] J. Chipps-Smith, 'Margaret of York and the Burgundian Portrait Tradition', in Kren (ed.), *Margaret of York*, pp. 47–57.

[136] Bod. Lib., MS Douce 365, f. 115.

[137] Chipps-Smith, in Kren (ed.), *Margaret of York*, p. 52.

around the time of the painting of this portrait, Richard translated the remains of Henry VI from Chertsey Abbey to St George's Chapel, Windsor, and he may have wished to be associated with a king with a posthumous reputation for sanctity. This portrait is also related to the Royal Collection portrait of Edward IV, copied *c.* 1534 to 1550 for another of Henry VIII's palaces from an original made shortly after Edward's death at the same time as Richard's portrait. The other portrait of Richard, in the possession of the Society of Antiquaries, is arch topped and shows Richard facing to the left (the heraldic right), and was faithfully copied between 1516 and 1522 from an original made during Richard's reign. It would have faced an arch-topped painting of Edward IV in one of Richard's palaces and demonstrated the continuity of his rule with Edward.[138] However both portraits emphasize the difference in personality between the two brothers. Edward's features show a smug, complacent, sensual though clever man. Both the Royal Collection portrait of Richard, despite the Tudor copyist's alteration of the setting of his eyes, and the Society of Antiquaries' portrait's faithful likeness, show a serious, determined man with anxious, careworn and hounded features that are entirely in accord with the tone of his private prayers and devotions. In the *Dialogue de la Duchesse de Bourgogne a Jesus Christ* (written for Margaret of York in 1470 by Nicholas Finet) Christ, to whom Margaret is shown praying, urges the duchess to devote herself to spiritual concerns as befits the sister of the King of England. Edward must have disappointed Margaret in this regard, but the portraits of the two brothers, both of which have Burgundian influences, assert that her younger brother lived up to these expectations.

This was given more specific expression, and in a more subtle way than a simple gesture of hands clasped in prayer would allow, in the rich symbolic details of flowers, jewellery, colour and clothing.[139] The key to the significance of these details lies in the *Liber, Specialis Gratie* of Bl. Mechtild of Hackeborn, an English translation of which, known as *The Book of Gostlye Grace*, was owned by Cecily Neville, her son, Richard, Duke of Gloucester, and his wife Anne

138 F. Hepburn, *Portraits of the Later Plantagenets* (1986), pp. 32, 71 ff.
139 P. Tudor-Craig, *Richard III* (National Portrait Gallery, 1973), pp. 92–3.

Neville.[140] The visions of St Mechtild coincide with the liturgical hours of the day and are full of details of court life; it is a work that is close to Richard's world. *The Revelations* are also rich in symbolism, the significance of which is explained to St Mechtild by Christ and the Virgin; and these explanations can be applied to the portraits of Richard III. The most striking aspect of both portraits is the prominence of red roses which occur in the Royal Collection portrait in the brocade red background; in the diamond-shaped lozenges, which contain in their corners fleurs de lys to represent the purity of the Virgin, that are interspersed with further pairs of roses in the king's collar; and in the centre of his hat badge. In the Society of Antiquaries' portrait they occur around the gold collar with garnets in the centre; the hat badge forms a prominent red rose, and gold roses, representing the sun and Christ, with five petals occur on the king's overcoat. Roses traditionally represented the Virgin and Christ: the red of the rose, alluding to Christ and the Virgin's suffering, and the five petals to the five wounds. The Virgin was known as the Lady of the Rose and prayers to her had been known since the twelfth century as roses. The primer, or the little office of the Blessed Virgin Mary, was known as a rose garden. By the fifteenth century there was a tight knot of associations of prayer and roses. It was recognized that the prayers one said formed a chaplet of roses which were worn by the Virgin and that they corresponded to the rosary beads.[141] Therefore when Richard chose to be depicted in a gold collar of roses it would have had specific associations of prayer and the rosary. At the time this portrait was executed there was a cult of the rosary throughout northern Europe: a confraternity of the Rosary was founded in Cologne in 1475 and a Yorkshire knight, Sir Robert Plumpton, was enrolled.[142] Richard's mother, Cecily, owned a large rosary of six sets of gold beads divided by square enamel stones from which hung a gold cross.[143] The significance of the

---

[140] The manuscript owned by Richard III and Anne Neville, which will be cited, is BL, Egerton MS 2006, edited by A. Halliwell as *The Booke of Gostlye Grace*. The Latin original *Liber Specialis Gratie* is printed in *Revelations Gertrudianae ac Mechtildianae*, Cura Solesmensium, 2 vols, Paris (1877).

[141] Eithne Wilkins, *The Rose Garden Game* (1969), pp. 106–10, 165–6, 173.

[142] *Plumpton Correspondence*, p. 50.

[143] E. Maclagan and C.C. Oman, 'An English Gold Rosary of about 1500', *Archeologia*, LXXXV (1935), pp. 1–22.

roses in Richard's portrait is revealed in a series of St Mechtild's visions. While praying to Our Lord to teach her how she should worship him she is granted a vision of Jesus, and from his heart springs a beautiful rose with five petals (echoed on Richard's coat) which represents the five senses through which Christ should be worshipped. The Virgin appears to Mechtild clothed in saffron embroidered with red roses which, the Virgin explains, represents the stability of patience that allows her to suffer all things; and in another vision Jesus explains to Mechtild that 'y am that am a rose ande borne without a thorne ande, prykkynde y am with many thornys'.[144] Roses were used in their religious as well as heraldic sense by the Burgundian painters employed in the household of Margaret of York and her step-daughter, Mary of Burgundy. In a votive portrait of Margaret in the Louvre, executed around 1468, showing her at prayer, she wears a collar of alternating red and white roses or marguerites to signify her descent from Edward III and Richard, Duke of York, and the sorrows and joys of the Virgin. These motifs occur in illustrations of Margaret at prayer: in the border of the image of her praying before Christ revealing his wounds to her there are five petalled roses.[145]

The predominant colours in Richard's portrait are red, which is so prominent in the jewelled roses and the background of the Royal Collection portrait; purple, the colour of Richard's doublet in the Society of Antiquaries' portrait; and gold: the overcoat of the Society of Antiquaries' portrait is plain cloth of gold and stylized acanthus leaves, that incidentally occur in the borders of Netherlandish books of hours of the 1480s illustrated by the Master of Burgundy; and gold also features in the jewellery, collars and hat badges and the doublet of the Royal Collection portrait. In the series of visions Mechtild is instructed by Jesus on the colours she should wear and their significance: purple to represent Christ's meekness; red the patience that allows him to take on all things hard and grievous which Christ showed when he took on himself man's humanity. These colours, Jesus informs her, should be surrounded by gold, representing the charity and love that Christ showed to all people on earth and

---

[144] BL, Egerton MS 2006, ff. 63v, 107r; *The Booke of Gostlye Grace*, pp. 199, 326–7.
[145] BL, Add. MS 7970, f. 1v; see also the borders of Bod. Lib., MS Douce 365.

which the worshipper should emulate. In another vision Christ appears in glory
to St Mechtild wearing a gold collar and a shield, under which there was a
beautiful rose to represent his great patience.[146] Gold is further emphasized in
the doublet in the Royal Collection portrait, which is possibly a piece of
armour,[147] and is without parallel in its display of gold circles that represent
Christ. When Richard therefore chose to wear for his portraits purple, red, gold
and a gold collar with roses, he was identifying himself with a patient Christ
who suffered and was misunderstood and rejected by others.

The jewellery in the portraits conveys the same message. The most
prominent items are the hat badges, which appear in the form of a rose in the
Society of Antiquaries' portrait and a crucifix in the form of a gold Greek cross
with a rose centre and pearls dividing the arms in the Royal Collection portrait.
The significance of the cruciform hat badge is explained in Mechtild's vision of
a gold cross. She is told that each person must bear their cross and follow
Christ: the right arm of the cross represents love of neighbour; the left, patience
in adversity, emphasized by the rose in the centre of Richard's cross and in the
other hat badge. The hat badges themselves are explained in Mechtild's vision
of a gold hat brooch which signified the way people's sins are transformed
through prayer.[148] Margaret of York's illuminator, the Master of Burgundy, was
aware of the symbolic significance of this cruciform jewellery, for it occurs in a
book of hours illustrated in 1485 for Englebert II of Nassau, Margaret's
lieutenant of the realm, and Philip the Fair, the son of her step-daughter, Mary
of Burgundy, on a page containing a prayer to St Catherine of Alexandria (one
of Margaret's patron saints). The illustrator shows Catherine pledging herself to
a life of chastity and prayer in a symbolic marriage to Christ and the cruciform
jewels relate symbolically to this picture.[149] Interestingly the hat Richard is
wearing closely resembles the hat of Englebert II in a panel portrait of *c.* 1480.
The importance of prayer is also emphasized by the pearls hanging down from

---

[146] BL, Egerton MS 2006, ff. 35r, 55r; *The Booke of Gostlye Grace*, pp. 112, 173.

[147] Hepburn, *Portraits of the Later Plantagenets*, p. 73.

[148] BL, Egerton MS 2006, f. 33v, 94r; *The Booke of Gostlye Grace*, pp. 123, 288.

[149] Bod. Lib., MS Douce 219, f. 40; Otto Pacht, *The Master of Mary of Burgundy* (1948), p. 38.

both hat badges and in the gold collar of the Royal Collection portrait. This is explained when Mechtild, listening to Psalm 148, 'praise him heavens, and your waters above the heavens', is granted a vision of pearls underneath water which betoken the virtues of the saints which are attained through prayer.[150] The Master of Burgundy frequently associated pearls with prayer, and in a book of hours owned by Charles the Bold and Margaret of York there is an illustration showing a pearl rosary on a prayer cushion near a book of hours before a window that overlooks Christ crucified. In the border of the miniature showing St Catherine of Alexandria being instructed to marry Christ there is, besides the cruciform cross that occurs in Richard's portrait, a pearl rosary.[151]

The other jewels in the portraits are the finger rings. The most prominent of these is the ring Richard places on the fourth finger of his left hand (the wedding finger) in the Society of Antiquaries' portrait. The Royal Collection portrait of Edward IV, the original of which may have faced a portrait of Elizabeth Woodville, shows Edward insouciantly playing with a ring that could be a wedding ring or a coronation ring, the symbol of his authority. The significance of Richard's more serious, determined treatment of his ring, in the Society of Antiquaries' portrait, can be explained in one of Mechtild's visions of the Virgin. Mary gives her a gold ring and Mechtild offers it to Christ who places it on his finger. Mechtild then desires him to return the ring to her as a symbol of her dispensation from sin and her marriage to Christ; she even asks him to give her a perpetual pain in this finger to remind her of this dispensation. Christ gives her a ring of seven stones to represent the seven articles of his godhead, including his sacrificing himself for man and wearing the purple and red clothes of his Passion.[152] Given that this portrait probably dates from 1485 after the death of Anne Neville during an eclipse of the sun, it is hard to escape the conclusion that Richard was not nervously playing with this ring, as a reading of Polydore Vergil implies, but consciously intending to quell rumours that he intended to marry Elizabeth of York and was stating his

[150] BL, Egerton MS 2006, f. 118r; *The Booke of Gostlye Grace*, p. 358.

[151] BL, Egerton MS 2006, f. 40.

[152] Ibid., f. 137r–137v; *The Booke of Gostlye Grace*, p. 408.

intention to put on the coronation ring, the wedding ring of England, and to pledge himself to Christ in suffering and prayer. A letter of exhortation by Mechtild to a nun on the meaning of the five fingers she joined to Christ's in prayer gives clues to the significance of the rings on Richard's right hand in the Royal Collection portrait. The little finger, onto which he is placing a ring, betokens Christ's meekness in coming to earth to serve others, and could therefore emphasize Richard's profession of his devotion to his kingdom and the common weal. The fourth finger, which also has a ring, represents the soul's devotion to God, and the thumb, which on Richard's hand bears a ring with a death's head, represents God's power and protection, and the soul's manly exercise of virtue and its refusal to despair of the mercy of God, who nevertheless allows the soul to be troubled and withdraws from it relieving comfort and grace.[153]

Taking all these things together, both portraits can be read as complex, symbolic representations of the self-image Richard wished (with the help of an artist influenced by painters associated with the court of his sister, Margaret) to convey to his people. A suffering, tormented man who, despite his bereavements, refused to despair of God's grace and who believed his sins would be forgiven through diligent prayer and Christ's intercession, and who sacrificed hopes of worldly felicity to enter a symbolic marriage to Christ, with whom he identified in his suffering, and whom he followed in dedicating his life to subjects who did not appreciate or understand his sacrifice. His identification with the line of David and Jesse is perhaps alluded to in the stylized acanthus foliage on his coat in the Society of Antiquaries' portrait; in this period the acanthus was a popular symbol of the rose bush and the tree of Jesse.[154] The image confronting us in these portraits is that of a man of prayer, a David whose strength of will and determination is in strong contrast to the soft, ineffectual piety that is stamped on the features of portraits of Henry VI.

In Shakespeare's *Richard III* Buckingham, when orchestrating the offer of the crown to Gloucester, says to the assembled citizens of London: 'O see, a book of

---

[153] BL, Egerton MS 2006, f. 186r–186v; *The Booke of Gostlye Grace*, pp. 542–5.

[154] Wilkins, *The Rose Garden Game*, p. 117.

[155] *The Arden Shakespeare: King Richard III*, A. Hammond (ed.) (1981), Act III, Sc. vii, 97–8.

prayer in his hand/True ornaments to know a holy man.'[155] For the audience of
the play this is a savagely ironic remark in the context of a scene displaying
ostentatious hypocrisy. Not all modern historians have shared the certainty of
the late Tudors that Richard III's ostentatious display of piety was hypocritical.
The roots of his spirituality lay in the religious culture of northern England,
especially in the use of private prayer and books of hours. To this extent his
piety was conventional and unexceptional. But prayer entailed the emotional
and personal involvement of the one who prayed. It is almost impossible to
determine with certainty what any individual brought to and sought from his or
her use of conventional prayers. But it can be argued that Richard III had
particular reason to identify with the David of the Psalms and to find solace in
them; especially to protect him from a world in which he perceived he was
surrounded by his enemies and misunderstood by his subjects. That he
perceived himself as a man of prayer is revealed in his surviving portraits. They
draw strongly on the iconography contained in the visions of St Mechtild and
portray a man in torment who refuses to despair of God's grace. Richard III's
tortured spirituality may not be what the Cambridge-educated clerical elite of
the late fifteenth-century north anticipated from their promotion of the practice
of private prayer among the laity, but it was nevertheless an output of the
distinctive religious culture of the late medieval north.

APPENDIX: SELECTED DOCUMENTS

1. THE APPEAL OF WILLIAM ROBYNSON, APPROVER, 12–14 JULY 1473

A full abstract translated from the Latin, with occupations, place- and personal names modernized, except where given in inverted commas.

Memorandum that William Robynson (hanged this term)[1] late of York, 'laborer', alias Robert Roberdson, late of York, 'laborer', on Friday after the quindene of St John the Baptist 13 Edward IV [9 July 1473] confessed at Westminster that he had committed divers felonies, became king's approver and for the good of the king and of his realm of England sought a king's coroner to be assigned to him. So John West, the king's coroner in King's Bench was assigned to record what he wished to say; and the approver was given the Monday, Tuesday and Wednesday after the quindene of St John the Baptist [12–14 July] to make his appeal.

On which days he came before the coroner in the custody of the marshal of the Marshalsea. On Monday he said that he and John Metcalf and John Tomson, both late of Northallerton, Yorkshire, both 'bocher', around the fifth day before the feast of the birth of Our Lord 10 Edward IV [c. 20 December 1470] made an assault on an unknown man called Stokysley [*sic*] at Northallerton Moor, Yorkshire, and feloniously plundered him of £55 8s cash; for which the approver appealed the said John Metcalf and John Tomson.

On Tuesday he said that he and John Colyn and Thomas Percy, both of Grinton in Swaledale, Yorkshire, both 'ffletcher', about the eighth day before the feast of All Saints 9 Edward IV [c. 24 October 1469] made an assault on a certain unknown 'hominem marchaunt'[2] at le 'Wodesyde' between Grinton and Marrick Abbey, and feloniously plundered him of £700 cash; for which he similarly appealed the said John Colyn and Thomas Percy.

Wednesday he said that he and Thomas Horseman of Nottingham, 'laborer', on Friday before the feast of Pentecost 12 Edward IV [15 May 1472] made an assault on a certain unknown canon between Pontefract and Wentbridge, Yorkshire and feloniously deprived him of a casket worth two shillings with £400 cash in it; for which he similarly appealed the said Thomas Horseman.

Asked by the coroner if he had any more to say, he said no; so the appeal was closed.

Dorse: note of delivery by the within-named coroner on the octave of Michaelmas [6 October]

(PRO, KB 9/334, m. 152)

[1] Inserted above the text. [2] Merchant man, or man walking?

2. A PRESENTMENT MADE AT THE ALLERTONSHIRE TOURN, THURSDAY IN PASSION WEEK, 1485

Translated from the Latin

The vill of Allerton (by one constable and four neighbours):

It is presented that Thomas Redeman and Christopher Radclyff with diverse unknowns in warlike array, to the number of three hundred men, on Saturday 26th day of October in the second year of the reign of the Lord King (1484), by force and in arms entered the liberty of St Cuthbert of Allerton and at Allerton made an attack and great affray upon all the inhabitants of the Town of Allerton and trespassed therein. John Vale, John Jakson, John Bynkes and Robert Founder were beaten, wounded and maltreated contrary to the peace of the Lord King.

(NYCRO, ZBD 52/3 (189443) fr.9.)

3. A LETTER FROM THE KING RECOMMENDING ROBERT NEVIILE TO DURHAM, 28 NOVEMBER 1437

Original English, with some modernizing of punctuation

Trusty and wellbeloved in god, we grete you wel. And signifie unto you that we have late understande of the/calling owt of this uncertyain & mortal lyf of the worshipful fader in god Thomas late Bisshop of Duresme/by whose decesse oure seid Cathedral Church is now viduate and unpourveid of a propre spouse and gouverneur/we havyng the prosperitee and good gouvernail of oure seid Church moch the more in oure tendre and specialle/Recomendacion Aswel for it is oon of the grettest and moost notable churches of oure patronnage within this/oure Royaume as for hit is nygh unto the marches of Scotland. For the which cause namely hit is right necessare/and expedient both for the wele of that countrey and of the said Church to set and pourvey of suche a notable/and myghty personne to be heed and Bisshop therof. as can and may puissantly kepe thayme best to the honnour of/god and defence of this oure Royaume we therfore booth for thees grete and notable consideracons & othre that moeven us/have finally ordeind and appointed the worshipful fader in god oure Righte trusty and welbeloved Cousin/Robert Bisshop of Salesbury to be translated unto oure seid Cathedral Churche of Duresme which consi/dering aswel his birth and kynsmen the which been of Right grete and notable estate as his grete vertues connyng & discrete providence aswel in spirituel as temporel administration and gouvernance is thought unto/us the moost convenient soufficant and hable prelate that we couth name or assign therunto. And therupon we/have writen oure Right specialle lettres of Recommendacion of him unto oure hooly fader the pope. Wherfore we desire/and prey yow hartly that conformyng yow hooly to oure entent as in this mater ye in your next election/wol by oon assent have oure seid Cousin of Salesbury in your

Right tendre Recomendacion unto thestat of/youre Bisshop and gouvernor wherin as in oure conceit oure said Church of Duresme/shal be of right notably pourveyed for to the worship of god and wele and proufit of the same and also of right/a souffisant fader and gouverneur. And over that ye shal doo unto us right grete an singlier/pleasure. Geven under oure signet at oure logge within oure parc of Wyndesor the xxviii day of November.

Dorse:

To oure trusty and welbeloved in god the priour & chapitre of oure Cathedral Church of Duresme.

(DCD, Locellus, XXV, 96)

4. ARCHIBALD WHITELAW'S ADDRESS TO KING RICHARD III, ADVOCATING THE STRENGTHENING OF PEACEFUL TIES BETWEEN THE ENGLISH AND THE SCOTS, 12 SEPTEMBER 1484[1]

Translated by David Shotter

Most serene Prince and King: of all the sovereigns whom I have known, you stand out as the greatest – in the renown of your nobility, in your sway over your people, in your strength of arms, and in the wealth of resources at your command. It is the usual practice of those who act as ambassadors to the courts of Kings and Princes to praise to the skies in highly elaborate orations the pre-eminent virtues[2] of those to whom they are sent, and with keen skill to plead to the last both their lofty praise and the mission despatched to them.

This, I believe, I must do to the best of my ability: for, although I have no rhetorical skill, I have been sent here by the order of my most serene Prince, together with my Lords here present who are his Highness's ambassadors, to lay this speech before you. For this reason I crave your Highness's indulgence should I fail to carry through to full satisfaction the task which I have been given and upon which I have embarked. But as I very rashly begin, it seems to me presumptuous that, although I myself can boast no glorious nobility, nor claim any distinction in learning, nor achieve any fluency of eloquence, I have come here to speak in the presence of one who is so esteemed in dignity and wondrous in majesty – and furthermore, of one who is attended by noble lords who are

[1] Translated from 'Oratio Scotorum ad Regem Ricardum Tertium pro face firmanda inter Anglos et Scotos. XII Sept. M.CCC.LXXIV', printed in *The Bannatyne Miscellany*, II, D. Laing (ed.) (Bannatyne Club, Edinburgh, 1836), pp. 41–8. I am extremely grateful to Professor John and Mrs Winifred MacQueen for many improvements to the first draft of my translation, and to Dr Alexander Grant for discussing the final translation with me and for adding some historical points in the notes.

[2] I.e. *virtutes*. In Whitelaw's usage, *uirtus* probably has the same meaning as the Renaissance Italian *virtù*: namely prowess, ability as a ruler, and political skill leading to success, as well as goodness. Throughout this translation I have rendered *virtus* as either 'virtue' or (less commonly) 'prowess'; in each case the wider sense should presumably be understood.

distinguished for the sublimity of the honours they enjoy, for the godlike quality of their eloquence and, equally, for their human wisdom. I see their gazes turned upon me alone, and I realise that there is no course of action which can in any way be affected by me in words, expressions or gestures, if it has not been deemed to deserve praise or condemnation by your Highness and by the great wisdom of your advisors.

But one consideration gives me consolation and support, namely your most celebrated reputation for the practice of every form of virtue, which has reached into every corner of the world; moreover, there is the excellent and outstanding humanity of your innate benevolence, your clemency, your liberality, your good faith, your supreme justice, and your incredible greatness of heart. Your wisdom is not just human; it is almost divine: for you make yourself not simply at ease with important individuals, but courteous to the common people, too. It is with such virtues and such lofty prudence as this that you impart improvement to everything that is uttered and spoken in your presence. As I make my address before you, in the name and on behalf of my most serene Prince, the King of Scots, who holds you in high affection, who loves you, and who strives for a close friendship and alliance with you, it is these virtues of yours that have made it possible for me to speak now, daring to rise above the level of my normal intellectual capacity. If I make a mistake at any point, then consider that it should be attributed to those heavenly virtues of yours, through which you have achieved fellowship and association with the celestial beings.

It is twenty-five years ago since I performed an ambassador's role to your illustrious father in Ireland, when a settlement was established and concluded, and confirmed by his seal and signature for himself, his heirs and successors;[3] I brought it back for my illustrious King and Prince, who was still alive then but has now ended his life of sacred memory.[4] But now I look for the first time upon your face; it is a countenance worthy of the highest power and kingliness, illuminated by moral and heroic virtue.[5] Fitting for you are the words which the poet Statius used of the noble prince of Thebes:

Never before has nature dared to encase in a smaller body such spirit and such strength.[6]

[3] For the Scottish embassy to Ireland for negotiations with Richard, Duke of York in 1459, see A.I. Dunlop, *The Life and Times of James Kennedy, Bishop of St Andrews* (Edinburgh, 1950), pp. 204–7, and R.A. Griffiths, *The Reign of King Henry VI* (1981), p. 813.

[4] I.e. King James II, who died in 1460.

[5] . . . *quam moralis et heroica virtus illustrat*: Professor MacQueen has remarked to me that this phrase particularly stands out as being typical of the Renaissance, and, for the general context, refers to E.R. Curtis, *European Literature and the Latin Middle Ages* (1953), ch. 9, 'Heroes and Rulers'.

[6] Statius, *Thebaid*, Book VI, ll. 845–6.

and again:

In his small body the greatest valour held sway.[7]

For you are the embodiment of military skill, prowess,[8] good fortune, and authority – all qualities which Cicero, in his eulogy of Pompey, declares should be sought in the best military leader. Nor are these the only virtues of generals which are commonly so regarded – there are also hard work in administration, bravery in the face of danger, application in developing a position, speed in execution, and care in forward planning. Nor is it virtue in warfare alone that must be sought in the greatest general; there are other important virtues too, which are the attendants and companions of virtue. How much pureness in heart is needed by one who is both King and general, how much self-control in all situations, how much good faith, how much liberality, how much intelligence, how much humanity. A general who is unable to control himself cannot control an army; nor can he be strict in passing judgement, if he fails to allow that others should be strict judges in his own case. In you, however, most serene Prince, all the requirements of a glorious King and general come together, in such a way that the words of no orator can add anything to your military or civilian prowess. As Virgil put it:

So long as rivers flow into the sea, so long as shadows move on the mountain-slopes; so long as the pole feeds the stars;[9] so long as the wild boar delights in the mountains and the fish in the rivers; so long as bees feed on thyme and grasshoppers on dew – your honour, your name and your glory will survive for ever.[10]

Were Cicero still alive, his skills would scarcely suffice to describe your virtues fully or sing your praises to the skies; still less should I with modest endeavour try you with excessive praise, or fail in my speech, or seem to have wished to flatter you – which I have done to no-one, nor wish to make a start in your case. But we must put these sentiments aside for another occasion, for my speech hastens on to express as succinctly as possible the central message of our legation.

Most serene Prince, it is the purpose of our embassy and mission that, with the Kings of England and Scotland joined in mutual love, affection, friendship and affinity, their subjects should enjoy the blessings and pleasures of peace and tranquillity. To be sure, it was conditions of peace that drew God down from heaven to earth, that made him man, so that, once made man, he could in a miraculous exchange turn us into gods. Moreover, he chose for the time of his incarnation, his arrival and his appearance on earth a period of peace, not of war; this was the peace that reigned when Augustus Caesar, having defeated Marc Antony by land and sea and routed Cleopatra,

---

[7] Ibid., Book I, l. 417.

[8] I.e. *virtus*.

[9] Virgil, *Aeneid*, Book I, l. 608–9.

[10] Virgil, *Eclogue*, V, ll. 76–8. Note that these two quotations are run together to make a single verse.

Queen of Egypt, held the whole world in tranquillity as a result of his prowess in war, and imposed the famous taxes and tributes. Truly, it was in peace that Christ was born; in peace that he was buried; in peace that he fell asleep; in peace that he went to his rest.[11] This was the last commandment of our Lord and Saviour, when he left this world to go to his Father: he enjoined peace on his disciples.

The King and the lords of the city of Rome built a temple to Peace, in which Peace and Good Faith were worshipped with high honours. Cicero, that master of Roman rhetoric and wisdom, declared that Peace and Concord were the foundations of all ordered government. And our Saviour calls peacemakers his sons and co-heirs in eternal life and happiness, and at the same time scatters those who thirst for war, and sends them far away from peace and tranquillity.

Most serene Prince, for a long time your subjects, who live within the borders of your realm, in their arrogance preferred war to peace; but now that they see their land lying uncultivated because of war they praise peace and condemn war and battles. They call you to brotherly love with your most noble Prince; it is a love which the nobles of your kingdom, in their wisdom and virtue, demand too. For there has been enough fighting, enough wrongdoing, enough Christian bloodshed in this most recent conflict – in which those who planned the death of all good men and the destruction of peace by force of arms, were immediately overwhelmed and put to flight, and now pay the penalty for their disturbance of the peace, suffering an exile which is worse even than death.[12]

These were the words which Virgil, through the character of Anchises, used to exhort the Romans to embrace the harmony of peace:

Do not, my children, let yourselves become used in your thoughts to such great warfare; nor turn your stout strength upon your own country's heart.[13]

He also said:

Romans, remember that it is your destiny to rule the people of the world with your command; your skill will be to impose the habit of peace, to spare the conquered, but to defeat in war those who prove intransigent.[14]

Statius echoes the same theme in his *Thebaid*, speaking thus to Polynices and his followers:

---

[11] The language used to describe Christ's death, resurrection and ascension appears odd, but there seems to be no other way to translate Whitelaw's words: *In pace profecto natus est Christus, in pace sepultus, in pace obdormuit, in pace quieuit.*

[12] This must refer to the flight to France of Alexander, Duke of Albany, after his defeat at Lochmaben on 22 July 1484: see A. Grant's essay, above (at note 83). In that case 'in their arrogance preferred war to peace', and 'land lying uncultivated because of war' presumably refer to the recent Anglo-Scottish warfare of 1480–2.

[13] Virgil, *Aeneid*, Book VI, ll. 833–4.

[14] Ibid., ll. 852–4.

Young men, control your spirits, and the wild fury that is eager for an foeman's blood.[15]

In the name of immortal God, what is more horrifying than war, or sweeter than peace? What is more terrifying than arms, or more pleasant than tranquillity? What is worse than the killing of one's fellow-men, or more natural than the saving of human life?

God established peace for the protection of mankind: it was the spirit of Satan that put warfare into men's minds. In time of war, all the land is left uncultivated and overgrown; curved sickles are forged into straight swords; vineyards are turned into thickets; and fields, grass and vegetation grow moist with the blood of men. The glory that is won by brute force does not last for ever; warfare gives a country a dreadful face – burned-out houses, sacked towns, and wrecked castles; human corpses lying scattered throughout the fields and streets; streams flowing with blood, and everything echoing with moans, crying and the wailing of women. Some flee from armed attacks, whilst others miserably expire racked by a variety of tortures. The ordinary husbandmen are left without the means to make a living, to cultivate the land, and look after their sweet wives and beloved children. No end will be found to every conceivable kind of cruelty, every form of crime and wrong-doing, every kind of violence, theft, pillaging, adultery, murder and rape. As Seneca says in one of his tragedies:

> There can be no moderation in the face of arms; nor can the anger of a drawn sword be easily assuaged, let alone stopped; for it is in the bloodshed that war delights.[16]

As Cicero put it, 'laws give way when faced with force'[17] – not, however, those ordained in Heaven, but those pronounced by men. There is no place for order, for reason, for fair-dealing or for a sense of duty; right and wrong, sacred and profane, lawful and unlawful – all of these are blurred in turmoil. Brute force holds sway; madness prevails; cruelty rages, and pillage is rife. Wrong-doing, crime, injustice – all sharpen their teeth in times of war; they open wide their throats and they raise up their gaping jaws and necks. They take pleasure in gathering booty together and engaging in plunder; to sum up everything in a few words, all that is beautiful collapses and falls into nothing.[18]

On the other hand, in time of peace, God is worshipped with particular fervour as the provider of peace; fair justice is powerful and effective; all virtue and good government shine forth. Husbandmen rejoice in peace: crops are sown, pastures thrive, vines are laden with grapes, and gardens are adorned

---

[15] Statius, *Thebaid*, Book VI, ll. 915–16.

[16] Seneca, *Hercules Furens*, ll. 405–7.

[17] Cicero, *Pro Milone*, sect. 10; also Lucretius, *De Rerum Natura*, Book I, l. 277.

[18] . . . *omnia bella corruunt, et ad nichilum prolapuntur*. Every other time *bella* is used in this speech, it means war. Here, at first sight, Whitelaw might appear to have been saying 'war corrupts everything, and brings it to nothing', which would sum the passage up perfectly; but unfortunately *prolapsor* cannot be translated in that active sense, and so I have followed the strict syntax, and rendered *bella* as 'beautiful (things)'.

with fruit and flowers. In farms, houses and towns, there is great plenty of material possessions; princes, nobles, merchants and the common people enjoy an abundance of gold, silver and jewels.[19] Sallust says that 'possessions grow slowly in peace-time, but are dissipated with great speed in time of conflict'.[20] Cicero believed that peace, which nothing should hinder, should always be a prime concern.[21]

But you know well that a lust for power and domination, which has led many mortal kings astray, has caused terrible wars amongst you princes. I implore you, dispel it from your minds with this agreement. Let every prince be content with the limits, bounds and confines of his own kingdom, so that he would rather retreat than advance; lest, contrary to the commandment of our Lord and Saviour, he steals other people's property in the presence of a judge who is rigorous as regards the restitution of stolen goods and encroachments. For the poison of exercising command, of dispute and discord, was devised by God, as Livy says, for the humiliation of mighty potentates. Thus, those kings who, as a result of long-enjoyed or suddenly-acquired affluence or of prosperous success have become overbearing, and who do not have a superior by whom their insolence could be checked, engage each other in fighting and combat, with the result that one or both of them is destroyed.

It is an unnatural thing that war should be fought between us – we who are bound together within a small island in the western sea, and who are linked by living in the same climate and in neighbouring lands, sharing similarity of physique, language, appearance, colouring and complexion. On the contrary, let virtue of spirit, love of God, and fear of our neighbours bond us together in a single fountain of goodwill. May you, most serene and godlike Prince, deal with the initiation of love and friendship between yourself and our Prince in such a way that not the least distinction will be made between English and Scots with regard to love, but rather that they may be seen to be joined together in one chain of love and goodwill.

Countless benefits will arise from the love of your people and ours, in union, sweet marriage, matrimony and kinship.[22] For just as when the weather roughens a quiet sea, and after the storm there is a sense of calmness and a joyous mood, so when war is transformed by the onset of peace it brings very much joy, and the bitterness at wrongs done is softened by what the Greeks call *amnestia*

---

[19] This striking description of the evils of war and the benefits of peace follows a common medieval and Renaissance *topos*, depicted most famously in the great fresco cycle, 'The Allegory of Good and Bad Government', painted by Ambrogio Lorenzetti in 1338–40 for the walls of the 'Hall of Peace' in the Palazzo del Comune, Siena. It is quite likely that Whitelaw went to Siena during the time he spent in Italy, particularly since it was the family home of the Pope at the time, Pius II (d. 1464) – the Aeneas Silvius Piccolomini who visited Scotland and met James I in 1435.

[20] Sallust, *Jugurtha*, sect. 10 (6).

[21] Whitelaw's Latin is obscure here: *pacique, nichil inhibitura sit, semper consulendum esse*. Here, *inhibiturum* has been read for *inhibitura*. I have been unable to find any specific passage from Cicero that Whitelaw may have been quoting.

[22] *Innumerabiles enim commoditates ex tui et nostri populi dilectionis, unione, dulci connubio, matrimonio, et affiniate*. A call for political union flowing from the marriage might be read into this, but the tenor of the rest of the speech makes that conclusion unlikely.

– a forgetting of injuries. This should be celebrated by a happy brotherhood between Princes. As Virgil said:

> Then wars will be put aside and the centuries of bitter conflict resolved: . . . the dreaded gates of war with their tight iron fastenings will be closed, and godless frenzy will sit inside on his murderous arms, letting forth a terrible roar from a bloody mouth, hands bound behind his back with a hundred bonds of bronze.[23]

My earnest wish is that the supreme provider of peace, whose role it is to confound war, may bring tranquillity to man's disturbed and troubled affairs; so that when this happens, harmony will continue to be enduring, stable and untroubled. May God himself, by his grace, guarantee that peace is held by an indissoluble bond, that no secret snares lie in wait to destroy it, that no perfidy shatters it, that no lurking deceptions disturb it, that no remnants of yesterday's hatred infect it, that no fraudulent tricks defile it, and that no memory of injuries tear it apart. On the contrary, may that agreement of the two Kings strengthen it, their affection bind it tightly, their love confirm it and their goodwill cement it, and may true brotherhood ratify it and guarantee it for all time.

That our embassy to you is pleasing and acceptable to God is proved by the kind, mild weather and the balmy conditions. These arguments, lavishing praise on a peace which all Princes should grasp, I have desired to present directly to you, Lord and most serene Prince; I have determined to be concise and to speak in terms that are easily assimilated, for I know that you are deeply involved in many enterprises in your kingdom and in public affairs. I trust that, because of your mild and clement temper, you will take these matters up in a kindly spirit, and improve upon them, knowing as you do how to make many things out of few.

I shall bring my speech to an end in this style of oratory; your kindness and gracious favour in listening have made it longer than was proper. I have learned from experience that all kings and princes take pleasure in a short speech. There are some matters which require a private audience: my Lords, who are here in the presence of your invincible Majesty, when witnesses have been excluded, together with those Lords of your Council whom you so order, will learn of these at greater length than has been possible in my simple speech.

I have spoken.[24]

Archibald Whitelaw's Latin: A Comment

The speech, which would have taken a little more than half an hour to deliver, is essentially simple in message and construction: it contains a long introductory section, the purpose of which is to flatter the English king (though not too tastelessly), to assure him of the ambassador's sincerity, and

---

[23] Virgil, *Aeneid*, Book I, ll. 291–6.

[24] The final word of the speech, in typical Ciceronian style, is *Dixi*.

to state his credentials (though not too forcefully). This is followed by the ambassador's chief message – the need for peace between England and Scotland, and the benefits that would flow from it.

Whitelaw had clearly read widely amongst classical authors, and obviously – following good classical practice – had mentally extracted from his reading the telling quotation to suit situations in which he might expect to be professionally involved. This displays an attitude to classical literature that is remarkably similar to that which characterised the schoolmaster and biographer, Suetonius. In the speech, Virgil, Statius, Seneca and Sallust are quoted, and there are allusions to Cicero and Livy. These are not overdone, but are brief, well-spaced, and appropriate to the context; their presence, of course, provides their own comment on Whitelaw's self-deprecation with regard to learning.

The style of the speech is modelled broadly upon that of Cicero, and there are occasions where rhetorical impact is gained by the juxtaposition of examples which are far in excess of what is required to clarify the meaning. Whitelaw does not, however, employ the common Ciceronian devices – which were certainly evident in the *Pro Milone*, a speech to which he here alludes – such as the introduction of sentences with questions like 'Who is there who does not know that . . .?' and statements like 'I will pass over . . .', which then proceed to detail the occasion. Possibly, Whitelaw found such devices too 'arrogant' for his taste or for the current purpose.

In a number of ways, Whitelaw's speech falls short of its model. His vocabulary indulges rather more in abstract nouns than Cicero's would have done in such circumstances. Whilst the syntax attempts to develop a Ciceronian periodic structure, this tends in places to become too convoluted – with a subsequent obscurity in precise meaning. This, and the looseness of structure which allows for frequent changes of nominatives within sentences, certainly blunts the impact which the Roman orator would have achieved. Since Cicero subsequently 'worked up' his speeches for publication, his impact cannot solely be ascribed to the immediacy of the occasion. In general – and that may be expected of a man steeped in classical scholarship – the style is more reminiscent of Cicero's philosophical and rhetorical treatises than of his oratorical productions.

The language and structure are learned rather than inspired; there is little sign of careful and telling balances or antitheses within and between sentences which gave Cicero's orations the impression (albeit calculated) of vigour and freshness. There are some examples of Ciceronian metrical cadences at sentence-ends, although it is not altogether clear that these were intentional.

In all, Whitelaw produces a Latin which is *studiedly* correct, but which lacks the impact of one with an essential *feel* for the language.

INDEX

The following abbreviations are used: Abp – Archbishop; Bp – Bishop; Cs – Countess; Dk – Duke; Ds – Duchess; Ea – Earl; Ld – Lord; Ly – Lady; Pr – Prince; Prs – Princess; Qn – Queen.